Health and Social Care
for Intermediate GNVQ

by Mark Walsh

Josephine de Souza

Collins Educational

An imprint of HarperCollinsPublishers

© Collins Educational 1996

Mark Walsh, Josephine de Souza and Pat NcNeill
assert the moral right to be identified as the authors of
this work.

Published by
Collins Educational Ltd
An imprint of HarperCollins*Publishers*
77–85 Fulham Palace Road
Hammersmith
London W6 8JB

First published 1996

Reprinted 1997, 1998

ISBN 0 00 329080 8

Commissioning editor: Richard Jackman
Designed by DSM Partnership
Cover designed by Trevor Burrows
Illustrations by Chris Keenan: Julia Osorno
Cartoons by Daniel Betts and Nathan Betts
Project managed by Susan Ross
Production by Mandy Inness
Printed and bound by Scotprint Ltd, Musselburgh,
Scotland

Contents

ACKNOWLEDGEMENTS

Thanks are due to Rick Jackman and Kay Wright at Collins Educational for their support and skill in coordinating and guiding the progress of the various contributors to the book, to Pat McNeill for his detailed comments, advice and contributions to various drafts of the text, and to Susan Ross and Sarah Brown for their impressively swift editing of the typescript. Karen Seymour's love, sense of humour and support are responsible for my part of the book being successfully completed.

Mark Walsh

I would especially like to thank Cynthia McLetchie-Rabess for her diligence and patience in proof-reading the typescript of chapter 1, Christine Fortune for ideas and suggestions, Olivia Simmonds for supplying useful information and names of contacts, David McArdle and Colin Smith for their help and advice, my family for their unstinting support, and Julia and Leah for their review of the completed text.

Josephine de Souza

The authors and publisher would like to thank the following for permission to reproduce photographs and other material:
Liam Bailey/Photofusion (p. 177)
Department of Health (p. 41 left)
Sally and Richard Greenhill (pp. 3, 15, 36, 56, 90, 92, 102, 103, 123, 133, 157, 175, 185, 201, 209, 213, 243 and 264)
Health Education Authority (pp. 41 right and 135)
Robert Isear/Science Photo Library (p. 20)
Charlotte Lippmann (p. 127)
Mothercare (pp. 88 and 95)
Susanna Rose (p. 173)
Susan Ross (p. 177)
St Bartholomew's Hospital, London/Science Photo Library (p. 115)

Thanks are also due to all those who gave permission to reproduce copyright material as shown in the sources.

Crown copyright material is reproduced with permission of the Controller of Her Majesty's Stationary Office.

Every effort has been made to contact copyright holders, but if any have been inadvertently overlooked, the publishers will be pleased to make the necessary arrangements at the first opportunity.

Introduction

What is a GNVQ?

The letters GNVQ stand for General National Vocational Qualification.

General   GNVQ courses provide a broad-based vocational education focused on work in a particular industry, such as health and social care.

National   A new national qualification introduced in 1992, the GNVQ is based on national standards, drawn up and published by the National Council for Vocational Qualifications (NCVQ).

Vocational Qualification   It is a vocational qualification which relates to the world of work and employment (in contrast to GCSEs and A levels, which are based on knowledge and the understanding of academic subjects).

What is Intermediate Health and Social Care GNVQ?

The Intermediate Health and Social Care GNVQ helps students reach, through practical investigation, an understanding of the ways in which people experience health and well-being and of how the health and social care services operate to prevent and respond to health and social care problems. The qualification offers students the opportunity to develop their skills, knowledge and understanding of health and social care and can be the basis for further education or entry into care work.

Much of your learning for this, and every, GNVQ will be achieved through carrying out your own enquiries and investigations, often in connection with assignments agreed with your tutor. These might include:

- ⊗ **carrying out research in libraries and resource centres**

- ⊗ **visiting care settings and talking to the people who work, or receive care, there**

- ⊗ **hearing about the experiences of patients, clients and care workers during interviews or arranged visits**

- ⊗ **conducting surveys of people's attitudes, preferences and opinions**

- ⊗ **using prepared case studies and undertaking role plays to gain more insight into health and social care situations**

- ⊗ **being able to arrange work experience with a local care organisation or provider.**

Overall, you will make an active investigation of the actual practice of health and social care work, presenting your findings in a variety of ways, including giving talks and presentations – two skills which are essential in the modern world of work.

CORE SKILLS UNITS

Each chapter in this book provides you with the background knowledge you need for one unit of your GNVQ. There are also three mandatory core skill units, which are the same for every GNVQ in every vocational area. These are:

- ⊗ **application of number:**
  - **– collect and record data**
  - **– tackle problems**
  - **– interpret and present data**

- ✪ **communications:**
  - **– take part in discussions**
  - **– prepare written material**
  - **– use images**
  - **– read and respond to written materials**

- ✪ **information technology:**
  - **– prepare information**
  - **– process information**
  - **– present information**
  - **– evaluate the use of information technology.**

The most important thing to remember about core skills is that they must be applied to work situations. You have to show that you have the skills, and that you can use them, and that you do this in the process of your other studies. There are no separate tests or exams in core skills. Instead, you demonstrate your skills while carrying out activities and assignments and by evidence you collect in your portfolio of evidence.

It is important to become familiar with the core skill requirements for the Intermediate Health and Social Care GNVQ. You should always check with your tutor to find out what core skills evidence you can claim in carrying out the activities and assignments in the book.

PORTFOLIO OF EVIDENCE

Your GNVQ assessment will be based on your collected 'portfolio of evidence', which will show that you have developed the skills and acquired the knowledge required by the qualification. Your portfolio has to be carefully planned, organised, maintained and indexed. The evidence you collect can take many forms, including:

- ✪ **written work (e.g. notes on a topic, a brief report, a detailed plan of a campaign or an example of a service provided)**

- ✪ **witness statements (e.g. written evidence provided by your tutor or some other person, perhaps an employer, who has witnessed you taking part in a discussion, or dealing with a patient/client, or making a presentation. It may also take the form of a video or audio recording of such events)**

- *presentations, group discussions and role plays (e.g. brainstorming ideas for an event)*

- *other evidence (e.g. letters, photographs, other audio or video recordings, or certificates which demonstrate that you have done other, relevant work).*

Your portfolio is unlikely, therefore, to be simply a file full of papers. It is much more likely to finish up as a box full of a variety of objects and documents. Everything you include, however, must be carefully recorded and indexed.

ACTIVITIES

Activities are exercises that should help you understand what you have been reading and to apply it to your own experience. You can complete many of the activities at your desk, perhaps by working with one or two others, by analysing case studies, documents and figures provided in the book. However, some activities involve enquiries or investigations outside the classroom. Whatever the type of activity, you will be given clear instructions on what to do.

An activity will sometimes act as a starting point for a portfolio assignment and, where this occurs, you may be able to include the evidence generated from carrying out the activity in your portfolio. Again, you will be given instructions whenever this is possible.

PORTFOLIO ASSIGNMENT

Portfolio assignments are more substantial pieces of work than activities. They may take any of the forms described under 'portfolio of evidence'. If you complete all the portfolio assignments in this book, you will have all the evidence you need to include in your portfolio for the four mandatory units.

The assignments also provide an opportunity for you to develop core skills and will ensure you meet the course grading themes:

- **planning**

- **information handling**

- ✪ evaluation

- ✪ quality of outcome.

The first three relate to the process of completing your coursework, and the fourth relates to the quality and content of the work you produce.

QUICK RESPONSE

The quick response questions that appear throughout each chapter are designed to help you to think about the issues raised by the topic you are studying. They should prompt you to express and discuss your thoughts and ideas but do not involve extensive writing or evidence generation.

TEST AND ASSESSMENTS

Each mandatory unit of the GNVQ requires you to sit an 'end-of-unit test'(with the exception of the communication and interpersonal relationships unit). This is designed to assess your knowledge and is taken under exam conditions. There are normally between 25 and 40 questions, and the test takes one hour. You will have several opportunities to take the tests, and, if you are unsuccessful at the first attempt, you may take the test again until you reach the required standard.

At the end of each chapter in this book, there are a number of questions which are designed to help you check that you have understood the knowledge you will need to pass these unit tests. The questions are not designed to be exactly like the actual unit tests (your tutor will be able to provide examples of these), but if you answer all the questions correctly, you will have a complete summary of the main points made in the preceding section of the book.

RECORD-KEEPING

You will appreciate by now that good record-keeping is an essential part of your GNVQ course, as it is in every area of your work and employment. You must keep records of your 'action plans' (and of any changes to these plans) and of all your studies, activities and assignments. You should also keep a record or index showing how the material in your portfolio is organised.

Good luck with your course!

Promoting Health and Well-being

CONTENTS

OUTLINE

This chapter aims to help you to develop knowledge and understanding of the basic factors that contribute to health and well-being.

The ways individuals are able to achieve, maintain and improve their personal health are discussed in the first part, which covers element 1.1. This focuses on aspects of lifestyle and health behaviours that promote health benefits and reduce risks to health.

In the second part – covering element 2 – you develop a plan that will improve the health of an individual. The purposes and methods of producing and presenting health advice to others are then explored.

The last part – covering element 1.3 – raises awareness of hazards to health and well-being, both in care settings and in the general environment. It covers the knowledge underpinning the development of skills for dealing with health emergencies.

PREVIEW

After working through this chapter you will be able to:

- ❂ **investigate the personal health and well-being of an individual**

- ❂ **present advice on health and well-being to others**

- ❂ **reduce the risk of injury and deal with common health emergencies.**

Health and social care workers have the overall aim of promoting the health and well-being of their clients. This requires a good understanding of the factors that contribute to health and of the risks that some features of people's lifestyle present. Care workers who can get their health messages across to patients, clients and members of the public are likely to increase the overall levels of health and well-being in the population. The methods by which this aim can be achieved are discussed. The ability to recognise and deal with health hazards and emergencies is also an important feature of any care worker's skills and ability.

INVESTIGATE PERSONAL HEALTH

HEALTH AND WELL-BEING

The term **health** means different things to different people. To one person, it may mean being free of injury or disease or simply not feeling unwell. To another person being healthy may mean being able to walk, run and carry out every-day tasks and responsibilities effortlessly.

These can be regarded as **negative** and **positive views of health**. The negative view emphasises that a lack of disease or illness is necessary for a person to be healthy. The positive view of health, which is taken by bodies such as the World Health Organisation, is that it is 'a state of complete physical, mental and social well-being, not merely the absence of disease or infirmity' (WHO, 1946). A positive view of health includes the physical, social, intellectual and emotional or psychological aspects of an individual's nature and experience. These different aspects of health are explained below.

Physical health: refers to the body and its working.

Social health: concerns the individual's involvement with other people in relationships.

Intellectual health: concerns the ability to learn, think and make judgements.

Emotional health: concerns the individual's ability to recognise his or her own feelings and to express them appropriately.

The term **psychological health** is often used to cover the last three areas.

 ACTIVITY

The following people have different lifestyles, attitudes and values. In some ways they may be healthy, in other ways they may not. Read through each example and answer the questions that follow.

Denise has a job as a stockbroker. She buys and sells shares and must reach certain targets each week. She works out at the company gym each morning and then works very hard from 7.30 am to 7.30 pm five days a week. She admits to feeling stressed most of the time. Before she goes home she usually goes for a few drinks with her colleagues to wind down. She has made a lot of money through her work but says that she has little time for other things.

Andy gave up his job as a business studies lecturer two years ago to live in France and write books. He used to spend a lot of the summer out of doors, cycling around the French countryside looking at the places and people he writes about. Last year he damaged his ankle in a fall and can't ride far anymore. Although he has made a few friends he rarely goes out socialising due to lack of money. In the winter he felt lonely. He caught pneumonia because he couldn't afford to heat his house. He is now working as a tourist guide to make some money to last until he gets a book published.

Belinda is a 19-year-old student of geology. She joined the rock climbing group at her university and went on most of the climbing trips in her first year. She recently went on a trip to Snowdonia. This time, she says, she 'just lost her nerve'. She got stuck on a cliff face and had to be taken off by rescue helicopter. She has been feeling 'on edge' ever since. This has resulted in her falling behind in her studies this term.

Samira describes herself as a 'housewife'. She is 23 and has two children under five. She lives on income support but gets help occasionally from her mother who lives a few miles away. She says that the children take up most of her time so she doesn't go out very often. Her favourite past time is television. After the children are in bed she likes to watch soap operas and quiz shows with a box of chocolates, some crisps and a few cans of lemonade.

Robbie is a packer in a factory. He says that his job is very boring most of the time. His life really revolves around sport and fitness training. He goes to a local gym five nights a week to do weight training. Before work each day he jogs or swims at the local pool. He cycles everywhere he goes. Robbie is very concerned about his diet and his physical appearance. He thinks about exercise even when he isn't doing it. He always wants to do more to improve his body. He has recently started taking anabolic steroids to help him build up his physique.

Norman is a church preacher. He says that he lives his life according to the Bible. He prays that God 'will punish sinners, like homosexuals, prostitutes and drug takers'. He believes that sex before marriage is a sin and that abortion is murder. He believes that God created all people but that 'they should not mix outside of their own race'. Norman is a keen golfer and plays a round with friends twice a week.

✕ **In what way is each person healthy or unhealthy? Make some notes of your own ideas.**

✕ **Discuss your ideas with other people in the class.**

✕ **What sort of approach to health are you using in making your decision about each person?**

The idea of **well-being** is used to refer to the way people feel about themselves. An individual is the only person who can judge his or her personal well-being. If people are feeling good then they will have a high level of well-being. If they have friends and are confident that their material needs (for food, shelter, warmth) are going to be met, then they will have a deeper and more lasting sense of well-being.

The terms 'illness', 'disease' and 'ill-health' are also commonly used in discussions about health. Often these three terms are used interchangeably to refer to an unhealthy state. However, there are important distinctions between them. **Disease** is a term used by doctors and other care workers to refer to an objective physical condition that can be seen and measured and which involves changes in the body's correct structure or working. An **illness**, on the other hand, is a subjective experience. A person with an illness may complain of feeling awful and have symptoms such as aches and pains or loss of his or her usual body functioning.

People can have a disease without feeling ill. This is one of the reasons for having screening programmes. Cervical smears, childhood blood tests and chest X-rays are all carried out for this purpose. Equally, at times people can feel ill without a doctor being able to find anything physically wrong with them. Often when people go to their GP complaining of feeling ill, the examination and the procedures carried out, such as chest X-rays and blood tests, may reveal that something is wrong. In this case an illness and a disease are present.

QUICK response

Using these definitions of illness and disease, identify times when you have experienced either.

ACTIVITY

Can you remember an occasion when you, or someone you know, had a disease without feeling ill? Can you remember an occasion when you felt ill but no one could find anything wrong with you?

How did others treat you in each case?

THE COMPONENTS OF A HEALTHY LIFESTYLE

Positive health and true well-being are achieved by finding a **balance** of the physical, social, emotional and intellectual aspects of our abilities and functioning in our lifestyle. It is easy to see that the absence of any one of these would contribute to ill-health. However, it is also important to realise that too much of any of these features of health may also be damaging to the individual. For example, individuals who spend every spare moment of their time in a gym may not develop their intellectual or social skills, and this will affect their overall well-being.

People also need to find a balance between activity and rest if they are to maintain a healthy lifestyle. Activity includes both work and recreation. Work may be paid or unpaid, professional, skilled, unskilled, or domestic (shopping, gardening, looking after children and the home). Recreation may include socialising and seeing friends, or physical exercise, or going to see a film. Rest includes both sleep and simple inactivity. Many people find it difficult to 'do nothing' but it is an important part of a healthy lifestyle though not if it is overdone!

DIET

The term **diet** refers to the type and amount of food regularly eaten and drunk. Eating a healthy, well-balanced and adequate diet on a daily basis is part of the process of achieving good personal health. A **balanced diet** is one which contains suitable amounts of each nutrient.

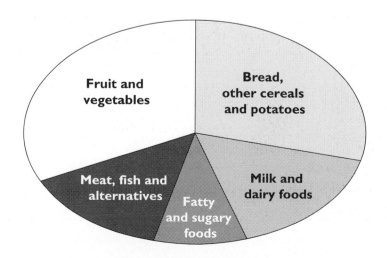

FIGURE 1.1: A well-balanced diet should include plenty of fruit, vegetables, bread, cereals, pasta and rice. Fatty and sugary foods, such as crisps, cakes and fizzy drinks should only be eaten occasionally in small quantities.

Nutrients are naturally occurring chemical substances found in different foods. They perform one or more of three functions.

1   They provide materials for building, repairing and maintaining body tissues.

2   They help to regulate body processes.

3   They serve as fuel to provide energy.

The food that we eat is composed of one or more of the following main nutrients:

- **carbohydrates**

- **fats**

- **proteins**

- **vitamins**

- **minerals.**

Fibre and water are also very important constituents of the food that we eat but are not counted as nutrients. **Dietary fibre** adds bulk to food and encourages the muscular movement (peristalsis) of food through the digestive system and intestines. Fibre is found in vegetables, fruit, wholemeal bread; pulses such as peas and beans; and in cereals such as oats, rice and bran. A lack of fibre in the diet can result in constipation and poor digestion of food.

Water is essential to life. About 80 per cent of the weight of a new-born child is made up of water. In adulthood water accounts for 75 per cent of body weight. Water is the main component of body cells and blood. It also helps to moisten and lubricate the lining of joints. Lack of water leads to dehydration and death.

Carbohydrates

Carbohydrates provide the body with energy. They are found in a large group of food stuffs which include sugars, starches and fibre. There are two main types of carbohydrate.

1   Foods containing sugar and sugar sources, such as jam, cakes and biscuits which provide the body with energy (in calories) but not with useful nutrients.

2 Starchy foods such as potatoes, rice and pasta which provide the body with a rich source of energy.

Fats

Fats also provide the body with energy but they have a much higher energy value than carbohydrates. There are two main types of fat.

1 **Saturated fats.** Animal fats are found in beef, lamb, pork, lard and dripping and in dairy products such as milk, butter and cheese.

Vegetable fats are present in foods such as coconut and palm oil and chocolate. It is important to limit the intake of these fats. Saturated fats contain a high level of **cholesterol**. This is the substance responsible for causing coronary heart disease. It causes the arteries to narrow and restricts the blood flow from the heart. In 1991 coronary heart disease was responsible for 174,358 deaths of people between the ages of 15–85 in England.

Saturated fats

2 **Unsaturated fats** are found in vegetable oils and products such as sunflower, corn or soya oils, special soft margarine, nuts, and oily fish such as herring. Included in these unsaturated fats are a special group called polyunsaturated fats or **polyunsaturates.** Unsaturated fats do not raise cholesterol in the same way as saturates. Our bodies need a small amount of polyunsaturated fats to help make and repair body cells.

Unsaturated fats

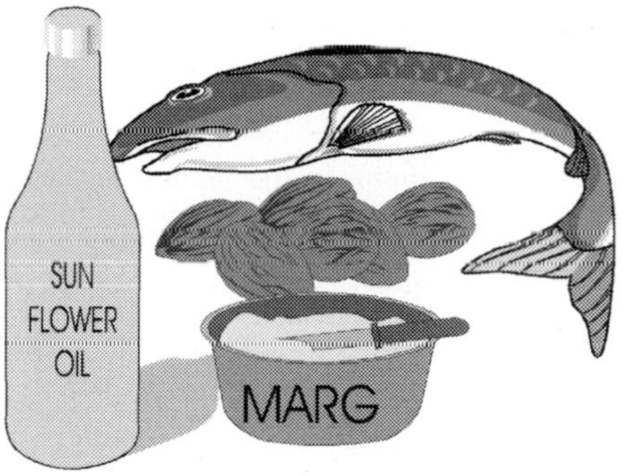

FIGURE 1.2: Examples of foods containing saturated and unsaturated fats

Proteins

Proteins provide the chemical substances needed to build and repair cells and tissues in the body. They are particularly important in childhood for building the brain, muscles, skin, blood and other tissues. Proteins are the building blocks of all the tissues in the body. They are made up of **amino acids.** An adult needs twenty-one different amino acids but the body can only make twelve of them itself. The other nine come from the food we eat. There are two kinds of protein.

1 **Animal protein** contains all nine essential amino acids. Sources of animal protein include lean meat, fish, egg-white, milk and cheese.

2 **Vegetable proteins** do not contain all the essential amino acids. Sources of vegetable protein include foods such as lentils, baked beans and soya beans. These contain a high level of essential amino acids. They are a good source of protein for those on vegetarian diets.

Vitamins

Vitamins help to regulate the chemical reactions that are continuously taking place in our bodies. They are found in most of the food that we eat. They are protective substances that combine with other chemicals to form **enzymes**. Enzymes cause chemical activities to take place. The body only requires a small quantity of each vitamin to keep it healthy and active. The human body cannot manufacture its own vitamins. A lack of any of them can result in deficiency diseases.

FIGURE 1.3: Vitamins and their effects

Name	Function	Sources	Deficiency effects
A	(Retinol) Prevents infection, keeps skin and bones healthy, helps with night vision.	Cheese, butter, oily fish, milk, carrots, spinach.	Inability to see in the dark. Dry, patchy skin. Unhealthy mucus membrane.
B1	(Thiamine) Needed for energy production in cells. Helps growth and repair of body tissues.	Milk, eggs, yeast products, nuts, liver, fish, beans, breakfast cereal.	Muscle weakness, skin problems, nervous disorders, beri-beri.
B12	Helps in the production of red blood cells. Helps growth.	As above.	As above.
C	(Ascorbic acid) Aids the healing of wounds and fractures. Keeps gums/teeth healthy. Protects against coughs and colds.	Fresh fruit and vegetables, especially citrus fruits.	Scurvy, slow healing of wounds and fractures.
D	Needed for strong bones and teeth. Aids the absorption of minerals.	Foods containing fat such as margarine, butter, oily fish and eggs.	Rickets in children, soft bones and muscle weakness in adults.
E	Needed to keep the skin supple and elastic.	Vegetable oils, wholemeal bread, rice, eggs, butter, green leaf vegetables.	Not yet known.
K	Needed to promote clotting of the blood when bleeding.	Liver, fresh green vegetables.	Bleeding under the skin. Blood slow to clot.

Minerals

Minerals are basic chemical **elements**, like calcium and iron which are found naturally in the soil and the air. Minerals are essential to life. They are needed to build and repair certain tissues and for control of body function. Some minerals, such as calcium, phosphorous, potassium, sodium and iron, are needed by the body in large quantities. Others, such as zinc and iodine, are needed in much smaller quantities. People get their mineral intake by:

- **eating vegetables which have absorbed minerals from the soil**

- **eating the meat of animals which have also eaten mineral-rich plants**

- **drinking water in which minerals are dissolved.**

Nearly all foods contain several minerals. The only ones in short supply are calcium, iron and fluoride.

Calcium is essential for strong bones and teeth, muscle contraction and maintenance of body fluids. Sources of calcium include milk, cheese, white bread, yoghurt, ice-cream, and green vegetables. A person who does not have enough calcium intake may develop weak bones.

Iron is essential for the production of haemoglobin in red blood cells. Sources of iron include red meat, egg yolk, green vegetables, liver, wholemeal bread, some breakfast cereals and potatoes. A person who does not have enough iron in their diet may develop anaemia.

Fluoride helps to produce strong healthy teeth. It has been added to the water supply in some parts of the United Kingdom and is an ingredient of toothpaste. A deficiency of fluoride can lead to mottling of the teeth and tooth decay.

☀ ACTIVITY

The diet record sheet opposite shows the weekend diet of the Riccio and Gregg families.

a Indicate which nutrients are contained in the foods eaten by the two families.

b Identify the effect of each nutrient on the body.

c How nutritional are the diets of each family?

d Do you think that they are balanced?

e Are there any deficiencies or excesses in their nutritional intakes?

Using examples from the record sheet write a paragraph explaining your views on these last three questions.

What advice would you give to the parents of Eva and Dean about the type of diet needed to promote healthy growth and development for their children?

Family	Day	Breakfast	Lunch	Snacks	Evening meal	Nutrients	Effect on body
Benito Riccio	1	Fried egg, toast, coffee	Ham roll, crisps, coffee	Doughnut, coffee	Pizza, salad, baked potatoes, orange juice, chocolate cake		
	2	Fried egg, bacon, toast, coffee	Meat pie, chips, can of soft drink	Cream cake	Meat lasagne, salad, orange juice, ice cream		
Maria Riccio	1	Boiled egg, toast, coffee	Crisps, coffee	Can of soft drink	Pizza, salad, baked potatoes, orange juice, chocolate cake		
	2	Toast, marmalade, coffee, orange juice	Ryvita and soft cheese	An orange	Meat lasagne, salad, orange juice, ice cream		
Eva (10) Riccio	1	Boiled egg, toast	Beef soup, bread	Chocolate bar	Pizza, salad, baked potatoes, orange juice, chocolate cake		
	2	Boiled egg, toast, can of soft drink	Meat pie and chips	Chocolate bar	Meat lasagne, salad, orange juice, ice cream		
Ronnie Gregg	1	Wholewheat cereal, coffee, whole milk	Chicken curry, rice, coffee	Chocolate bar	Fish fingers, chips, peas, coffee, apple pie, cream		
	2	Wholewheat cereal, coffee, whole milk	Cheese sandwiches, crisps	Nothing	Baked vegetables, baked potatoes, water, fruit salad		
Angela Gregg	1	Grapefruit and sugar, orange juice	Ham salad, boiled potatoes	Apple	Fish fingers, chips, peas, coffee, apple pie, cream		
	2	Grapefruit and sugar, orange juice	Low-fat yoghurt, apple	Apple	Baked vegetables, baked potatoes, water, fruit salad		
Dean (10) Gregg	1	Sugar-coated cereal, milk, sugar	Chips, beefburger, beans	Can of soft drink	Fish fingers, chips, peas, coffee, apple pie, cream		
	2	Sugar-coated cereal, milk, sugar	Beefburger, chips, beans	Can of soft drink	Baked vegetables, baked potatoes, water, fruit salad		

INDIVIDUAL NUTRITIONAL NEEDS

Individuals need food in sufficient quantities to survive. It is a basic and fundamental human need. A lack of nutritious food over a period of time can adversely affect health and physical performance. The amount of nutritious food needed varies from person to person. It is dependent upon:

- ✪ age

- ✪ gender

- ✪ body size

- ✪ height

- ✪ weight

- ✪ the physical and climatic conditions in which the person lives

- ✪ whether the person is living an active or a sedentary life.

For example:

- ✪ **Children need greater amounts of some nutrients than their size would indicate, because they are growing.**

- ✪ **Pregnant women need extra energy and increased amounts of certain nutrients to nourish themselves and their baby.**

- ✪ **In cold weather the body must have additional nutrients because it uses more energy to stay at the same temperature.**

- ✪ **Physical work or exercise requires more energy than resting.**

- ✪ **A man's body has a greater percentage of muscle tissue than a woman's. Men need more calories to keep their tissues healthy.**

Some groups of people have **special diets**. These require them to leave out or include specific food groups to meet their personal values or special physical needs.

- ✪ **Vegetarians do not eat meat or fish. Meat is a main source of protein for many people. Vegetarians can still obtain all their nutrients from a diet containing no meat. Their proteins can be obtained from cereals, beans, eggs and cheese.**

- ✪ **Vegans, who eat no animal products at all, can obtain all the essential nutrients provided their vegetable diet is varied.**

✪ **A pregnant or nursing mother should eat and drink sensibly, in order to provide adequate nutrition and fluids for herself and her child. This is necessary for the child's growth and development, to maintain the health of mother and baby, and to prepare the mother for labour and confinement.**

ACTIVITY

Plan a week's menu for each of the following people.

✪ **A woman in the first three months of pregnancy. You should include sources of all the necessary nutrients that make up a balanced diet.**

✪ **A toddler of 18 months to 2 years. Include breakfast, mid-morning snack, lunch, tea and supper.**

✪ **An elderly woman who has walking difficulties but who is able to move slowly around her home.**

✪ **A male teenager, aged 15, who is sports captain at school.**

EXERCISE

Physical activity contributes to good general health. To offer the most benefit, physical activity needs to be undertaken regularly. Exercise is one of the components of a healthy lifestyle. The type and level of exercise individuals do will depend on their age, gender, and other physical factors. Moderate exercise can be undertaken by older, and less physically mobile people, or by people with disabilities. More vigorous and energetic exercise will be undertaken by the person who is well and more physically able.

Exercise has many health benefits. It:

- ⊗ **is great fun and a good way of socialising**

- ⊗ **enables the individual to feel more energetic**

- ⊗ **helps relaxation and reduces or relieves stress**

- ⊗ **increases stamina for daily living**

- ⊗ **helps to control and maintain a healthy body weight**

- ⊗ **improves the ability of skeletal muscles to extract oxygen from the blood, reducing the demand for blood flow**

- ⊗ **reduces the risk of heart attacks**

- ⊗ **strengthens muscles, joints and bones**

- ⊗ **improves the staying power of muscles**

- ⊗ **helps the heart to work more efficiently**

- ⊗ **improves circulation and helps to reduce the risk of heart disease**

- ⊗ **increases suppleness and mobility as the body ages.**

FIGURE 1.4 Activities to improve health and fitness

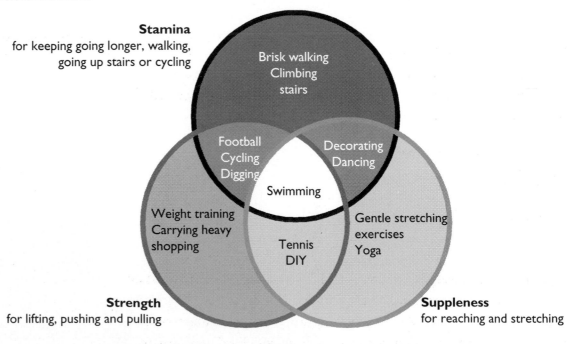

Stamina
for keeping going longer, walking,
going up stairs or cycling

Brisk walking
Climbing
stairs

Football
Cycling
Digging

Decorating
Dancing

Swimming

Weight training
Carrying heavy
shopping

Tennis
DIY

Gentle stretching
exercises
Yoga

Strength
for lifting, pushing and pulling

Suppleness
for reaching and stretching

Source: Health Education Authority, *Becoming More Active*, 1995

Activity	Stamina	Muscular/ strength	Suppleness flexibility	Coordination
Aerobics	*****	**	**	****
Badminton	***	***	****	*****
Bowls	*	**	***	***
Cricket	**	*****	**	****
Cycling*	*****	*****	**	****
Dancing	****	*****	****	*****
Fitness class	****	*****	****	****
Football	****	*****	****	****
Gardening	***	****	**	***
Golf	**	**	***	****
Hill walking	***	**	*	**
Horse riding	*	****	*	****
Jogging	****	****	**	**
Netball	***	****	****	*****
Rowing*	*****	*****	**	****
Running	*****	*****	**	**
Squash	****	****	****	*****
Stair climbing	****	***	*	**
Swimming*	*****	*****	*****	*****
Tennis	***	****	****	*****
Walking briskly	***	**	*	*
Weight training	**	*****	*	****
Yoga	*	**	*****	***

* no real effect
** beneficial effect
*** good effect
**** very good effect
***** excellent effect

* energetically

Source: Health Education Authority, *Becoming More Active*, 1995

FIGURE 1.5: The health benefits of a variety of exercise activities

Research evidence suggests that physical inactivity, or drastically reduced levels of activity, can lead to ill-health and disease. Physical inactivity is responsible for an increase in the risks of:

- **coronary heart disease**

- **stroke**

- **obesity.**

The Allied Dunbar National Fitness Survey (1995) identified several barriers which prevent people from taking more physical activity. They include insufficient time, dislike of sport and fear of injury. The survey found that an estimated 70 per cent or more of both men and women in all age groups were below the acceptable activity level necessary to keep them physically fit.

ACTIVITY

> **Elsie Stevens** is a 60-year-old woman. Recently retired from her job as a secretary, she has decided that she needs to get fit to make the most of her retirement. Elsie currently does no exercise. She is 1.68 metres tall and 12.7 kg overweight. In her youth Elsie was a keen swimmer and also enjoyed walking.

What types of exercise would you recommend for Elsie as a way of reducing her weight and getting fitter? Suggest three things that she could do, explaining how these particular choices would benefit her.

Plan a three-month exercise programme for Elsie based on the range of facilities available in your local area. Set out your programme in a table form.

Calculate the cost of your programme for Elsie. You should include any equipment costs, hire charges and admission charges but not travel costs. You should note that Elsie is eligible for pensioner rates.

REST AND SLEEP

People need to **rest** on a daily basis to maintain their health and well-being. Babies, young children, older people and pregnant women require a period of rest during the day. Most healthy adults and older children need rest only at the end of their active day. At nurseries and toddler groups it is routine for children to have a sleep to enable them to feel refreshed and relaxed for the afternoon activities. Some older people are less energetic and tend to feel tired more quickly than teenagers and younger adults.

There are two different kinds of sleep.

1 **Non-rapid eye movement sleep** occurs when a person first falls asleep. Activity decreases and the muscles are greatly but not completely relaxed. The heartbeat and breathing slow down and the eyelids remain quite still. The depth of sleep then increases.

2 **Rapid eye movement sleep** occurs when the person's eyes move jerkily under their closed lids. The heart and respiratory rates quicken and the muscles, particularly in the neck, are completely relaxed. This is the sleep in which dreaming occurs.

On going to bed drowsiness is followed by the first kind of sleep. After about 90 minutes the second type of sleep occurs.

Sleep patterns

Sleep patterns develop gradually. New-born babies sleep for brief periods throughout the day and night. By the age of three months they have learned to sleep through the night. By the age of six, most children will have given up daytime sleep. The amount of sleep required varies according to age. A 4–year-old child sleeps an average of ten to fourteen hours a day, and a 10–year-old about nine to twelve hours. Most adults sleep from seven to eight and a half hours every night. Others require as few as four or five hours or as many as ten hours each night. Most people find that they need slightly less sleep as they grow older. A person who slept eight hours a night at age thirty may need only seven hours at age sixty.

People deprived of sleep lose energy and become quick-tempered. After two days without sleep, lengthy concentration can become difficult. Through pure determination a person may perform tasks well for short periods but they will be easily distracted. Other adverse effects of sleep loss include:

- ✪ **making mistakes during routine tasks**

- ✪ **experiencing slips of attention**

- ✪ **dozing off for periods of a few seconds or more**

- ✪ **falling asleep completely**

- ✪ **having difficulty thinking, seeing and hearing clearly**

- ✪ **experiencing confusion.**

> **⚡ QUICK response**
>
> **At what age do you think a child should be allowed to decide his or her own bed-time?**

DRUG USE AND MISUSE

Drugs are chemical substances which affect the body's chemistry and functioning. They are widely used and available in the United Kingdom. They can be obtained by:

- ✪ **a doctor's prescription – medicinal drugs used for medical treatment**

- ✪ **purchasing them over the counter from a chemist – medicinal drugs or substances such as alcohol and tobacco which are used in social situations**

- ✪ **illegal purchase – controlled drugs or non-prescribed medicinal drugs.**

USING DRUGS FOR MEDICAL TREATMENT

Some of the medical profession's most valuable tools are the drugs that have been developed to treat specific illnesses and diseases. Many of these drugs can only be legally prescribed and used by doctors in medical situations. Other 'over-the-counter' drugs may be purchased without a doctor's permission.

MISUSE OF DRUGS INTENDED FOR MEDICAL TREATMENT

Any drug may cause harm if it is used improperly. As well as treating illness, some drugs produce physical and psychological **side-effects**. Some of these are very serious and can be life-threatening where the drug is misused. Certain drugs that are intended for specific medical use are frequently misused. These drugs may be obtained legally, on prescription, or illegally. They are shown in Figure 1.6.

Type of drug	Example	Effects/dangers
Barbiturates	Seconal	Normally used for severe sleeping problems or to stabilise epilepsy. Users can develop physical and mental dependence.
Tranquillisers/Benzodiazepines	Valium	Used to counteract anxiety. If used over a long period users can come to depend on them rather than on non-drug coping methods.
Anabolic steroids	Stanozolol	Abused by some athletes and bodybuilders. While they can increase muscle size in underweight/unwell people, they also stimulate aggression and can cause depression, jaundice and reproductive problems in men and women.
Amphetamines	Dexedrine	These drugs have very limited medical use. They are occasionally used to control hyperactivity in children and severe, chronic sleepiness in adults. They cause dependence and a range of physical and mental problems, including paranoia.
Opiates	Morphine	These drugs have a medical use as painkillers. Morphine may be abused because it gives the user a feeling of euphoria and mental well-being. It is very addictive. Overuse can cause nausea, breathing problems and vomiting.

Most of the drugs shown in Figure 1.6 can be obtained illegally. Taken over prolonged periods, it is easy to become psychologically dependent upon them. People who try to stop taking them may suffer very unpleasant side-effects and withdrawal symptoms.

FIGURE 1.6: Misuse of drugs intended for medical treatment

MISUSE OF ILLEGAL DRUGS

Non-prescription drugs are substances used to produce feelings of mental pleasure, stimulation and physical energy. These drugs have some short-term effects that users find pleasurable. However, their longer-term effects present major risks to users because of their damaging impact on physical health and on social, psychological and financial well-being.

The Misuse of Drugs Act (1971) bans the non-medical use of certain drugs, referred to as **controlled drugs**. The sale or possession of a controlled drug with intention to supply is a criminal offence and can result in very severe penalties.

FIGURE 1.7: Controlled drugs

Cannabis (dope, pot, hash, grass) is the most commonly used of the illegal drugs. It is a hard brown resinous material or herbal mixture. It causes users to feel more relaxed and talkative, reduces their ability to carry out complicated tasks and induces a sense of well-being with a heightened perception of music and colour.

Amphetamines (speed) are the most common illegal stimulant. They are usually found as a white or brown powder but can be in pill or capsule form. Amphetamines can be sniffed or injected and are addictive. They cause the user to experience disturbed sleep, loss of appetite, increased breathing and heart rate, a rise in blood pressure and sometimes feelings of acute anxiety and paranoia.

Magic mushrooms are hallucinogenic. They are a type of mushroom containing a substance similar to LSD. They grow wild in parts of the United Kingdom. It is not illegal to pick and eat them raw. The mushrooms contain the drug psilocybin, which causes an hallucinogenic effect. They give the user varying experiences, from visions of joy and beauty to over excitement after high doses. They may induce vomiting and severe stomach pains.

LSD (d-lysergic acid diethylamide) is another commonly used hallucinogen. It is a manufactured substance. Minute quantities of LSD are impregnated into small squares on blotting paper which are then dissolved on the tongue. These may induce distortion of vision and result in a feeling of being outside the body. 'Bad trips' can lead to depression, dizziness and panic attacks.

Ecstasy (methylenedioxymethamphetamine) is found as white, pink, or yellow tablets or as coloured capsules. Their effects can include a feeling of energy with heightened perception of colour and sound. They can also cause the user to feel hot and thirsty and lead them to consume dangerously large quantities of fluids.

Cocaine is a powerful stimulant with properties similar to those of amphetamines. It is a white powder made from the leaves of the Andean coca shrub. Sometimes users inject it but more often it is inhaled. Users experience feelings of mental exhilaration and well-being, an indifference to pain and illusions of physical and mental strength. Cocaine is highly addictive and induces dependence. Severe anxiety and panic are two of its side-effects.

MISUSE OF SOLVENTS

After alcohol and tobacco, solvents are the main drugs that young people are most likely to experiment with. Most solvents and the solutions they form are liquids, but there are some solutions of gases or solids. Solvents have many industrial and scientific applications. They are used in the production of cleaning fluids and in ink and paints. Solvent-based products that are available and which are misused are:

- **aerosol sprays (for example hair sprays or pain relieving spray)**

- **butane gas (used as cigarette lighter fuel)**

- **solvent-based glues**

- **dry-cleaning fluids**

- **paint and paint thinners**

- **correction fluids**

- **petrol.**

The Intoxicating Substances Supply Act (1985) makes it an offence to supply substances which the supplier knows, or has reasons to believe, will be used to achieve intoxication by a young person under the age of 18. The law, although mainly directed at shopkeepers, could be applied to anyone who sells or gives a young person a solvent-based product. Solvent misuse has a number of effects and dangers which are similar to those associated with alcohol.

- **Butane gas, sprayed in the mouth, cools the throat tissues causing swelling and perhaps suffocation.**

- **Some solvents contain poisonous substances such as lead.**

- **Solvents induce a feeling of recklessness, making the user less able to deal with danger.**

- **Solvents are flammable. There is an increased fire risk if the user is smoking.**

- **Hallucinations may be caused.**

- **Disorientation may increase the risk from hazards in dangerous environments, for example, railway lines.**

- **Long-term use can cause damage to liver, kidneys, lungs, bone marrow and nervous system.**

USING TOBACCO AND ALCOHOL

Tobacco and alcohol are widely available in the United Kingdom and are part of many people's lifestyle. Both tobacco and alcohol are drugs that can have negative effects on personal health. Because of the evidence linking the use of both these substances to ill health and disease, they can only legally be bought by adults. The use of tobacco is now less widespread and socially acceptable than it was twenty years ago.

TOBACCO

The smoking of tobacco, usually as cigarettes, is currently a major cause of ill-health, disease and death in the western world. It is a major cause of preventable disease and early death in the United Kingdom.

The health problems associated with using tobacco include:

- **coronary heart disease**
- **stroke**
- **high blood pressure**
- **bronchitis**
- **lung cancer.**

The harmful substances contained in tobacco and cigarette smoke affect the health of the person who is smoking and the health of non-smokers breathing in the smoke. These substances include nicotine, carbon monoxide and tar.

Nicotine
Nicotine is a powerful, fast acting and addictive drug. When smoked it is absorbed into the blood stream and its effects on the brain are felt seven to eight minutes later. The immediate effects of absorbing nicotine into the blood are:

- **increase in heart rate and therefore an increase in blood pressure**
- **increase in hormone production**

FIGURE 1.8: Percentage of cigarette smokers* in Great Britain, 1972–95

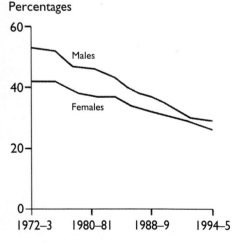

Percentages

* People aged 16 and over, except 1972 which is aged 15 and over
Source: *Social Trends 26*, 1996

- ☹ constriction of the small blood vessels under the skin

- ☹ changes in blood composition with possibility of formation of blood clots in the vessels

- ☹ changes in appetite, either an increase or a decrease.

Carbon monoxide

Carbon monoxide is a poisonous gas which is found in high concentrations in cigarette smoke. It combines readily with **haemoglobin**, the substance in the blood that carries oxygen. Because carbon monoxide combines more easily with haemoglobin than oxygen, the amount of oxygen carried to the lungs and tissues is reduced. A reduction in oxygen supply to the body affects the growth and repair of tissues, and the exchange of essential nutrients.

Carbon monoxide can also affect the activity of the heart. The changes in the blood that are associated with poor diet and smoking may cause fat deposits to form on the walls of the arteries. This can lead to hardening of the arteries and to circulatory problems.

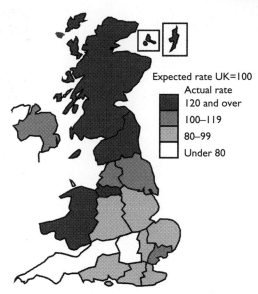

Expected rate UK=100
Actual rate
120 and over
100–119
80–99
Under 80

Source: *Social Trends 26*, 1996

FIGURE 1.9: Lung cancer: by region, 1989

Tar

Tar contains many substances known to cause cancer. It damages the **cilia**, the small hairs lining the lungs that help to protect them from dirt and infection. As a result, smokers are more susceptible to throat and chest infections. About 70 per cent of the tar in a cigarette is deposited in the lungs when cigarette smoke is inhaled.

Smoking during pregnancy

When women smoke during pregnancy, the ability of the blood to carry oxygen to all parts of their body is reduced. This affects the flow of blood to the **placenta** which feeds the foetus. Mothers who smoke are at risk of suffering spontaneous abortions. Babies born to women who smoke can be premature, underweight and are more prone to upper respiratory tract infections.

Passive smoking

Passive smoking means breathing in other people's cigarette smoke. This may be smoke from the burning end of the cigarette (side stream smoke) or smoke inhaled and exhaled by the smoker (mainstream smoke). As this smoke is not being filtered, it is worse than smoking

itself. Passive smoking can result in nose, throat, and eye irritation, headaches, dizziness and sickness. Conditions such as asthma and other allergies are usually made worse.

ALCOHOL

Alcohol is a socially accepted drug which is widely used in the United Kingdom. Research shows that 98 per cent of the adult population use alcohol. There is a huge industry involved in the production and sale of alcoholic drinks.

Sensible drinking in small quantities can be a pleasurable social experience. When consumed in large quantities, however, alcohol can have an adverse effect on personal health. Safe limits of alcohol consumption have been published by the Health Education Authority and are supported by health care professionals. The recommended limits are 28 units of alcohol for men and 21 units for women. Intake up to these limits should be spread throughout the week, with one or two drink-free days.

FIGURE 1.10: Consumption of alcohol above sensible levels, in Great Britian, 1994–5

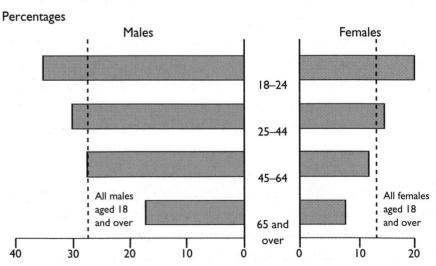

Note: Maximum sensible levels in 1994–5 were 21 units per week for a man and 14 for a woman.

Source: *Social Trends 26*, 1996

The effects of alcohol on the body

Alcohol is rapidly absorbed into the bloodstream. Nearly all the alcohol that a person drinks has to be burnt up by the liver. The rest is disposed of either in sweat or urine. The body gets rid of one unit of alcohol in one hour. The amount of alcohol that is concentrated in the body at any one time depends on:

- **how much a person drinks**

- **whether the stomach is empty or full**

- **the height, weight, age and sex of the drinker.**

Smaller or lighter than average people, younger or older people and people who are not used to drinking are more easily affected by alcohol.

Alcohol is a **depressant**. It reduces certain brain functions and affects judgement, self-control and coordination. It is because of this that many fights, injuries and accidents result from excessive use of alcohol.

SEXUAL BEHAVIOUR

Reproduction is an important reason for being sexually active. It is the only natural way in which humanity reproduces itself. Developing a sexual relationship with another person is also a way of expressing intimate feelings. Choosing to be sexually active involves taking some personal risks, for example, unwanted pregnancy. These risks can be minimised by taking certain precautions. The main risk to health that sexual activity presents is from sexually transmitted diseases.

There are at least thirty different types of sexually transmitted disease. They affect about one million men and women in the UK every year. Research shows that young people between the ages of 15 and 30 are most likely to be affected. Figure 1.11 summarises some of the different types of sexually transmitted diseases, their causes, symptoms, and treatment.

Disease	Symptoms	Cause	Treatment
Thrush (Candida albicans)	A thick, white discharge from the vagina, itching, swelling, soreness and pain around the vulva and on urination	Candida	Anti-fungal creams, pessaries or tablets inserted into the vagina
Genital warts	Small hard spots on the lips or inside of the vagina or around the anus. In men they may appear on the penis or scrotum	Virus transmitted through intimate physical contact	Ointments can be applied to infected areas or the warts may be removed by freezing, burning or surgery
Genital herpes	A burning sensation and pain in the infected area. Small red bumps develop into blisters or painful open sores on the penis or in the vagina and around the genitals	Herpes simplex virus transmitted through intimate contact	Drug treatment, either an ointment or tablets
Gonorrhoea	Pain or burning sensation when urinating. Also discharge from vagina or penis. Women may also have pain in the lower abdomen	A bacteria transmitted by intimate physical contact that grows rapidly in moist warm areas such as the cervix	Antibiotic drug treatment
Hepatitis B	Flu-like symptoms two to three months after contact with the infection. Jaundice later appears with yellow discolouration of skin and eyes	A virus in the blood or other body fluids transmitted by intimate physical contact	Bed rest, plenty of fluids. Vaccinations are recommended
Pubic lice	Itching in the pubic area. Lice eggs on the base of pubic hairs	Lice mites laying eggs and being transferred during close physical contact	Medicated lotions and shampoos
Syphilis	A painless sore on the penis, vulva, vagina, cervix, tongue or fingertips two to six weeks after contact with the infection	Bacteria transmitted during intimate physical contact	A course of penicillin treatment

FIGURE 1.11: Sexually transmitted diseases

Sexually transmitted diseases can affect both men and women heterosexuals or homosexuals. A person can become infected with a sexually transmitted disease after one act of unprotected sex with an infected person. The risk of contracting infection is not confined only to people with many sexual partners, although they do run a greater risk.

United Kingdom Thousands	1986	1991	1994
Males			
Wart virus	46	55	55
Non-specific urethritis	–	58	53
Chlamydia	–	19	19
Herpes	11	12	13
Candidiasis	13	11	11
Gonorrhoea	28	12	8
Syphylis	2	1	1
Trichomoniasis	1		
Females			
Wart virus	30	39	42
Non-specific urethritis	–	19	18
Chlamydia	–	22	21
Herpes	9	12	16
Candidiasis	56	54	60
Gonorrhoea	18	8	4
Syphylis	1	–	1
Trichomoniasis	14	6	5

Source: *Social Trends 26*, 1996

FIGURE 1.12 New cases seen at sexually transmitted diseases clinics in the UK, 1986–94

HIV AND AIDS

The newest and most challenging sexually transmitted disease is the Human Immune-deficiency Virus (HIV). This is the virus which causes Acquired Immune Deficiency Syndrome (AIDS). The virus, a simple living organism, gets into the blood stream and attacks and destroys the body's natural defence mechanisms. HIV can be transmitted through three different routes.

1 **Unprotected sex** involving penetration (anal or vaginal) and the release of infected semen or vaginal secretions into the body. People who do not use condoms and spermicides during sex run a higher risk of catching the virus through this route.

2 **Infected blood** can enter the body through a cut or other wound. People who inject drugs and use unclean needles and syringes run a high risk of catching the virus through this route.

3 **During pregnancy**, before, during or after birth, an infected mother can pass on the virus to her baby through breast milk or blood.

Many people who have HIV (are HIV positive) have no symptoms of illness and live healthy lives for many years. Some have never developed AIDS and continue to be healthy. Others may present symptoms of illnesses and be unwell due to the virus. By the end of June 1995 a total of 11,051 cases of AIDS had been reported in the UK and there were 7,571 related deaths (Figure 1.13). A total of 24,453 people were reported to have been infected by the HIV-1 virus at the end of June 1995 in the UK.

| | AIDS | | | | Reports of HIV-1 infected persons | |
| | Cases | | Related deaths | | | |
	Males	Females	Males	Females	Males	Females
Probable HIV exposure category						
Sexual intercourse						
Between men	8,101		5,725		15,001	
Between men and women	782	627	433	333	2,000	2,280
Injecting drug use (IDU)	449	202	292	118	1,885	859
Blood						
Blood factor	493	6	424	5	1,218	11
(e.g. haemophilia)						
Blood/tissue transfer	39	71	26	48	77	85
(e.g. blood transfusion)						
Mother to child	81	82	42	40	152	149
Other/undetermined	100	18	76	9	621	115
All categories	10,045	1,006	7,018	553	20,954	3,499

Source: *Social Trends 26*, 1996

FIGURE 1.13: AIDS cases and related deaths and reports of HIV-1 infected persons in the UK to end June 1995

The following measures can be taken to reduce the risk of contracting HIV in the care workplace.

- ✪ **Practise good basic hygiene, regularly washing your hands.**

- ✪ **Cover all existing wounds or skin lesions with waterproof dressing when in contact with body fluids or bleeding wounds.**

- ✪ **Avoid contamination of clothing by using protective garments, such as aprons.**

- ✪ **Follow approved procedures for sterilisation and disinfection of instruments and equipment.**

- ✪ **Follow correct procedures for the safe disposal of contaminated waste.**

- ✪ **Avoid using sharp instruments wherever possible.**

- ✪ **Follow safe procedures for handling and disposal of needles and other sharps.**

- ✪ **Clear up all spillages of blood and other body fluids promptly and disinfect surfaces thoroughly.**

ACTIVITY

Most of us are aware that certain behaviours pose health risks. For example, there are well-known risks associated with drinking too much alcohol and smoking. People still do these things despite knowing that their behaviour goes against current health advice.

Why don't people:

- ✪ **take enough exercise?**

- ✪ **eat a balanced diet?**

- ✪ **avoid using potentially harmful substances (drugs, alcohol, tobacco) to excess?**

- ✪ **engage in safe sexual practices?**

Discuss your ideas about each of these in a small group.

Produce spidergrams like the one below to show what you came up with.

?
? ?
? **Why don't people take enough exercise?** ?
? ?
?

HEALTH AND HYGIENE

PERSONAL HYGIENE

Good personal hygiene is a basic element of health and well-being. The main purpose of washing and cleaning regularly is to control the growth of bacteria, fungi and viruses that can cause illness and disease. The body provides the necessary conditions for the growth of bacteria and fungi. These are:

- ✪ **moisture from sweat**

- ✪ **warmth from body heat**

- ✪ **food from the dead cells and waste products in sweat.**

Washing and cleaning the body on a daily basis is essential to achieve good hygiene standards. The areas of the body that most need cleaning are those where sweat is excreted. These are under the arms, the groin area, the feet and the scalp and hair.

DENTAL CARE AND HYGIENE

Daily dental care is an important part of personal cleanliness. Brushing the teeth properly and using dental floss keep the teeth clean, help to prevent decay and gum disease.

Tooth decay begins with small holes, **cavities**, which appear in the enamel. The cavities are caused by bacteria on the tooth surface. Certain bacteria are naturally present in the mouth to act on the food we eat. In breaking down the food the bacteria produce an acid. This acid attacks the enamel on the teeth causing it to dissolve away in patches, forming cavities. The cavities reduce the distance between the outside of the tooth and the nerve endings. The acids produced by the bacteria irritate the nerve endings and cause toothache.

The best way to prevent tooth decay is to avoid eating sugar. The large amount of refined sugar in western diets causes a high level of tooth decay. Brushing with a fluoride toothpaste helps to increase the resistance of the enamel to bacterial acids. Regular visits to the dentist will ensure adequate dental care.

SKIN CARE AND HYGIENE

The skin forms a protective barrier for the body against bacteria and other chemicals. Waste products are excreted through the skin. Glands in the skin release sweat containing waste products when the body becomes too hot. Harmful organisms may invade the body through areas where the skin has been broken. Others remain on the surface of the skin and dirt and debris accumulates in large quantities.

A daily bath or shower keeps the body free from dirt and odour. It also helps to prevent the skin infections that may develop if bacteria are allowed to grow and multiply on the skin.

HAIR CARE AND HYGIENE

Hair is protected from damage by a substance called **sebum**. This is the greasy substance that occurs naturally in everyone's hair. When we comb our hair the sebum is spread through it. Washing the hair also removes the sebum. While hair must be washed and dressed regularly to remove dirt and the bacteria that use the sebum as food, a balance must be found between washing and combing the sebum through the hair.

 ACTIVITY

Sandra Davis is a single mother of three children. She has just got a job and needs to arrange child care for the time that she will be at work. You are one of three people who have answered her advert for a childminder for Dion, aged 3, Sonia, aged 6, and Jay, aged 9. In the interview she has explained the arrangements. They would arrive at your house at about 8.30 am. Sandra would pick them up again after work at 4 pm Sandra's next question is: 'What will you do to ensure that each of my children maintains good personal hygiene throughout the day?'

Write an answer explaining what you think the priorities are and indicate what you would do to set and maintain standards of good hygiene practice for each child.

PUBLIC HYGIENE

The term **public health** refers to all the actions taken to maintain and improve the general health of a community. The local authority environmental health department ensures that standards of hygiene are maintained in places such as restaurants, pubs and hairdressing salons.

Food preparation

Cleanliness of the kitchen and kitchen equipment is vital for safe food preparation. The area where food is prepared should be cleaned at regular intervals to reduce the amount of dirt brought in. Refrigerators, ovens, floors and other equipment used in direct handling of food must receive thorough and regular cleaning.

Strict guidelines for food preparation and storage are enforced by local authority environmental health officers. General cleanliness of the entire building, and the adequate provision of washing and food storage facilities are important to prevent food-borne illnesses and diseases. To ensure the reduction of risk and to minimise contamination of food, the following measures should be observed.

- ✪ **Wash hands before and after the preparation of food.**

- ✪ **Follow the storage guidelines on the package.**

- ✪ **Quickly cool and refrigerate left-over food.**

- ✪ **Allow food removed from a refrigerator to thaw out to room temperature.**

- ✪ **Store meats in the bottom of the refrigerator.**

- ✪ **Cover or tie back hair.**

- ✪ **Keep cuts and wounds covered.**

- ✪ **Avoid food preparation if you are suffering from any type of infection or infectious disease.**

- ✪ **Clean surfaces on which food is prepared after use.**

- ✪ **Use a separate preparation board for poultry products.**

⚙ ACTIVITY

Dave's Downtown Diner is a popular meeting and eating place with students from a local college. Dave employs a number of students who work part-time in the kitchen and serve customers. The diner sells mostly fast food like burgers, pizza, sandwiches, tea and coffee and soft drinks. All are prepared in the diner's kitchen. There are twenty tables, each with a quick turnover of student customers. As part of Dave's drive to offer a quality service hygiene has become a priority. He would like a set of written guidelines that he could give to his staff to prompt them to maintain good standards.

Produce a set of hygiene guidelines for staff working at Dave's. They should be easy to follow and should cover the do's and don'ts of good practice about:

- ✪ food preparation and handling
- ✪ personal cleanliness
- ✪ environmental cleanliness.

HYGIENE IN CARE SETTINGS

Health workers who care directly for patients in various settings must take precautions, and observe recommended basic hygiene practices, to counter the risk of infection. Nurses, doctors and other health workers in accident and emergency departments and those involved in surgical, gynaecological and obstetrics procedures must take all precautions to avoid risks of infection because they are likely to come into contact with body fluids and open wounds.

In care settings health workers can protect themselves and their clients from the risks of infection by:

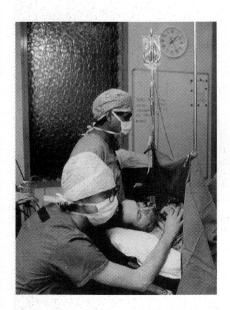

- ⊗ washing their hands after using the toilet or helping another person to do so, when changing beds or touching used bed linen, and before eating or preparing a meal for themselves or others

- ⊗ wearing disposable gloves, aprons and other protective clothing when dealing with body fluids and wounds

- ⊗ putting used linen and clothes in the correct bags to protect laundry workers

- ⊗ using the correct bags and bins to dipose of waste; dressings and other clinical waste should always be put in bags that will be incinerated

- ⊗ reporting broken equipment, spillages and pest infestations immediately

- ⊗ always following hygiene rules when storing and preparing food

- ⊗ reporting outbreaks of illness from infection immediately.

📖 📖 📖 PORTFOLIO ASSIGNMENT 📖 📖 📖

WHAT IS A HEALTHY LIFE?

INTRODUCTION

This assignment gives you the opportunity to interview an individual about his or her lifestyle and ideas about health. As it is quite a personal topic you should approach your volunteer sensitively and be careful about how you use and present the information that he or she reveals to you.

Task 1

Identify a volunteer who is willing to talk to you about his or her health behaviour. Explain to the person that your questions will be on topics such as diet, exercise and recreational behaviour.

Task 2

Compile a questionnaire for your volunteer to fill in. The areas that you need to cover include:

- exercise

- diet (adequate, balanced)

- rest and relaxation

- tobacco and alcohol use

- sexual behaviour.

You should ask your volunteer about his or her attitudes and actual behaviour. Your questionnaire should produce a picture of the person's lifestyle.

Task 3

Write a review of your findings which:

- Describe the person's health behaviour. What is the person's diet made up of? What exercise does he or she take? Does the person smoke or drink? If so how much? How does the person use his or her leisure time?

- Explain the risks and benefits associated with the person's different health behaviours. In what ways is your volunteer living a healthy life? Are there areas that are not so healthy?

- Explain why a balanced lifestyle is important for the person.

PORTFOLIO ASSIGNMENT

USE AND MISUSE OF DRUGS AND OTHER SUBSTANCES

INTRODUCTION

This assignment gives you the opportunity to describe the use and effects of drugs and other substances.

Task 1

Most high streets have a pharmacy, or chemist shop that sells drugs intended for use as medical treatment. Some of these drugs are available 'over-the-counter' while others require a doctor's prescription . Find out about five drugs in each of these two categories and produce a table like the one below, outlining your findings.

Name of drug	Main intended use of drug	Effects on user

Task 2

Medicinal drugs are prescribed for specific uses and should only be used in the way that the doctor prescribing them says. There are a number of dangers involved in misusing these drugs. Identify some of the ways people misuse prescribed drugs and the possible consequences. Present your findings in the form of a poster warning people about the dangers of misuse.

Task 3

There are some categories and compounds of drugs that have no accepted use in medical treatment. Many of these are available as 'street drugs' and are bought and used illegally for leisure purposes or because the user has become addicted to them. Find out about five of these drugs and produce another table like the one above, outlining your findings. You should use the accepted generic name of the drug (for example, amphetamine) as well as any nickname that it is known by (for example, speed). You should refer to the possible effects that the drugs have on physical, social, emotional and intellectual life.

PRESENT ADVICE ON HEALTH AND WELL-BEING TO OTHERS

LEADING A HEALTHY LIFE

In the first part of this chapter we examined a number of health issues. We looked at the benefits and risks to health associated with modern lifestyles. Your understanding of the need to maximise the benefits and minimise the risks in your lifestyle choices will help you to make an assessment of the health and well-being of your own health.

Some of the aspects of your lifestyle that affect your personal health include :

- ✪ **exercise habits**

- ✪ **dietary intake**

- ✪ **smoking habits**

- ✪ **rest/sleep patterns**

- ✪ **relaxation/leisure patterns**

- ✪ **alcohol intake**

- ✪ **sexual behaviour.**

It is possible for everyone to assess their own health and to develop a personal plan to improve on important aspects of health. We are now going to work through the way this can be done.

PERSONAL HEALTH ASSESSMENT

The state of a person's health can be assessed by **measuring** and **recording** some of their physical characteristics and patterns of behaviour. These individual measurements are then compared against a **standard scale**.

Personal characteristics that are often measured and compared include height, weight and indicators of physical condition such as pulse rate and blood pressure.

Certain health behaviour patterns can also be recorded for the same reason. These include dietary intake, amount of exercise taken and alcohol and tobacco use. Personal habits and patterns of behaviour can again be compared against tables and scales of recommended intake, to assess the extent to which they are healthy.

When assessing an individual's health it is necessary to take age, gender, sex, social class and ability/disability into consideration. As no two people are ever exactly alike, these measures should only be used as a guide to health status.

FIGURE 1.14: A height/weight chart

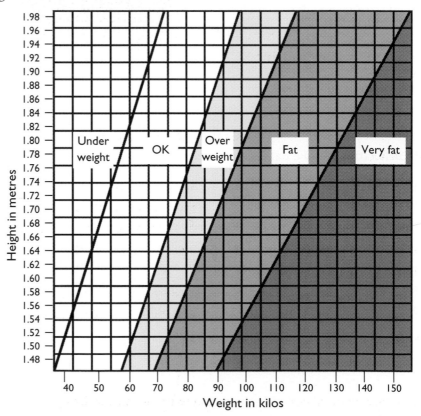

PRESENTING HEALTH ADVICE TO OTHERS

Health promotion is a growing area of health care work. Most of the health promotion that is carried out is done by government health promotion agencies. They use different media, such as newspapers, pictures, television and radio to put health messages across. You have probably seen evidence of many different health promotion campaigns in newspapers and magazines, on television or in booklets and posters. You may have come across them at your local leisure centre, sports ground, health centre, library, shopping centre, health food shop, school, college, home for the elderly, nursery, or youth club. You may have felt that some of these campaigns were aimed at people of your age-group or background.

Name ——————— Date ———————

TARGETING HEALTH PROMOTION ADVICE AND INFORMATION

Health promotion campaigns target specific groups in the population as well as the general public. The groups in the community which need specific advice on health topics are known as **target groups**. The health promotion message and the methods used to put it across must appeal to the group to whom it is targeted.

There are many areas of health promotion which may be suitable to a specific groups needs. These might include:

- ✪ **how to lose weight safely and quickly**

- ✪ **information about how to use the local health services**

- how to lead an active life after disability

- cutting down on salt, or increasing fibre, intake

- keeping warm in winter

- preparation for retirement

- the benefits of exercise

- maintaining personal hygiene

- preventing dental problems

- getting the best out of sport and leisure facilities

- how to maintain desired weight in pregnancy.

ACTIVITY

Choose any one of the following topics around which to develop a health message targeted at children.

- Dental health.

- Balanced diet.

- Smoking.

- Exercise.

- Personal safety.

Identify a goal that would promote good health and well-being in a group of children aged 7 to 9.

What methods could be used to get this message across to children of this age?

PRODUCING HEALTH PROMOTION ADVICE

Careful planning and preparation are essential for successful health promotion. Once a health promotion topic has been identified, the promotion team needs to:

- identify the key aims (what you want to do) and objectives (what you want to achieve) of the campaign

- decide the best way of putting the health message across

- identify all of the resources needed to deliver the health promotion message

- decide how the effectiveness of the campaign will be evaluated (judged).

When planning a health promotion campaign for a specific target group, the reasons for the campaign must be clearly identified from the outset. Reasons could be:

- to provide advice and support

- to supply information

- to help people to change or modify health-related behaviour.

ACTIVITY

Advertisements and promotional campaigns try to put across a distinctive message. They do this in subtle ways and in very strong, obvious ways. They try to persuade the person who is reading or watching the message to either do something or to think something.

- Make a list of the features you believe are important in making persuasive communications like adverts and health campaigns effective.

- What is your favourite advertisement/health campaign? Identify the features you like and which make it memorable.

- Design a poster that aims to influence the reader's behaviour toward something that you consider to be a risk to health. Try to incorporate all the features that you believe are important and which attract you to your favourite advert/campaign.

CHOOSING A PRESENTATION FORMAT

Once a health promotion team has completed the above process, they will undertake some research and investigation into the topic. The health promotion campaign will be more effective if it is well prepared. Some of the possible sources of information that might be used include:

- **your local health promotion unit**

- **leaflets, posters, charts, booklets, books**

- **GP surgeries and health centres**

- **the special educational needs coordinator at your school or college**

- **cuttings of newspaper articles.**

Health promotion can be delivered in various ways. Methods that have been used include:

- **poster campaigns**

- **talks and lectures**

- **information films and videos**

- **booklets and leaflets**

- **games and role plays.**

The health promotion team will need to choose the delivery method that will be most effective in reaching its target group.

ASSESSING THE IMPACT OF HEALTH PROMOTION ADVICE

There are various ways of assessing how health promotion advice has been received and understood. The key is to gain feedback from the target audience on the effectiveness of the presentation. By acting on the feedback received health promoters will be able to improve subsequent campaigns.

The impact of, say, a health promotion session can be assessed by verbal methods, such as asking questions at the end of the presentation to check understanding. It can also be assessed by written methods, such as questionnaires designed to find out the target group's views on the topic and the presentation.

Questionnaire

Evaluation of a health promotion session on: _____

Please can you complete the following questionnaire to help in the assessment of the impact of this session and the design of further sessions. Tick the appropriate box .

1 I found the session   very useful   ☐

                       useful   ☐

                       not useful   ☐

2 The most valuable part was:

_____

3 The least valuable part was:

_____

4. The session was   too long   ☐

                  too short   ☐

                  just right   ☐

5 The session added to my existing knowledge.   Yes   ☐

                                                No   ☐

6 The session will affect my behaviour.   Yes   ☐

                                                No   ☐

7 I will act on the advice.   Yes   ☐

                                                No   ☐

8 If you had to change any part of the session which would you change, how and why?

_____

_____

9 Any comments.

_____

_____

Thank you for completing this evaluation form.

PORTFOLIO ASSIGNMENT

DEVELOPING PLANS FOR IMPROVING HEALTH

INTRODUCTION

This assignment gives you the opportunity to look at your own health compared to standard measures and to develop a plan to improve your health in a more informed way.

TASK 1

Collect information about yourself and your lifestyle to use as the basis for your health assessment. Carry out and record the following measures.

Physical measures	Lifestyle measures
Your height (no shoes)	Average number of hours of sleep per night
Your weight (no shoes)	Average number of units of alcohol per week
Your blood pressure (if possible)	Average number of hours watching TV per week
Your pulse rate before exercise	Average number of minutes of exercise per week
	The number of cigarettes you smoke per week

Design your own record sheet to note the results.

TASK 2

Make a record sheet with headings like those shown below. On it record your dietary intake. Record all of the food and drinks that you take over a three-day period. Remember to record the snacks that you have as well as meals.

Day	What did I eat?	What nutrients did it contain?	How many calories are there in it?

TASK 3

Find out how your results compare to those recommended for someone of your age and physical characteristics. Write a short report to indicate:

- which of your measures are outside the limits recommended

- which of your measures match the recommendations

- which aspects of your health you feel that you need to improve.

PORTFOLIO ASSIGNMENT

TASK 4

Use the information from your health assessment to make a three-month plan of health improvement. Produce a written personal health plan which covers the following points.

- What your priorities for action are.

- Your short-term targets to achieve over the next two weeks.

- Your medium-term targets to achieve over the next three months.

- The ways you are going to try to achieve your targets.

- How you will reassess your health status during the three months.

One way of doing this is to present the information as a table like the one below.

Target	Priority	Methods	Assessment method
Improve diet	Increase vitamin C intake	Eat more fruit and vegetables daily	Record in diary – compare month 1 and 3 amounts

PORTFOLIO ASSIGNMENT

HEALTH PROMOTION

INTRODUCTION
This assignment gives you the opportunity to plan and present a health promotion campaign targeted at a specific group.

TASK 1
Form a health promotion team of four to six people. The team will work together to plan, produce and present a health promotion campaign. You will have to arrange and take part in team meetings to ensure that the work is co-ordinated and that you think things through together. You may like to elect a chairperson and notetaker for each meeting, or perhaps keep the same one for the whole time the group is together. It will be easier and more productive to work with roles that you have agreed before your meetings.

TASK 2
In your group think about the potential topics and groups that you could develop a health promotion campaign around. Your campaign will be called Keeping Well and Feeling Fit. Your topic could be an aspect of diet, exercise, recreation or relaxation. Keep minutes of the meeting and notes about any ideas and decisions. You should decide on a target group and a topic by the end of this meeting.

TASK 3
As a group, list and discuss the different forms of presentation format that can be used to get a health promotion message across. A live presentation, a poster-based display, a video or a booklet are all potential methods that you could use to get your message across. Discuss the pros and cons of each for your topic and target group. Make notes on these. Again keep minutes of the meeting's ideas and decisions. You should decide on a health message and two presentation formats that you will use by the end of this meeting.

TASK 4
As a group carry out all of the activities necessary to produce a health promotion campaign for your target group. This will involve researching, finding, collecting, developing and producing materials to get your message across. You will have to agree who will do what within the group, set deadlines and arrange additional meetings as you need to. Remember to keep notes about what you are doing and how it is going. These can be used in your portfolio.

TASK 5
In your group, think of a way of assessing the impact of your campaign on members of the target group. Present your health promotion campaign, Keeping Well and Feeling Fit to your target group. Everybody in the group should play a part in doing this. Collect your assessment information together and write it up in your evaluation.

TASK 6
If you were to present the same message to the other target groups referred to in the range how would you need to adapt and change your presentation to get the message across? Briefly describe and explain the changes that you would make.

REDUCE RISK OF INJURY AND DEAL WITH EMERGENCIES

HAZARDS, RISKS AND HEALTH EMERGENCIES

Accidents happen every day, in the home and garden, on the roads, in people's workplaces and in the places where people go for fun and recreation. They result in injury, disability and death, and affect people of all ages. The every-day environment is a potentially dangerous place. However, many accidents can be prevented, and injuries reduced, if the environment is made safer and people made aware of the hazards and risks that they face in different situations.

Risks and **hazards** are different concepts. A hazard is anything that is considered a danger to health, safety and life. For example, the following present hazards to certain people in the situations mentioned.

- **Obstructions or potholes in unlit streets.**

- **Unprotected derelict buildings and buildings sites.**

- **Walking or playing by the local canal.**

- **Open-air swimming pools and uncovered garden ponds.**

- **Unattended railway crossings.**

- **Kitchen knives and electrical equipment left around the home.**

- **Crowded, noisy school playgrounds.**

- **Chemicals, such as bleach or detergents, kept in unlocked cupboards.**

A risk is the possibility of meeting danger or suffering harm if a person does something when faced by a hazard, or fails to do something to minimise the danger from the hazard. Hazards may carry different levels of risks to different people. For example, a young child who is unable to swim and who does not understand the dangers of deep water is at high risk when playing alone by the local canal. The local canal is still a hazard, but presents fewer risks, to an adult who is able to swim and who knows about the dangers associated with falling into deep water.

ACTIVITY

Look again at the list of hazardous situations above.
Identify one person who would be at high risk and another who would be at low risk in each situation, explaining why the risk would vary.

MAKING DECISIONS ABOUT RISK

In every-day situations people have to take calculated risks. For example, in certain forms of sport, such as boxing, rugby or skiing athletes may risk injury to achieve their best performance. Similarly, a frail elderly person at home may risk falling downstairs to reach the kitchen to prepare a meal or simply because he or she wants to stay at home to retain personal independence.

In care settings workers need to try to balance risks against benefits. Something that may be hazardous may also have health benefits if dealt with safely. For example, medicines are potentially very dangerous if they are not administered and stored correctly. They are also potentially very beneficial when they are used correctly.

IDENTIFYING HAZARDS AND REDUCING RISKS IN EVERY-DAY SITUATIONS

A great number of the injuries that occur each day are caused by hazardous conditions in the home. People are most familiar with their home environment but also overlook the hazards that exist there. People are also at risk of injury from the hazards that exist in other every-day situations. Many of the accidents and incidents that cause injury are avoidable. By identifying and understanding hazards and taking basic precautions, the risks that they present can be reduced. When the risks associated with a hazard are reduced, accidents are less likely to happen.

The following activity gives you the opportunity to identify the hazards in your everyday environment, to say who is at risk from the dangers these hazards pose and to explain how the hazards can be reduced.

ACTIVITY

Complete the following table by giving examples of the hazards
and risks associated with the common aspects of each setting.

Setting	What are the hazards?	In what way(s) are they potentially harmful?	To whom are they a risk?
In the home and garden from: appliances/tools dangerous substances electrical equipment poisonous plants loose-fitting carpets rubbish			
On the road as a: pedestrian cyclist driver passenger			
In social settings as a: sports person worker (for example from floors, chemicals, passive smoking, lifting)			
In the local environment from: pollution playgrounds rivers and canals			

Those at higher risk are babies which have just begun to crawl,
toddlers, older people and those with special needs such the
partially sighted, or the hearing impaired.

The idea of safety should be given priority in all care work, but
particularly when caring for children, older people and others
who may not be able to judge risks to themselves or who are
less able to notice or deal with danger.

PATTERNS OF ACCIDENTS RESULTING IN INJURIES AND DEATH

Figure 1.16 shows the recorded pattern of accidents that resulted in injuries and death between 1986 and 1994. Figure 1.17 shows the death rates for accidents involving people under 15, people aged 15–24, and those aged 65 and over in England. It also shows the accident reduction targets set by the government for the year 2005.

FIGURE 1.16: Car driver casualties in the UK

	Percentages		
	1986	1991	1994
Males			
17–21	23	22	18
22–39	45	46	47
40–59	22	22	23
50 and over	11	11	11
All males (000s)	61.1	66.4	70.1
Females			
17–21	20	20	16
22–39	40	50	53
40–59	24	24	25
50 and over	7	6	7
All females (000s)	32.5	45.5	54.7

Source: *Social Trends 26, 1996*

a

All persons under 15

FIGURE 1.17: Death rates for accidents, England, 1970–90

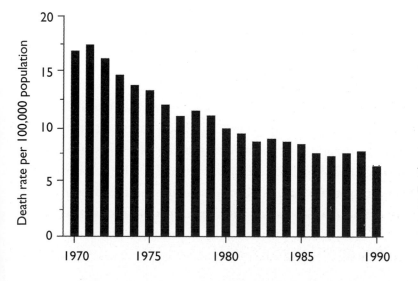

Target for 2005: 33% minimum reduction from 1990 rate

b

All persons aged 15–24

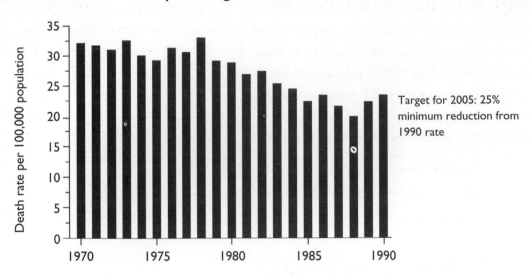

Target for 2005: 25% minimum reduction from 1990 rate

c

All persons aged 65 and over

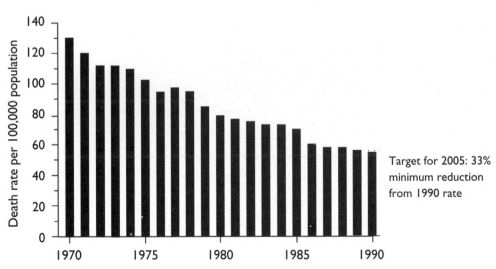

Target for 2005: 33% minimum reduction from 1990 rate

Source: *Health of the Nation*

There are many situations in which people can reduce the risk of injury from accidents. The government has developed national targets for the reduction of death and injury from accidents as part of its effort to improve the general health of the population of the United Kingdom. Its proposed targets for accidents are outlined in a document available from many clinics, health centres and health promotion units called *Health of the Nation*. The targets for accidents in *Health of the Nation* are set out below.

A reduction in the death rate for accidents among children aged under 15 by at least 33 per cent by 2005. This means reducing the death rate from 6.7 people per 100,000 of the population in 1990 to no more than 4.5 people per 100,000 by 2005.

A reduction in the death rate for accidents among young people aged 15–24 by at least 25 per cent by 2005. This means reducing the death rate from 23.2 people per 100,000 of the population in 1990 to no more than 17.4 people per 100,000 by 2005.

A reduction in the death rate for accidents among people aged 65 and over by at least 33 per cent by 2005. This means reducing the death rate from 56.7 per 100,000 of the population in 1990 to no more than 38 people per 100,000 by 2005.

 ACTIVITY

You are a care assistant working in a residential home for the elderly. Decorators are about to start work painting the clients' bedrooms and refurbishing the kitchen. All of the ten residents are over the age of 65. Several of them have mobility problems and use electric wheelchairs to get around. Others are confused and tend to wander and pick up objects that they find. Most have poor eyesight and slower reactions than younger people.

Produce a list of guidelines for the decorators. They should highlight the potential hazards that their work may present to the residents and give advice on how to reduce the risk of accidents resulting from their tools, materials, behaviour and general activity.

Produce your guidelines in the form of an easy-to-read sheet like that suggested below.

What is the potential hazard?	What can be done to reduce the risk of accidents?

RESPONDING TO EMERGENCY SITUATIONS

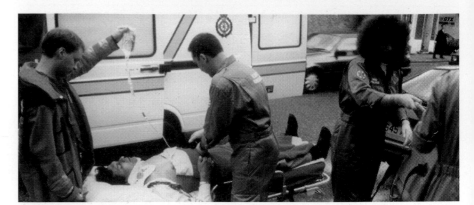

Health emergencies occur unexpectedly and may present major and life-threatening injuries and problems. The scene of a health emergency could be your home, school or college, a local street or your place of work. If you are at the scene of a health emergency you may be called on to help. You will be more capable of helping and coping if you know something about the role and responsibilities of a first-aider.

ROLES AND RESPONSIBILITIES IN HEALTH EMERGENCIES

To be an effective helper in an emergency situation a person must be able to:

- **assess the emergency**

- **maintain their own safety**

- **make contact with the emergency services**

- **give accurate and useful information to the emergency services**

- **support the casualty physically and emotionally**

- **appreciate their own limitations**

- **know when to intervene and when to wait for more skilled help to arrive.**

There are a huge number of possible emergency situations in which a casualty may require first aid. While each situation varies, the aims of the first-aider are always the same. These are defined by first-aid organisations such as the St John Ambulance Association and the British Red Cross, as:

- ⊗ **To preserve life.**

- ⊗ **To prevent deterioration of a casualty's condition.**

- ⊗ **To promote recovery.**

Each emergency situation is unique. Competent first-aiders are able to respond to the wide variety of situations that might confront them because they follow a standard emergency procedure.

STAGES OF RESPONDING TO EMERGENCIES

Emergency situations can be frightening and stressful for bystanders and people who arrive at the scene to offer help. By following a standard procedure the first-aider can act quickly and effectively, despite the stress and anxiety they may experience. There are four basic stages to an effective emergency response.

1 Assessing the emergency situation.

2 Making the area safe.

3 Assessing the casualty's condition.

4 Getting help from the emergency services.

ASSESSING THE EMERGENCY SITUATION

In the first stages of responding to an emergency it is important to be as calm as possible and to try and understand what has happened. Try to work out what is going on and whether it is safe for you to approach the scene. You need to decide whether:

- ⊗ **there is any continuing danger**

- ⊗ **anyone's life is in immediate danger**

- ⊗ **there are any other people around who could help**

- ⊗ **more skilled help is needed.**

If there are bystanders who can help, tell one of them to go and phone for emergency services as soon as you realise that their assistance is needed.

MAKING THE AREA SAFE

It is vitally important that you make sure that you remain safe and that you reduce the risks posed by any hazards. You will not be of much use if you become a casualty yourself.

If there is continuing danger from hazards at the scene of the emergency you need to reduce the risks they pose and make the area as safe as possible. Again, people who are at the scene of the emergency may be able to help or tell you how to deal with continuing dangers.

The key rule for making the area safe is always remove the danger from the casualty where possible. Only remove the casualty from the danger as a last resort.

ASSESSING THE CASUALTY'S CONDITION

You must assess the condition of casualties carefully. Prompt assessment is crucial to recovery. You should quickly establish the condition of the casualties at the scene of the incident. Make a mental note of all the people who are hurt. You should begin assessing the casualties' condition as you approach them. Make sure there is no continuing danger to yourself or to the casualty when you approach.

Your assessment involves finding the answers to a few basic questions.

Is the casualty conscious?
What should I do?

If the casualty is talking, sitting or standing they are conscious. Talk to them if they are. Ask about, and listen to their history of the event. Reassure them throughout the time that you are with them.

If the casualty is lying or sitting motionless they may be unconscious. Try to get them to respond by shouting and shaking them firmly but not roughly. If they respond to you, do the above. If they are not breathing and/or have no pulse, you should open their airway, begin mouth-to-mouth breathing or massage their heart until ambulance paramedics arrive to take over.

What injuries might the casualty have?
What should I look for?

Head injuries/concussion
Look for signs of confusion, bumps or wounds to the head. Ask if they have a headache or blurred vision. Check to see if there is any sign of blood or other fluid from the nose, mouth or ears. Ask the casualty if they can see and hear normally.

Neck or spinal injuries
Gently and carefully feel down the neck and spine for swelling and areas of tenderness. Try not to move the casualty.

Chest injuries
Touch the collarbone, the ribs and the breastbone, noting any tenderness or signs of deformity. Ask the casualty if they have any pain in these areas and whether they feel pain when breathing in or out.

Arm, wrist and hand, and leg and foot injuries
Ask the casualty if they have any pain in these areas and to show that they can move the joints of each limb. Look to see if there are any signs of deformity or swelling by comparing the body part on one side with the other.

Wounds
Look for signs of blood loss on the casualty's clothes, body or on the surface they are on. Check carefully for objects (metal, glass, knives) that may be stuck into the skin.

GETTING HELP FROM THE EMERGENCY SERVICES

Emergency help can be obtained from the ambulance, police and fire services in all parts of the country. It can also be obtained from the mine/mountain/cave rescue services and the coastguard in areas of the country where particular hazards exist.

For all services, help is obtained by dialling the emergency 999 number from any phone. Calls are always free of charge. If you have to phone for help use the nearest telephone, even if it means going to the nearest house or to a public place like a shop, pub or newsagent to ask. The most important thing is to get help quickly.

Calling for an ambulance

To call an ambulance you must dial the 999 service. When the operator answers he or she will initially ask you:

- **which service you require – fire, police or ambulance**

- **the number of the phone you are using.**

The operator will then put you through to the ambulance control room. A second operator will ask for the following information:

- **the address and location of the accident (details of nearby landmarks will help)**

- **the nature of the incident**

- **the number of people involved**

- **their condition (for example whether they are bleeding, unconscious or in shock)**

- **whether there are any continuing hazards at the scene (for example, fire, electrical faults, or chemicals).**

BASIC LIFE-SAVING TECHNIQUES

We are now going to look at two body processes, breathing and circulation, and the reasons why a number of basic life-saving techniques work as a temporary substitute when they fail. We will look at the basic first aid involved in opening and maintaining airways, placing a person in the recovery position, carrying out cardio-pulmonary resuscitation and controlling bleeding.

You will need recognised first-aid training and a qualification before you are able to take on the full responsibilities of a competent first-aider. Courses that offer training in, and assessment of, first-aid skills are approved by the Health and Safety Executive. They can be undertaken in some schools and at many Further Education colleges. They are also held at local branches of the St John Ambulance Association and the British Red Cross Society.

THE PROCESS OF BREATHING

The human body needs oxygen to sustain life. The oxygen that the body uses is obtained from the air around us. Fresh air is a mixture of gases. This mixture is introduced into, and used by, the body through the breathing process (Figure 1.18). Breathing has two functions.

1   To transfer oxygen from the air outside the body to the lungs where it can be collected by the blood and circulated throughout the body.

2   To allow carbon dioxide, a waste product of the body, to be expelled.

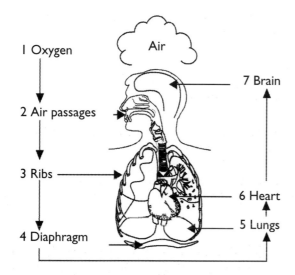

FIGURE 1.18: The respiratory system

Related problems (causes of asphyxia)
1   Insufficient oxygen
2   Obstruction, choking, smothering, strangling, hanging
3   Crushing, penetrating injuries, stove-in chest
4   Paralysis
5   Drowning, gas/smoke inhalation
6   Heart attacks
7   Poisoning, stroke, fits, electrical injury

When we breath an exchange of gases occurs in the body. Those gases that are useful, and which are needed, are transferred into the body and those that are not useful are expelled. The exchange of gases takes place in the cell linings of air sacs known as alveoli, in the lungs. Oxygen is transferred through them into the blood. Oxygenated blood is then pumped by the heart to the various tissues around the body.

While 21 per cent of fresh air is oxygen, only 5 per cent of it is used by our own bodies in breathing. When we exhale we breathe out 16 per cent oxygen as well as carbon dioxide. The amount of oxygen breathed out is enough to resuscitate another person whose heart and breathing have stopped and who is no longer conscious.

THE CIRCULATION OF BLOOD

Blood is circulated around the body through a system of arteries, veins and capillaries after being pumped by the heart (Figure 1.19). Blood is pumped through the heart to the lungs where it picks up oxygen and loses carbon dioxide. Arteries carry the oxygenated blood from the heart to the various tissues. Deoxygenated blood returns to the heart to pick up more oxygen through the veins.

FIGURE 1.19: Blood circulation

■ Oxygenated blood
■ Deoxygenated blood

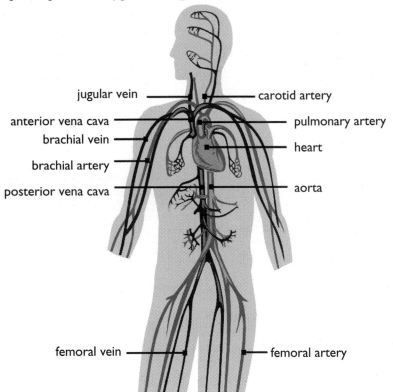

jugular vein — carotid artery
anterior vena cava — pulmonary artery
brachial vein — heart
brachial artery
posterior vena cava — aorta

femoral vein — femoral artery

A normally healthy heart beats about seventy times a minute when the person is at rest. It beats faster when individuals exercise. Each beat provides the body with the oxygen needed to sustain life. This beating is recorded through the pulse rate.

The blood pressure is a measure that records the pressure at which the heart pumps blood out into the arteries over the continuous pressure of blood in the arteries.

Circulation problems are potentially very serious. They can occur because:

⊗ **the heart stops beating**

⊗ **blood is lost from the circulation.**

When the heart stops beating there is an immediate and very serious health emergency. External chest compression should be used to maintain circulation, otherwise the person will die. External chest compression technique is described later in this chapter.

BASIC LIFE-SAVING TECHNIQUES WHEN THE CASUALTY IS UNCONSCIOUS

In some health emergencies you may come across somebody who is already unconscious. In others the casualty slips gradually into unconsciousness following an accident or because of illness or injury. The general procedure for treatment of an unconscious person is the same for all emergencies. You should check the airway, breathing and circulation (ABC) of the casualty (Figure 1.20).

1 Check for breathing by putting your ear close to the person's mouth and nose for a few seconds. Look for movement of the chest and abdomen and listen for breathing sounds.

2 Check the circulation by feeling for the pulse at the carotid or radial artery for at least five seconds.

3 Make sure the air passages are not obstructed. Clear the mouth of any debris (mucus, blood, vomit and any detached teeth).

FIGURE 1.20: Checking a person's ABC for the presence of breathing and pulse

1 Checking for breathing

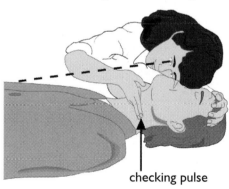

checking pulse

2 Checking pulse

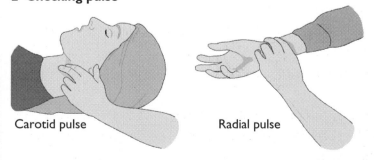

Carotid pulse   Radial pulse

3 Checking air passages are clear

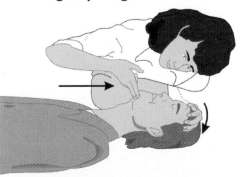

There are three possible sets of findings when you follow the ABC procedure.

1 The casualty is breathing and has a pulse.

2 The casualty has no pulse and is not breathing.

3 The casualty has a pulse but is not breathing.

In the first situation you should examine the casualty for further injuries and place the individual in the recovery position until skilled help arrives. In the other situations the following techniques should be used to restart breathing and/or circulation.

Opening an airway

To open the airway you should first:

- ⊗ **support the nape of the neck**

- ⊗ **press the forehead gently so that it is tilted backwards**

- ⊗ **push the chin upwards.**

If the person is capable of breathing this may be all that is necessary. He or she will gasp and start breathing again when the airway is opened. At this point, you can place the casualty in the recovery position (Figure 1.21). A lot of lives have been saved by knowledge of these two simple techniques.

FIGURE 1.21: The recovery position

Preparing the casualty

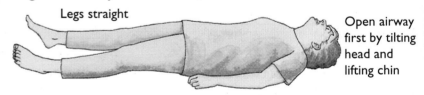

Legs straight

Open airway first by tilting head and lifting chin

The recovery position

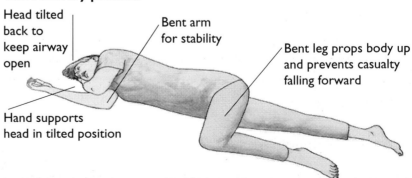

Head tilted back to keep airway open

Bent arm for stability

Bent leg props body up and prevents casualty falling forward

Hand supports head in tilted position

The purpose of the recovery position is to put the unconscious casualty in a safe position. It prevents the tongue blocking the airway and allows fluids to drain out of the mouth, so avoiding choking.

To turn a person lying on the back into the recovery position follow the steps below.

- **Kneel beside the casualty. Open the casualty's airway by tilting back the head and lifting the chin.**

- **Straighten the casualty's legs.**

- **Place the casualty's arm nearest to you at right angles to his or her body – the elbow should be bent with the palm of the hand facing upwards.**

- **Bring the casualty's far arm across the chest and position the back of the casualty's hand on his or her cheek – hold it in this position while you grasp the far thigh.**

- **Roll the casualty towards you.**

- **Adjust the casualty's upper leg so that the hip and knee are bent at right angles.**

Emergency resuscitation

If breathing begins to fail or stops you must immediately check the casualty's ABC and prepare to start emergency resuscitation. You must act quickly. It is essential for the brain to be continuously supplied with oxygenated blood. If totally deprived of oxygen for more than four minutes, the brain is likely to be permanently damaged.

During resuscitation the speed with which the first few breaths are given is the most important single factor in ensuring success. Various methods can be used, but the most effective is mouth-to-mouth breathing combined with cardiac compressions.

Mouth-to-mouth breathing

If a casualty stops breathing he or she may still have a pulse. Sometimes the person does not as the heart has also stopped beating. In either situation mouth-to-mouth breathing can inflate the lungs with enough oxygen to save life.

If the casualty is not breathing:

- **ensure he or she has a clear airway (see the procedure above)**

- loosen the person's clothing at neck and waist

- keep the person's head tilted backwards and begin mouth-to-mouth breathing if he or she does not start breathing when the airway is opened. (Do not try this on a conscious person.)

If the casualty is an adult:

- **Open your mouth wide and take a deep breath.**

- **Pinch the person's nostril together with your fingers.**

- **Seal your lips round the person's mouth.**

- **Blow into the person's lungs until the chest rises.**

- **Remove your mouth, and watch the chest fall.**

- **Repeat and continue inflations at your natural rate of breathing.**

Give the first few inflations as rapidly as possible to saturate the blood with oxygen. Repeat this process ten times to fill up the lungs with oxygen. The rate should be approximately ten breaths per minute. If the chest fails to rise there is an obstruction. Ensure that the head is tilted well backwards, turn the casualty on his or her side and thump the person's back. Check for, and remove any foreign matter from the back of the throat. If the heart is beating normally, continue to give mouth-to-mouth oxygen until natural breathing is restored.

If the casualty is an infant or young child lips should be sealed around both nose and mouth. Blow gently into the child's lungs until the chest rises.

External chest compression

By combining external chest compression with mouth-to-mouth breathing, the first-aider can supply the casualty with enough oxygen to sustain life when the person's own breathing and circulation have stopped. To carry out external chest compression the following procedure should be followed.

- **Place yourself at the side of the person.**

- **Feel for the lower half of the breastbone.**

- **Place the heel of your hand on this part of the bone keeping the palm and fingers off the chest.**

☺ **Cover the hand with the heel of the other hand.**

☺ **With the arms straight, rock forwards pressing down on the lower half of the breastbone.**

In adults, the pressure should be repeated at least 60 times per minute. With children up to 10 years old light pressure of only one hand is sufficient at 70 to 80 times per minute. In infants, very light pressure with two fingers is enough, at 100 times per minute. Although the pressure differs according to the age of the person it must always be firm and controlled. Erratic or violent movements may cause further damage to the ribs or to internal organs.

External chest compression works because the first-aider is able to artificially push oxygen-carrying blood around the body. By pushing down on the breastbone pressure increases in the chest. This pushes blood out of the heart. Releasing the breastbone allows the chest to rise and blood to re-enter the heart.

 ACTIVITY

Read the case studies and answer the questions that follow.

Emergency at the beach

Judith Fisher felt that she was quite a good swimmer. She often swam at her local swimming baths, but had never swum in the open sea before. On a school field trip to the Cornish coast with her teachers and school friends she had to use a canoe to paddle out to a small island 500 metres offshore. On the way back, about 200 metres from the beach, her canoe capsized. Bruce Treharrock, the local life guard, saw this from his observation post and responded immediately. Judith was trapped upside down in the water for a couple of minutes before he rescued her. When he got her back to the shore she was unconscious.

a **What would you expect Bruce to do as part of his first-aid routine when he reached the shore with Judith? Describe as many of the aspects of his role and personal responsibilities as you can think of.**

b **If there were no life guards on the beach and you saw Judith's canoe capsize, what would you have to think about and do to ensure that help was provided safely and quickly?**

c **If Judith had stopped breathing and you could find no pulse, what techniques could be used to try and restore breathing and circulation? Explain how to perform the techniques and why they work when performed properly.**

Responding to a heart attack

David James is a 45-year-old pub manager. He is a smoker, is 6.5 kg overweight and has not done any regular exercise for the last ten years. David is currently in hospital following a serious heart attack at work. A customer found David slumped outside the toilets. His heart stopped beating briefly when the paramedic staff arrived but he was revived on the way to hospital. David says that he was unaware of what was happening to him when he was having his heart attack and doesn't understand why it happened to him.

a **Which aspects of David's lifestyle may have contributed to him having a heart attack?**

b **What were the main first-aid responsibilities of the customer who found David?**

c **What techniques would the paramedic staff have used to revive him?**

d **Find out what the key signs and symptoms of a heart attack are.**

WOUNDS AND BLEEDING

Haemorrhage is another term for bleeding. Blood can be lost through wounds inside or outside of the body. Blood loss that occurs through wounds inside the body is known as **internal bleeding**. Blood lost through wounds outside of the body is known as **external bleeding**.

GENERAL SIGNS AND SYMPTOMS OF BLEEDING

Internal	External
gunshot wounds	lacerations
stab wounds	incised or clean cuts
perforated stomach	grazes
broken bones	bruises

FIGURE 1.22: Causes of bleeding

Signs and symptoms of bleeding will vary according to the person and the severity of the bleeding. They will include:

- **pale or ashen skin colour**

- **cold and clammy skin**

- **rapid pulse becoming weaker**

- **fainting and dizziness**

- **restlessness**

- **nausea**

- **shallow breathing sometimes accompanied by yawning and sighing**

- **air hunger respiration (gasping)**

- **thirst.**

Blood lost from a capillary will ooze. Blood lost from a vein will pour steadily. Blood lost from an artery will spurt in time with the beating of the heart. Minor blood loss from capillary wounds will tend to clot and stop by itself. Blood lost from arteries and major veins is much more serious and may require emergency treatment.

Internal bleeding occurs when the organs of the body, for example the liver, spleen, or stomach, are damaged by injury or illness. The amount of blood lost in this way is more difficult to quantify than with external bleeding. Some may be vomited or coughed (visible internal bleeding) depending where the person is bleeding inside the body.

FIRST AID FOR BLEEDING

When dealing with wounds it is important to observe the precautions covered in the first part of this chapter to prevent contamination by infections carried in the blood.

Minor external bleeding

The following procedure should be observed.

- ✪ **Reassure the casualty.**

- ✪ **Wash the wound under running water if it is dirty.**

- ✪ **Protect it with a sterile swab.**

- ✪ **Clean the surrounding skin.**

- ✪ **Dry the skin with cotton wool.**

- ✪ **Apply a dressing and bandage firmly in position.**

- ✪ **Place the person at rest, raise the injured part and support it in position, unless there is a fracture.**

Severe external bleeding

The following procedure should be observed.

- ✪ **Apply direct pressure to the bleeding point with fingers for 5–15 minutes to stop bleeding immediately.**

- ✪ **If the wound area is large, or there is an object embedded in the skin, press the sides of wound gently but firmly together.**

- ✪ **Call for medical assistance urgently.**

- ✪ **Lay the person down comfortably and elevate their legs.**

- ✪ **Raise and support the injured part.**

Blood loss is usually controlled relatively easily by the use of pressure. However, bleeding might not always be controlled by direct pressure on the wound. As an alternative you may have to apply indirect pressure at the appropriate **pressure point** (Figure 1.23) between the heart and wound for no more than 15 minutes. A pressure point is where an artery can be compressed against an underlying bone. By doing this the first-aider can prevent the flow of blood through the artery to the wound.

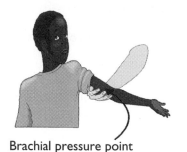

FIGURE 1.23: Pressure points

Brachial pressure point   Femoral pressure point

Internal bleeding

The following procedure should be observed.

- ✪ **Obtain medical aid immediately to combat shock.**

- ✪ **Place the person at rest with their legs raised.**

- ✪ **Loosen all tight clothing.**

- ✪ **Reassure the casualty.**

- ✪ **Check them for other injuries.**

- ✪ **Protect them from cold.**

- ✪ **Check and record their pulse and respiration every 10–15 minutes.**

- ✪ **Save all specimens (for example, urine) produced by the casualty.**

- ✪ **Do not give them any food or fluid by mouth.**

Nose bleeds

Nose bleeds that occur from the front part of the nose are very common and easy to treat. In children, they are due to blowing the nose too hard or to picking dry crusts. They may be associated with conditions such as hay fever. Severe, sudden, nose bleeds in the elderly may be due to medical conditions such as high blood pressure. The following procedure should be observed.

- ⊗ **Sit the person down with his or her head bent slightly forward.**

- ⊗ **Ask the person to breathe through the mouth.**

- ⊗ **Ask the person to pinch the soft part of the nose for about 10 minutes.**

- ⊗ **Loosen clothing around the neck and waist.**

- ⊗ **Instruct the person not to blow the nose for several hours.**

- ⊗ **Do not disturb the clot that forms.**

- ⊗ **If the bleeding does not stop within a reasonable time, or if it recurs, advise the person to seek medical help.**

ACTIVITY

An emergency at the supermarket

It was Keiran's first day working on the meat counter at the supermarket. Jean, his supervisor, said that he was a bit nervous but a good worker. Things started to go wrong when a customer asked Keiran to trim the fat off a piece of meat that she wanted. Keiran began to do this, slowly and carefully. The customer then spoke to him, asking him to hurry up. Keiran looked up at her nervously. As he did so he accidentally pushed the knife across his fingers where he held the meat. He shouted out in pain and dropped the knife. Jean said, 'There was blood everywhere, I didn't know what to do next.'

a **What should Jean have done in response to this accident? Describe her first-aid role and responsibilities. You should indicate both what she should and shouldn't do.**

b **How could a first-aider control Keiran's bleeding and ensure that the risk of infection in this situation was minimised?**

c **All places of work should have a first-aid box with equipment in it. Find out about and list the items that it should contain.**

SHOCK

Shock is a condition resulting from reduced supply of oxygen to the body tissues because of a lack of blood supply. It may occur because of:

- severe wound injuries

- severe pain

- sudden illness.

The signs and symptoms of shock are the same as those of severe bleeding, except that the person may become unconscious and may stop breathing. The aim of first aid is to ensure an adequate blood supply gets to the brain, heart and lungs. A first-aider should:

- reassure the person

- lay the person down on his or her back on a blanket if the condition allows

- keep the person's head low, turned on to one side, with legs raised unless a fracture is suspected

- keep the casualty warm

- loosen any tight clothing

- establish the cause and treat it

- check and record breathing and pulse rate every 10 minutes

- place the casualty in the recovery position if breathing becomes difficult, or if he or she become unconscious.

You should not move casualties unnecessarily as this will increase shock. They should not be given hot water bottles or anything to drink. They should not be allowed to smoke.

PORTFOLIO ASSIGNMENT

CARRYING OUT A HEALTH AND SAFETY INSPECTION

INTRODUCTION

This assignment asks you to carry out a health and safety assessment on your own every-day surroundings. You will need to identify as many potential hazards in different locations as you can.

TASK 1

Carry out a survey of hazards in your local area. Cover the places where you go regularly and where you spend most of your time. Make sure that you cover your home, the roads you use and cross, your work or education enviornment and places where you relax or exercise.
You should make a survey sheet like the one below to record your findings.

TASK 2

Write a report identifying the main hazards in your area to:

- children

- the elderly

- teenagers

- adults.

Your report should indicate what the hazards are, how they might affect people's health and how you think the risks could be reduced.

What is the hazard?	Where is the hazard?	Who is it a hazard to?

PORTFOLIO ASSIGNMENT

RESPONDING TO HEALTH EMERGENCIES

INTRODUCTION

This assignment gives you the opportunity to produce a short information film, video or role-play demonstration for young people that informs them about basic first-aid methods.

TASK 1

Form a group of four to six people. Your group will plan, perform and produce a video or role play aimed at teenagers, about:

- opening and maintaining airways

- using the recovery position

- stopping bleeding.

You will need to think about how you will present this information in an interesting way. For example, you could present it in a drama style following characters through a short story, or you could use a documentary style with more formal presentations.

TASK 2

You will need to hold planning meetings to discuss and negotiate about how you will complete the required work. Everybody in the group should play some part in planning, performing in and producing your film. You should keep notes about your group meetings and about your contributions to them.

TASK 3

Produce a 5–10 minute information video or role play that:

- demonstrates how to open and maintain the airway of an unconscious casualty

- demonstrates how to put someone in the recovery position

- demonstrates how to control bleeding from a serious wound

- explains the physiological basis of these techniques

- informs and encourages teenagers with no previous first-aid knowledge about when and how these techniques should be performed.

Your film must be factually correct. It should also appeal to the target audience and get your point across clearly.

TASK 4

Show your film or role play to a group of teenagers. Get them to appraise it and make comments on its usefulness. Encourage them to ask, and be prepared to respond to, any questions raised.

✔ MULTIPLE CHOICE QUESTIONS

These questions are designed to test your knowledge and understanding of chapter 1. There is only one correct answer (A, B, C or D) to each question. You can check your choices with the answers given at the back of the book.

1 **People who have a very stressful job could balance their lifestyle by:**

A taking more tranquillisers

B doing a lot of exercise before and after work

C finding time for rest and relaxation

D drinking plenty of alcohol when under pressure

2 **Which of the following refers to passive smoking?**

A smoking without inhaling

B smoking when you are alone

C sharing other people's cigarettes

D breathing in the tobacco smoke produced by other people

3 **Which of the following dietary measures could be taken to improve health?**

A reducing the amount of saturated fat eaten

B increasing the amount of sugar eaten

C avoiding eating protein foods

D all of the above

4 **What is the recommended maximum number of weekly units of alcohol for women?**

A 4   C 36

B 11   D 21

5 **The type of drugs that are prescribed by doctors to counteract infections are known as:**

A anti-psychotics

B antibiotics

C anti-depressants

D analgesics

6 **The sale of cannabis, a controlled drug, is regulated in the United Kingdom by:**

A the Children Act 1989

B the Intoxicating Substances Supply Act 1985

C the Drugs Misuse Act 1971

D the Medicines Act 1971

7 **Which of the following foods are sources of protein?**

A soya beans

B beef

C pork

D all of the above

8 **What is the main function of carbohydrates in the diet?**

A to make food taste nicer

B to build and repair body tissue

C to provide energy for the body

D to strengthen bones and teeth

✔ MULTIPLE CHOICE QUESTIONS

9 Which of the following would provide a healthy dietary intake for a child at school?

A a meal that contains mainly fried foods

B a meal that contains green vegetables and fruit

C a chocolate snack bar

D a packet of crisps and a can of soft drink

10 Identify the essential dietary component which is **NOT** a mineral in the following list:

A calcium

B fibre

C iron

D potassium

11 HIV is spread by contact with infected body fluids. The risk can be reduced by:

A using the contraceptive pill

B sharing needles with drug users

C reducing the number of sexual partners and using a condom

D not using gloves and masks during surgical procedures

12 The main purpose of regular washing and personal care is to:

A keep the skin moist and supple

B smell nice to others

C control the growth of bacteria, fungi and viruses

D look attractive

13 The naturally produced substance that protects the hair is known as:

A conditioner

B serum

C shampoo

D sebum

14 A cyclist is knocked off his bike in front of you as you wait to cross the road. The car that knocked him off doesn't stop. What should your first response be?

A phone the police from the nearest phone

B pull the cyclist on to the pavement

C stop the oncoming traffic

D start resuscitation immediately

15 In which of the following situations would you place the casualty in the recovery position?

A if she was unconscious but had a clear airway and good pulse

B if she had no pulse and was not breathing

C if she had a fractured arm

D if she was bleeding from an artery

16 A pressure point occurs:

A when blood is lost through an artery

B where an artery can be compressed against an underlying bone

C where a bone breaks in two

D when blood clots at an open wound

✔ MULTIPLE CHOICE QUESTIONS

17 **A person has an open wound from which blood is spurting out in time with the heart. Where is this blood being lost from?**

A an artery

B a bone

C a vein

D a capillary

18 **How could a health promotion officer best present advice on dental care to a group of 5–year-olds?**

A by using a questionnaire

B by presenting information in pictorial form

C by giving them a talk or lecture

D by using books or leaflets developed for GNVQ students

19 **A person who drinks excess alcohol on a regular basis is at risk of developing:**

A asthma

B liver damage

C a stroke

D schizophrenia

20 **Which of the following would help to prevent obesity in the long term?**

A a reduction of water and salt intake

B walking upstairs instead of using the lift

C cutting down on smoking

D a healthy diet and fitness programme

Influences on Health and Well-being

CONTENTS

OUTLINE

This chapter is designed to help you to understand health and well-being by considering personal development, interpersonal relationships and relationships within society.

The first part – covering element 2.1 – requires you to explore characteristics of different stages in the life span and some of the major events that may affect individuals. You are also encouraged to appreciate how your own view of yourself influences your health and well-being.

The second part – covering element 2.1 – focuses on the nature of interpersonal relationships and their influence on health and well-being. Here, the main focus is on the role of the family.

The final part – covering element 2.3 – requires you to investigate relationships in society and the different roles individuals adopt. You are also asked to consider the impact of socio-economic factors on the choices which individuals can make and ways they may influence health and well-being.

PREVIEW

After working through this unit you will be able to:

- ⊗ **explore the development of individuals and how they change**

- ⊗ **explore the nature of interpersonal relationships and their influence on health and well-being**

- ⊗ **explore the interactions of individuals and ways they may influence health and well-being.**

A number of factors contribute to our growth and development as individuals. The different relationships we are part of, the social groups that we belong to and the types of social experience we have shape us into the people we are at various times in our lives. In this chapter we look at the main features and processes of human development. We also consider the relationships that are formed as we develop, and explore the links between the process of development, individual relationships and the experience of health and well-being.

Explore the Development of Individuals and How They Manage Change

Growth, Development and Change Through the Life Span

In this section we will be looking at how people develop and change throughout their lives. People go through a number of developmental stages as they grow and mature. We experience growth and development in our physical, emotional and social, and intellectual capabilities. **Growth** refers to the increase in physical size or mass that we achieve as we grow into adults. It occurs because of the influence of hormones, nutrition and exercise. **Development** refers to the change in the complexity and sophistication of our capabilities that we experience as we mature into adulthood. People can develop their skills and abilities through practice and training. The term **maturity** refers to genetically programmed changes that unfold as we reach different ages. Girls don't have to be taught how to grow breasts and boys don't have to practise growing facial hair. These changes occur as a result of maturation.

> **QUICK response**
> Can you think of any other changes that you have experienced as a result of maturation?

The life span and the life cycle

The term **life span** refers to the period of time that people live, from their birth to their death. The **life cycle** refers to the predictable stages of growth and development that people pass through during their life span.

Compared to many other species, and also to our ancestors, modern human beings have a relatively long life span.

The life span of human beings has increased over the last hundred years. Figure 2.1 shows that while people are living to an increasingly older age, women are still living longer than men. Male children born in the period 1990–92 have an expected lifespan of 73.4 years compared to 79 years for women born during the same period.

FIGURE 2.1: Changes in life expectancy, 1891–1992

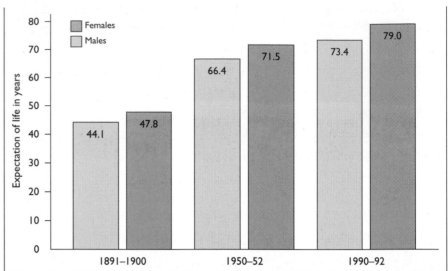

Source: Office of Population Censuses and Surveys

QUICK response

Make a list of factors that you think might have contributed to the extended life span shown in the bar chart.

ACTIVITY

Think of six people you know from different age groups.
Describe each person's:

Ⓢ **physical appearance**

Ⓢ **state of health**

Ⓢ **interests**

Ⓢ **main ambitions**

Ⓢ **talents and weaknesses.**

In completing the activity you will have seen that there are plenty of differences between the people in your list. The differences will be greater between people whose ages are very different. People have individual characters, different in many respects from those of even their closest friends and family members. However, biologists, psychologists and sociologists have identified common patterns and factors in all our experiences of growth and development.

INFLUENCES ON GROWTH AND DEVELOPMENT – 'NATURE' AND 'NURTURE'

People are said to develop through the combined effects and interaction of nature and nurture. **Nature** refers to our internal, genetic inheritance. We all inherit certain characteristics, abilities and predispositions from our biological parents. There is very little that we can do to change these inherited features. They are given to us by nature as chromosomes and express themselves as we mature into adults.

The environment in which we live also has a powerful influence on the person we become. This is what is meant by **nurture.** Environmental influences include culture, the social groups that we belong to, and the physical circumstances in which we live. Living in poor housing conditions and not having enough food to eat are factors associated with poor growth in children and illness in all age groups. Nurture has a very powerful effect in shaping our social, emotional and intellectual development.

ACTIVITY

Produce a list of:

⊗ the environmental influences that have played a role in your development

⊗ the characteristics you possess that you feel are inherited.

Organise your list under the following headings:

⊗ physical

⊗ social

⊗ emotional

⊗ intellectual.

PHYSICAL GROWTH AND DEVELOPMENT

Most of the physical growth and change that people experience is predictable and is part of a natural human process of ageing. In the early stages of the life cycle a person grows in size and develops physical abilities and attributes as the body matures. For example, a child of two naturally develops what are known as 'gross motor skills', such as being able to stand, walk and climb steps, as their bones and muscles grow to the required size and are able to support them. Initially, their 'motor', or movement, skills are clumsy and unsophisticated. As the child's body systems mature they develop 'fine' motor skills, such as the ability to tie their shoe laces and do up their buttons.

The patterns of physical growth, with some examples to illustrate the changes that occur throughout the life cycle in relatively wealthy countries such as Britain, are illustrated below.

INFANCY TO CHILDHOOD

Infancy to one year

Children are born with a number of basic physical reflexes – they can breathe, blink their eyes, distinguish colours and smells and will suck when something is pushed into their mouth.

By the end of its first year a child will weigh three times its birth weight, be one and a half times as tall, have a comparatively smaller head, have a more solid physical frame and have developed gross motor abilities.

From 1 to 4 years

Physical growth is slower than the previous stage. Children begin to draw as a result of improved hand-eye coordination. Finer movements are still difficult for 3-year-olds. Many will still have difficulty doing up buttons and shoe laces. Because their motor skills have developed substantially, children have a greater need for physical activity. They are extremely mobile and enjoy movement. Children develop and learn a lot of physical skills through movement.

From 4 to 6 years

In this stage children learn to run, jump, hop and ride a bicycle as a result of their increasing balance control. In contrast to the previous phase, 4–6-year-olds are no longer top heavy as they have lost their baby fat and are more physically coordinated. Learning activities in many reception and early infants classes are often directed towards refining and expanding coordination and fine motor skills. At the end of this phase growth in physique begins to increase.

From 6 to 12 years

Physical growth progresses slowly and gradually in this phase until puberty begins in about the twelfth year. Children increase their muscle tissue and become taller, stronger and more robust. Children now have much more distinct physical features than they did in the previous phase. For example, they will have developed the facial features that change very little throughout their adult life.

Adolescence

Adolescence begins at the age of 12 and ends somewhere between 16 and 22. In terms of physical features and growth, adolescence is a very active phase.

At about the age of 11 for girls and 13 for boys there is a growth spurt, when their bodies begin to grow and change very rapidly. This stage of maturation is called puberty. In boys, the first indication of puberty is the growth of testes, the scrotum and pubic hair. They grow body hair (face, chest and in the armpits) and their voice gets deeper. In girls, puberty begins with the growth of pubic hair and breasts start to become more noticeable. These changes are followed by the growth of the uterus and vagina. An increase in the activity of hormones causes these changes to occur. The two glands that affect this are the pituitary and thyroid glands.

Adulthood

Physically, young adults are in the prime of their lives. The first half of young adulthood, from early twenties to early thirties, is characterised by maximum physical performance. In the second half of this phase, from about 30 to 42, there is an increase in fatty tissue, people move more slowly, and take longer to recover from their efforts. Men can also start to lose their hair or go grey and women start to get wrinkles around the eyes as their skin becomes less supple.

Mid-life

People in this age-range, from their forties to late fifties, generally undergo a lot of physical change. Many people experience diminishing abilities and a decline in their physical performance when compared to earlier phases of their life. Hormonal changes lead to the menopause in women.

Old age

Old age can be divided into two periods. The 'young old' are people in their early sixties to early mid-seventies. There is also another increasingly large group of 'old old' people. These are people living into their late seventies, eighties and nineties. The process of physical ageing quickens form the age of abut 55. People change in appearance (wrinkles, grey/white hair, decrease in height), experience sensory changes (hearing and sight impairments) and internal physical decline (poorer heart/lung function, muscles wastage, brittle bones/stiff joints).

THE ROLE OF HORMONES IN GROWTH AND DEVELOPMENT

Hormones are chemical secretions that pass directly into the blood from the endocrine glands. The two main glands that secrete hormones affecting growth and development are the **thyroid** gland and the **pituitary** gland. Several different hormones are secreted by each of these glands. Some of the different hormones and their effects are described in Figure 2.2.

FIGURE 2.2: Some hormones and their effects

QUICK response

Where are the pituitary and thyroid glands located?

Gland	Hormone	Function/effect
Pituitary	Prolactin	Stimulates milk production by mammary glands
	Growth hormone	Stimulates general body growth
	Lipotropin	Increases the rate of use of stored fat
	Gonad-stimulating hormone	Regulates the development of reproductive organs
Thyroid	Thyroxine	Controls the rate of growth and the rate at which glucose is used to release energy

ACTIVITY

Look at the following information on growth of an individual from infancy to adulthood.

a Produce a graph of the person's growth pattern using the figures.

b What do the data tell you about the person's pattern of growth? Write a paragraph explaining the figures.

Age	Height gained per year (cm)
0–1	22.5
1–2	20.0
2–3	17.5
3–4	9.0
4–5	7.5
5–6	7.5
6–7	7.0
7–8	7.0
8–9	6.0
9–10	6.0
10–11	5.0
11–12	5.0
12–13	8.0
13–14	8.0
14–15	12.5
15–16	12.5

EMOTIONAL AND SOCIAL DEVELOPMENT

Emotional and social development occurs throughout the life cycle as individuals make and experience different types of relationship and social situation. As with physical growth there are general patterns of development. These reflect the type of experience that we have at different stages of the life cycle and how much we have learnt and matured as a result of them.

The general pattern of social and emotional development is illustrated with examples in the section below. Although this looks at 'typical' development there will be variations in speed and the extent of development between individuals of the same age even when they are of the same sex, members of the same family and have the same social background.

INFANCY TO ONE YEAR

Early social and emotional development plays an important part in future relationships and social behaviour. Ideally children should develop feelings of trust and security early in their lives. This is known as **attachment** and links the child to its parent or main care-giver. The return of this emotional linking by the parent or care-giver is known as **bonding**. Attachment and bonding provide the link between baby and adult through which a first relationship is built.

In their first year children will have a small 'social' circle of people to whom they are attached. These people provide the child with a basis of security and safety from which they can explore the world around them. By the age of six months, bonding with immediate care-givers has become very strong. After this point babies may become very distressed if they are separated from the people to whom they are especially attached, and may cry if a stranger talks to them.

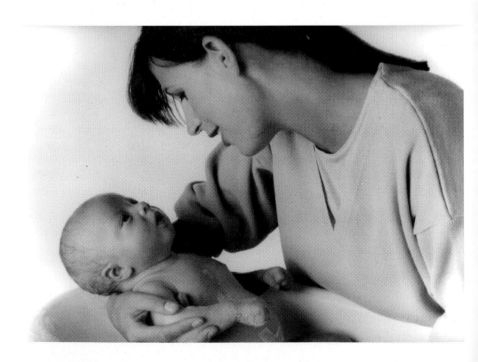

ACTIVITY

Read the brief descriptions of mother-baby relationships that follow. Identify the ones which you feel will form a strong and successful bond and explain why you think this will happen.

- **Kelly feels that she understands her baby and can easily tell when a cry is because of hunger, pain or because the baby is frightened.**

- **Jenny thinks that all cries are the same and feels that babies should not get picked up just because they cry.**

- **Beatrice is angry that she has had another baby as she cannot cope with her other children. She looks after his physical care but only talks or cuddles with him when she is in a good mood.**

- **Helen is enjoying life with her new baby. She feels comfortable and happy with her and already feels as if they are friends.**

Kelly and Helen are more likely to develop a strong, positive bond with their babies than the other mothers. The quality of the bond is influenced by four main things.

1 How sensitively the mother understands and responds to the baby's needs.

2 The personality of the mother.

3 The consistency of the care that the baby receives.

4 The baby's own temperament.

From 1 to 4 years

As with the first year of life, social and emotional development in this early phase is extremely important. Children increase their social relationships by including brothers, sisters, relatives and perhaps

QUICK response

Having a baby is often a major life change for the mother. Make a list of the factors that you feel would be most important in helping her to cope with the pressures that result from having a baby.

neighbour's children in their social circle. The nature of the social contacts that children have at this stage are influenced by their developing communication skills. Children are increasingly able to look at the world from the perspectives of other people as they progress through this phase. This is demonstrated by the changing way in which children in this age group play – see Figure 2.3.

0–1 year	Solo play (child playing alone). 'It's difficult for me to think of people other than myself so I like to play on my own. I learn through exploring everything around me.'
2–3 years old	Parallel play (child plays alongside but not with another child). 'I'm still mainly interested in myself and I can't see the sense of sharing yet. I am interested in other people so I like to be near them. I learn by imitating other people.'
3 years old	Associative play (child beginning to play and communicate with other children). 'I'm beginning to understand how they feel and to be sympathetic, so that makes it easier to play with other children. I learn a lot by imitating and pretending to be people who are important to me.'
Over 3 years old	Cooperative play (child playing a game involving cooperation, for example building a house to play in). 'I am beginning to see that it's important to share and help other children. I realise that if I cooperate with the other children we have more fun and do more interesting things.'

FIGURE 2.3: Stages of play from infancy to 4 years old

Social relationships can be important for children for a number of reasons.

⊗ **It is satisfying and fun to have friends.**

⊗ Social relationships give children the opportunity to develop their linguistic and intellectual skills and develop their moral and emotional frameworks.

⊗ Joining in games and other physical activities with other children develops physical skills and abilities.

Successful social relationships among children are encouraged by:

⊗ secure attachment in their early years

⊗ opportunities to mix with other children, especially where they involve activities that require cooperation

⊗ the personality of the child – children who are friendly, supportive and optimistic make friends more easily than children who are negative and aggressive.

⚡QUICK response
What could parents and carers do to promote the development of friendliness and optimism in children?

From 4 to 6 years

At this stage of development a child needs to resolve a number of social and emotional challenges. Going to school means being with other children and listening to people who are not parents or close family members. Children must begin to learn to solve their own problems and acquire the communication skills and social behaviours needed to build relationships with a broader range of people. The child's social world is expanding rapidly.

From 6 to 12 years

In this age group there is a reduction in **dependence** on family members. Relationships with friends, teachers and other adults will have become more important. Friendships with other children become closer and last much longer. Children use these friendships to understand how people relate to each other. In the later part of this phase friendships become more stable and important. By the age of eleven to twelve, friends often share emotions and swap secrets, helping each other to develop social skills such as listening. Primary school experiences are very important in promoting social and emotional development within this age range. Schools often deliberately promote 'appropriate' social behaviours and values, such as 'caring for others', 'trying hard', and 'not behaving aggressively'. Children in this phase begin to develop more complex social images of themselves and to identify with particular social groups.

ADOLESCENCE

The need for an **identity** and a sense of social and emotional 'belonging' are important concerns in this phase. People tend to experiment with their relationships and to explore the different, positive and negative, emotions that result from personal relationships. This experimentation can include making decisions about whether or not to engage in sexual activity as a part of intimate, personal relationships. In this phase of social and emotional development, individuals tend to gain greater understanding of the thoughts, feelings and motives of others.

ADULTHOOD

Because of the huge diversity of experience among people in this phase it is very difficult to generalise about what happens in terms of social and emotional development. People tend to develop as a result of work, relationship and maturation influences. This phase tends to revolve around people trying to achieve their position in society and their ambitions in life.

MID-LIFE AND OLD AGE

Social and emotional development take on a new importance in this phase of life. People tend to be more reflective, reviewing their achievements, or lack of them, and their relationships. They often try to come to terms with the changes occurring in their relationships with partners, grown-up children and friends. People continue to develop and change emotionally as they experience events such as children leaving home, becoming grandparents and perhaps retiring from work. People may have more leisure time in which to build relationships with friends and family members. However, they may also experience insecurity and loneliness if their social contacts are reduced by retirement or bereavement.

INTELLECTUAL DEVELOPMENT

Intellectual development refers to the development of thinking, memory and language abilities. Like social and emotional development this is a life-long process. During infancy and childhood our natural abilities are maturing. With the aid of learning experiences, through formal education and informal learning from others, we develop and extend our intellectual abilities

INFANCY TO ONE YEAR

Early intellectual, or cognitive, development is mainly a matter of maturing. In a very short space of time children see and experience a large number of things for the first time in their lives. Young children are very quick to use these new experiences to acquire a better insight into the world around them.

FROM 1 TO 4 YEARS

In this phase of intellectual development the acquisition and use of language is very important. The way that children think about and see the world also changes in this phase. They are more physically active and independently mobile and are expanding their social circle.

FROM 4 TO 6 YEARS

School-age children begin to organise their thinking more. Their speech becomes more sophisticated and they often accompany their actions with a description of what they are about to do. This 'thinking out loud' gradually disappears as thinking becomes more complex and abstract.

FROM 6 TO 12 YEARS

At this stage of their intellectual development children are expected to learn and deal with a lot more information about the world. Learning and intellectual development becomes more systematic. Children are now able to concentrate more and to follow instructions. They learn to think about how and why things happen in specific situations but cannot necessarily apply this to other similar situations. For example, they might wash their hands before meals because they obey the rules of hygiene but won't necessarily apply these rules when they use the toilet.

ADOLESCENCE

Intellectual development in this phase changes mainly because of the emergence of abstract thinking. A person who can think abstractly can think about things that aren't actually there and things that don't actually exist. For example, algebra equations involve abstract thinking and so does thinking about the beginning of the universe. Abstract thinking is considered to be the final stage of thought development. An important feature of this process in adolescence is that the adolescent's values become increasingly consistent. This process is not completed in adolescence however, and lasts through the whole of life.

ADULTHOOD

Young adults have usually reached abstract thought, have a memory functioning at its peak and can think very quickly. Compared to older adults, people in this phase lack experience of the world. In the second half of this phase the capacity for quick, reactive thought begins to slow down and memory starts to become slower.

MID-LIFE

The main feature of intellectual development at this stage is a further slowing in reactive thinking. This does not mean that people are any less capable, just that they may require more time to perform the same intellectual activities as younger adults. Because older people have a greater breadth and depth of knowledge gained from experience they tend to use this to be more analytical and reflective in their thinking.

OLD AGE

Older people maintain and use their intellectual abilities in much the same ways that adults and middle-aged people do. Both the young-old (60–75) and the old-old (75+) need and enjoy activities in their lives that are intellectually stimulating. There are many negative ideas about older people's intellectual abilities. While it is true that a minority of people develop dementia and have memory problems, the majority of older people do not and can perform the same intellectual activities as younger people, if a little slower.

ACTIVITY

Think of six people you know who fall into either the young-old or old-old age categories. Identify whether, and in what ways, their intellectual abilities have changed as they have got older. You should identify areas in which age has enhanced their abilities as well as areas in which their abilities may have deteriorated.

LANGUAGE DEVELOPMENT

Care-givers responsible for young children have an important role to play in helping them to learn to communicate well and to use language in a wide variety of ways. While children do not actually use their first proper words until they are about one-year-old, babies are developing communication skills almost straight from birth. The initial communications of babies are in the form of smiles, movements and noises that are part of a conversation with a care-giver. The baby is already able to give and receive information and to communicate feelings.

QUICK response
How does a baby communicate its feelings without the use of language?

Young children move rapidly through the different stages of language development, from babbling at 8–10 months, to their first words between one and two years of age, to sentences from 18 months. By two and a half, children are learning a few new words a day so that by three they have a vocabulary of about a thousand words. At this point children will be using language for a variety of purposes.

Although children can talk effectively by the time they are three, it is not correct to think that language development ends there. Language learning continues throughout childhood and people continue to refine their use of language throughout life.

ACTIVITY

Look at the following development information about four children of varying ages. Write a short paragraph about each indicating:

- whether their development is appropriate so far

- what other significant milestones you would expect each to have passed

- which areas require further attention or may be a cause for concern for each child.

Dennis (age 3)

- Can talk clearly and pronounce most words correctly.

- Can feed himself but needs help to get dressed and use the toilet.

- Is continent during the day but sometimes wets the bed at night.

- Can pedal a tricycle.

- Is 15 kilos in weight.

- Can count to ten and recognise his name in writing.

Simon (age 15)

- Can run 100 metres in 13 seconds.

- Voice has recently broken.

- Has begun to develop muscular mass around his arms and legs.

- Has pubic hair growth around his genital area and along his jaw line.

- Has difficulty reading and writing.

Pritpal (age 7)

- Can speak and write in two languages.

- Has some of her front teeth missing.

- Is 1.22 metres tall.

- Has not yet started menstruating.

- Does not have any breast development or pubic hair growth.

- Weighs 38 kilos.

- Often feels insecure and lives with foster parents.

Rosie (age 14)

- Speaks and writes her first language fluently.

- Is 1.57 metres tall.

- Weighs 53 kilos.

- Started menstruating at the age of 13.

- Has few friends out of school and is an introverted person.

Throughout this element we have been exploring the various predictable developmental changes which take place from birth to late childhood. All of these present a challenge to people at different points in the life cycle. Here is a summary of some of the ways we can help each other enjoy these changes and challenges.

- **By ensuring that people of all ages feel valued and important.**

- **By encouraging individuals to have a strong self-concept.**

- **By understanding what changes to expect so that we can look for and give suitable support.**

- **By providing a warm, secure and stimulating environment for other people in our lives.**

- **By making time to listen to other people.**

- **By encouraging successful language and communication skills so that people can express their anxieties.**

- **By helping individuals to feel in control of their lives.**

DEVELOPMENT OF THE SELF-CONCEPT

 ACTIVITY

Think about your main features and characteristics (for example, your height, gender, eye-colour, where you live, personality), and produce a self-portrait. You may use both words and pictures to express your perception of the essential you at this point in your life.

The self-portrait that you produced in the above activity describes your present **self-image**. How you see yourself is important. It has an effect on the way you form and contribute to your relationships with others. For example, if you see yourself as a popular and likeable person you will tend to be more outgoing and confident than if you see yourself as shy and uninteresting to others.

ACTIVITY

How do you feel about yourself as a person? Write some comments about:

- the things you like about yourself

- the things that you would like to change if you could

- the things that you are good at

- the things that you feel weaker at.

The information that results from questions such as those in the activity above, is a reflection of your **self-esteem**. A person's self-image combines with their self-esteem to make up their **self-concept**.

$$\text{Self-image} + \text{self-esteem} = \text{self-concept}.$$

The self-concept is important for us as individuals. There are a number of reasons why.

1 Individuals' self-concept is the essence of who they are. Having a strong self-concept gives us psychological security.

2 How we feel about ourselves affects the way others view us.

3 Having a positive and strong self-concept gives us a solid base from which to cope with future change.

People who have a negative self-concept may talk and behave in ways that lead to a 'self-fulfilling prophecy'. If, for example, you feel that you are boring and have little to offer, you may start to walk, talk and act in ways that confirm this. You may only see evidence of this being true and ignore evidence that contradicts it.

FACTORS AFFECTING THE SELF-CONCEPT

Self-image develops and changes as we **age** and gain in **maturity**. Our self-concept evolves and changes as we gain experience of the world and find out how others view us and about how we react in different situations. The image that you have of yourself today will not be the image that you reflect upon when you are forty, sixty or eighty years old. For example, our self-image and evaluation of our physical capabilities changes as we experience health, fitness, illness and disability at different points in our life cycle.

The factors that influence this process of change and development include:

- **the variety of social experiences we have, such as our educational and work experiences**

- **the effect of wider social attitudes, towards our gender, appearance and cultural origins for example**

- **the results of the process of maturing, such as physical ageing and gaining emotional complexity.**

Education

Education, particularly the things that teachers tell you about yourself and the way that they treat you, can affect your self-concept at a time when people are very open to suggestions about 'who' and 'what' they are. For some, educational success forms a positive self-image and high self-esteem. For others, school can be a more negative experience which leaves them feeling less capable and critical of themselves and their skills.

Relationships

People go through a number of phases of emotional and sexual development as they experience **relationships** and good and bad periods in their life. Simply because they grow older they adapt their outlook and behaviour to take account of the thoughts and feelings that they have. For example, young people who have a strong self-concept of themselves as 'young, free and single' learn new things about themselves and have to adapt their self-concept when they form an intimate, long-term partnership or get married.

Appearance

How we see and present ourselves, and how we feel others view us, play a big part in our overall self-concept. People tend to be more sensitive to this influence on their self-concept in their later adolescence and adult years. As people get older, physical appearance and the way that we present ourselves has a smaller impact on self-concept.

Culture

Culture, especially ethnic identity, affects our self-concept by influencing our feelings of belonging and our ideas about membership of different social groups. Culture and ethnic identity give us a sense of shared values. They can also lead to people being treated differently, perhaps in a discriminatory way, and thus influencing their sense of self-worth.

Work

Work is a very important influence on self-concept formation. One of the questions most commonly asked by people meeting for the first time is 'what do you do'? Our work status is a central feature of our lives. It becomes a part of our self-concept when the work that we do reflects aspects of us as individuals. For example, a person who answers that he is 'a home help with the elderly' is likely to have a very different self-concept to a person who answers that she is 'a politician'. The absence of work, when people are unemployed or retired for example, can be damaging to people's self-esteem.

THE IMPACT OF MAJOR EVENTS AND CHANGE

People may experience major events, also known as **life events**, at predictable times in their lives. They may also experience them as sudden, unexpected events. Major events in an individual's life have a direct impact on the person involved but can also, directly and indirectly, affect other people. For example, when a child first starts school both the child and its parents, or carers, will be affected by such a big change in their regular daily routines and life generally.

PREDICTABLE LIFE EVENTS

Predictable life events involve personal and social transitions. They are often turning points at which we start and finish major experiences in life. Examples of this type of life event occur throughout our life cycle and are expected milestones in our personal and social development.

Starting school

This is one of the first predictable life events for all children. Beginning primary school is a turning point in children's lives. It involves spending time away from parents and introduces them to a wider circle of people and to new patterns of behaviour and social situations. For many children this predictable life event is initially quite difficult to deal with. It is eventually successful because of the support received from parents, brothers and sisters and teachers. At eleven years old most children change from primary to secondary school. This change can be as difficult to adjust to as starting primary school was at a younger age.

 ACTIVITY

Ffion Robbins is 11 years old. She lives in a small village in North Wales with her parents and two younger brothers Tom, aged 8, and Geraint, aged 6. Her grandparents live ten miles away and are regular visitors. Ffion is about to finish at Wylfa Primary School and move to Glan Aber Comprehensive School in September. She knows everyone at Wylfa as all the children come from the same village and her teachers have been there since she started. She doesn't want to leave her primary school and admits to being scared of going to 'the big school', as she calls it, eight miles away. Ffion's best friend at school, Rhian, goes to swimming club with her, and they both belong to the same church group. Rhian is going to a different school in September.

⊗ **Describe the ways Ffion is about to experience life events in the next few months.**

⊗ **What type of help and support might she need as she experiences change in her life?**

⊗ **If you were one of Ffion's parents, what would you tell her about the likely impact of changing schools on her friendship with Rhian?**

Starting work

In Britain schooling is compulsory up to the age of 16. Everybody finishes school and studying at some point in their life. Most people go on to start work in either paid or unpaid employment. This is another major event in most people's lives. Starting work imposes different responsibilities and expectations on us. It is a point at which young people are required to function more independently of supportive parents and teachers.

Leaving home

As people establish more personal and financial independence from parents they usually broaden their social relationships, find work or take up a place on an educational course in a different part of the country. They reach a point where they either choose to, or have to, leave home. For some people this transition is the point at which they feel they have established their independence. For others, the changes that result from leaving home are not as positive. Experiences can include loneliness, lack of support and poverty. Whether the consequences are initially positive or negative, the experience of leaving home is a major event that will always be memorable for many people.

Marriage

Marriage is a life event that is generally viewed positively and which is celebrated by thousands of people each year. Marriage involves a major adaptation in personal relationships and behaviour for the couple. Ideally it establishes a deeper emotional and psychological commitment between them. Marriages also alter family relationships. The roles of family members change and new members are introduced into family groups. For example, in-laws become part of a wider family network and relationships between original family members may weaken because of the practicalities of a son or daughter moving away to live with their new partner.

Having children

Whether a couple are married or not, having children introduces major change into people's lives. Parenthood involves a change in role for both partners in a relationship and introduces new personal responsibilities and financial pressures. Decisions must be made about how to bring up the child, about how the work involved should be divided and about the need to provide on-going, nurturing love and financial support for the child. This can be seen as offering positive, enjoyable experiences but can seem a burden sometimes.

Changing job

Many people change jobs in the course of their career. Sometimes this change is planned as part of a career strategy. For others change is made out of necessity or because better opportunities arose at particular points. Whenever people change jobs they end some working, and perhaps also personal, relationships and begin new ones. New work roles can involve new responsibilities. It might mean learning new skills and acquiring new knowledge. Changing job can be a positive or negative life event depending on the effect that it has on the individual's social, financial and emotional life.

Moving home

This is recognised as a stressful life event for many people. A person's home is usually a place that they associate with safety, security and stability in their lives. Moving home means a break with the past and perhaps with friends, neighbours and the security of familiar surroundings. The practical demands of organising the removal of possessions, arranging finance to cover the cost of moving, and perhaps buying a house or flat, add to the emotional strain associated with this life event.

Retirement

Retirement is the point at which people end their working career. In Britain the retirement age for men is currently 65 and for women 60 years of age. Retirement is a major change as it requires an adjustment in daily routine, an alteration in status and has an impact on social relationships and on the person's financial situation. For people who have been very committed to their work and whose work provided their social life, retirement can give too much time to fill. For other people who have planned for their retirement and who have other interests and friendships, retirement can offer new opportunities and be welcomed as a positive life event. Retirement can cause financial problems. State and occupational pensions are likely to provide less money than a work salary. For many older people retirement can be the beginning of financial hardship.

Death

Death is inevitable. It marks the final predictable life event for all of us because we all know that one day each of our lives must end. Most people expect and hope to die painlessly in old age. Its impact is felt by people who have family, personal, work and friendship relationships with the deceased person and is felt most strongly in the period shortly after the person's death. Death is marked by all religious faiths with rituals and services that celebrate the life and achievements of the deceased person.

UNEXPECTED LIFE EVENTS

Unexpected life events happen to everyone. Events such as redundancy, serious illness, disability, divorce and bereavement can happen unexpectedly and are not usually welcomed.

Redundancy

Redundancy happens when an employer decides that a job is no longer required and ends the worker's contract of employment. It is different to dismissal, or 'sacking', as people who are made redundant lose their jobs through no fault of their own. Because of rapid changes in technology, changes in organisational structures and the economic recession over the last ten years, redundancy has been a relatively common experience. It can have a major impact on individuals as they lose their salary and find their financial situation insecure. It may break up firm friendships and leave people feeling as though they have no clear or valued role in life.

Serious illness

People who have serious illnesses, such as heart attacks, multiple sclerosis or cancer, may find themselves unable to carry out their usual daily routines. They may need additional practical help and emotional support and sometimes experience physical pain or mental distress as a result of their illness. Serious illnesses that occur suddenly also have an impact on those who have relationships with the individual affected. For example, the lifestyle of all the members of a family in which a child is suffering from leukaemia is altered. Their lives can be lived around meeting the needs of the child and responding to the effects that the illness has on them.

Disability

Some people inherit or are born with physical and learning disabilities. Other people acquire their disability as the result of an accident or because of their lifestyle. For example, people who drink alcohol to excess may be disabled by road traffic accidents, fights or the effects of large amounts of alcohol on the body.

People who become disabled must adapt their skills and lifestyle to cope with their situation. A disability can cause practical problems, such as whether they can work. It may also induce psychological stress and alter personal relationships that existed before the person had a disability. Friends, family and colleagues will also be affected. They will need to adjust their relationship to take account of the disabled person's new situation.

Divorce

Divorce is a relatively common experience in Britain today. People do not marry intending to get divorced. The breakdown of marriage, and the process of divorce, have an emotional impact on the couple concerned as well as financial and practical consequences. Separation will probably mean having to find separate accommodation and independent sources of income. Where the couple have children the impact of their divorce will be felt by the children because of new living arrangements, changing relationships and sometimes the need to adapt to new step-parents.

FIGURE 2.4: Divorce in England and Wales, 1961–90

	1961	1971	1976	1981	1986	1987	1988	1989	1990
Petitions filed (thousands)	32	111	145	170	180	183	183	185	192
Decrees nisi granted (thousands)	27	89	132	148	153	150	155	152	158
Decrees absolute granted (thousands)	25	74	127	146	154	151	153	151	153
Persons divorcing per thousand married people	2.1	6.0	10.1	11.9	12.9	12.7	12.8	12.7	12.9

Source: *Social Trends 23*, 1993

Bereavement

The death of some people may be anticipated and prepared for because of their greater age or because they have a terminal, or life-threatening, illness. While their loss is anticipated it may still be hard to accept and deal with emotionally. Bereavement can be even more traumatic and psychologically difficult when a person's death is unexpected and occurs suddenly or dramatically, for example because of accidents, serious injuries or suicide. To those who remain, the sense of loss can cause both short- and long-term problems of acceptance and adjustment.

ACTIVITY

☉ **Which of the following life events are predictable and which are unpredictable? Make a list.**

1 Becoming a parent.
2 Moving to a new house.
3 Starting school.
4 Getting married.
5 Getting your first job.
6 Being promoted.
7 Leaving home.
8 Getting divorced.
9 Retiring from work.

10 Going bankrupt.
11 The death of a loved one.
12 Taking exams.
13 Losing your job.
14 Learning to read/write.
15 Going into care.
16 Winning the National Lottery.

☉ **At what life stage are the above life events most likely to occur? Match them in the table.**

Life stages	Life events
Infancy to childhood	
Adolescence	
Adulthood	
Mid-life	
Old age	

METHODS OF MANAGING CHANGE CAUSED BY MAJOR EVENTS

Major events in our lives, such as going to school, starting work, marriage, divorce and bereavement all mean experiencing change. Change can be beneficial when it helps us to move on, to acquire or improve on skills, experience and knowledge. For people to benefit from the changes that major events offer, they need to work out ways of coping and adapting. There are a number of common methods of managing change including using family support, social support, and seeking professional help where necessary.

People are **supported** by their friends, their families and by care workers in different ways. For example, the emotional support that a person's family provides meets the need for love, affection and stability.

FAMILY SUPPORT

Family support is often the first form of help that people seek when they experience a major event. Families may be able to provide practical and emotional support at times of stress, change and crisis and are the source of a lot of informal care for people in all age groups. People need support from their families at different stages in their lives. Marriage is a major life event in which individuals may be supported emotionally and financially by their parents. Similarly parenthood and bereavement are occasions when family members may need to support each other emotionally and financially.

SOCIAL SUPPORT

Social support is useful in enabling people to adapt to the personal and emotional changes that a major life event cause. It may take the form of practical help and advice from people such as work colleagues and friends. It may also be offered by organisations such as the Citizens Advice Bureau, Relate (the marriage guidance agency) and MIND (the mental health charity). This enables an individual experiencing a major life event or change to obtain information, guidance and use opportunities to talk through different options available to them.

PROFESSIONAL SUPPORT

Help can be obtained from medical and social care workers who are trained and qualified to deal with complex difficulties that families and friends are unable to help with. Where people need financial help and advice, support is available from professionally qualified advisers, banks, building societies and government departments such as the Department of Social Security.

ACTIVITY

This activity asks you to think about different ways of managing and coping with change. Our reactions to change are important as they affect our health and well-being. Failing to adapt can lead to physical, psychological, social and financial problems.

Individually, identify ways of coping with the changes that may result from each of the major events listed below. Write down examples of the three types of support that someone might need to cope with the situation.

- ☺ The break-up of a marriage or long-term relationship.

- ☺ Leaving school or college with no job to go to.

- ☺ Moving to a new area of the country with your family.

- ☺ Being involved in a car crash.

- ☺ Losing your sight.

- ☺ Being promoted to a very responsible position at work.

- ☺ Leaving home to go to university or to live with friends.

- ☺ The birth of your first child.

- ☺ Being made redundant shortly after the birth of your first child.

- ☺ Failing to get the exam grades that are needed for a job or course.

- ☺ The death of a close relative or friend.

- ☺ Being diagnosed as having a serious illness.

- ☺ The onset of puberty.

- ☺ Winning the National Lottery jackpot.

- ☺ Emigrating to another country.

- ☺ Being sent to prison.

- ☺ Starting employment.

- ☺ Moving from primary to secondary school.

- ☺ Getting married.

- ☺ Getting into serious debt.

- ☺ One of your parents developing Alzheimer's disease.

- ☺ Retiring from work after 40 years in the same job.

- ☺ Beginning college.

Discuss your ideas with a partner, explaining the reasons for your decisions.

PORTFOLIO ASSIGNMENT

DEVELOPMENT DURING DIFFERENT LIFE STAGES

INTRODUCTION

Individuals develop and change in various ways as they pass through different life stages. These changes are easier to cope with if they are explained and prepared for in advance. This assignment gives you the opportunity to describe the main characteristics of development and the factors that influence self-concept.

Task 1

Write a 500-word article for a magazine read by young people aged 11 to 13 that explains the physical, social, emotional and intellectual development that occurs in childhood, adolescence, adulthood, mid-life and old age. Your article should be illustrated with pictures, diagrams or photographs.

Task 2

What do you think and feel about your own identity or self-concept? Take some time to think about this. Then write down your ideas in response to the following statements.

- I see myself as...

- My family see me as...

- My friends see me as...

- The things that I most like about myself are...

- The things that other people most like about me are...

- The aspects of my self that I would most like to change are...

- The aspects of me that other people would most like to change are....

Present your ideas in any form that you feel is appropriate. You may use pictures, line drawings and words to express the way that you see yourself and feel that others see you.

Task 3

What has made you the person that you are today? Think about your past experiences and identify the important events and people in your life so far that have influenced the way you have developed.

The influences that you may wish to consider might include:

- family relationships

- early childhood

- school

- friendships

- the effects of your gender, race and religion

- your physical appearance and other people's reaction to you

- your work experiences

- any major events in your life.

Present your ideas in the form of a life chart that covers the following stages.

- Infancy to childhood.

- Adolescence.

- Adulthood.

Again you should use a mixture of written and illustrative information to present your ideas.

PORTFOLIO ASSIGNMENT

EXERIENCING LIFE EVENTS

INTRODUCTION

A life event is a major, significant turning point, event or incident that affects the way that a person experiences life. This assignment gives you the opportunity to explore with others their life event experience and the effect that this had on them.

Task 1

Think of as many different life events as you can that you think would have an effect on an individual's life. Divide your list into predictable and unpredictable events.

Task 2

Find two volunteers who are willing to be interviewed by you about a significant life event that they have experienced. (You will need to do this carefully and avoid pressurising them.) These people could be someone in your family or a friend you know well. They should be clear about the purpose of the interview and about which life event you wish to discuss before you begin. The two interviewees need to be of different gender or ethnic origin or age.

Task 3

Interview your volunteers about their life events. You will need to compile appropriate questions and find a way of recording the information that they give you. The main areas that you need to cover include:

- their background

- the nature of the life event

- their thoughts and feelings about the life event

- their methods of coping with the life event.

Remember to keep copies of questions, any tape recordings and your notes. These can be used in your portfolio as evidence.

Task 4

For each person, use the information collected in your interview to produce a case study describing the life event experienced and the way the person coped with it. To maintain confidentiality you should change the names of your volunteers.

EXPLORE ᴛʜᴇ NATURE ᴏꜰ INTERPERSONAL RELATIONSHIPS ᴀɴᴅ ᴛʜᴇɪʀ INFLUENCE ON HEALTH ᴀɴᴅ WELL-BEING

THE RANGE OF RELATIONSHIPS IN DAILY LIFE

A relationship is founded on a connection between an individual and another person or group of people. For example, there is a connection (and so a form of relationship) between you and the rest of your class at school or college. There will also be a relationship between you and the person whom you most trust and confide in. The connections, or relationships that we have with others are made in a number of different areas, or contexts, of daily life. The three main contexts in which we form relationships are:

- in the family

- at work

- in our broader social circle.

FAMILY RELATIONSHIPS

The experience of living as a part of a **family** is something that most people will have at some time in their life. The family is a very important social unit both for the individual and for society as a whole. It is the main focus of many people's lives. It would not be correct to think of 'the family' as referring to one particular form of social relationship. Although the stereotype of the family is of a married couple with two children, there are in fact many variations in family structure as shown in Figure 2.5.

FIGURE 2.5: Types of family structure

⚡ QUICK response

Which types of family structure match those you have lived in?

Structure	Characteristics
Nuclear family	One man, one woman and their dependent children
Extended family	A nuclear family with other relatives living as part of the family (for example, grandparents, aunts and uncles)
Lone-parent family	A single parent and their dependent children
Reconstituted family	Two parents who may or may not be married and whose dependent children are step- or half-brothers and sisters with another parent living outside of the family following break-up of the original family through separation or divorce

FIGURE 2.6: Families by types of household and ethnic group

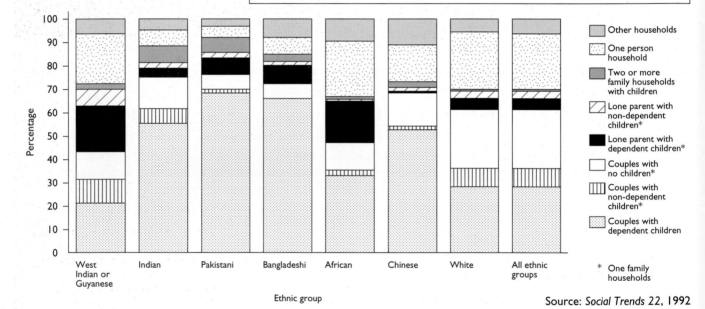

Source: *Social Trends 22*, 1992

GENOGRAMS

Genograms are a type of diagram used to show the structure of a family and the relationships between the different members. They show family trees in diagram form. The symbols that are used in genograms are shown in Figure 2.7.

In a genogram the original parents are shown at the top and the relatives who follow underneath. Look at the example in Figure 2.8.

We can see that Harry and Sally got married. They had two children, George and Delia. When George and Delia grew up they got married to Jean and Victor. Delia has had one child called Patrick, and Jean has had two children, Ben and Jenny.

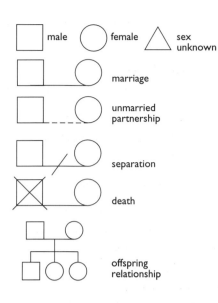

FIGURE 2.7: Symbols used in genograms

male   female   sex unknown

marriage

unmarried partnership

separation

death

offspring relationship

FIGURE 2.8: Example of a genogram

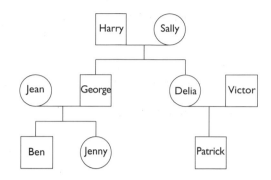

ACTIVITY

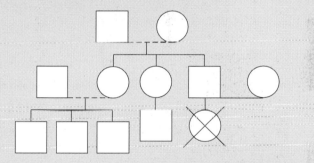

1 **Read the genograms above and identify the relationships and make-up of each family. You should write the primary relationship that each person has in the family (for example, mother, son, father) next to the appropriate box.**

2 **Using the following list of family members, make a genogram of the Carver family.**

   Raymond – grandfather

   Anna – grandmother

   Scott – son of Raymond and Anna

   Gina – Scott's wife

   Ian – son of Raymond and Anna

   Angela – Ian's girlfriend who lives with him

   Maxine – daughter of Raymond and Anna

   Mia – partner who lives with Maxine

   Chris – son of Gina and Scott

   Peter – son of Gina and Scott

   Pamela – daughter of Ian and Angela

   Colin – son of Maxine.

3 **Make a genogram of your own family. You should include the current ages and first names to make the diagram more interesting and easier to follow. If you come across a type of relationship or situation that is not covered by the above symbols you should develop your own, but remember to say what they stand for in a key at the end.**

THE ROLE OF THE FAMILY IN SOCIETY

Many people see the family as the cornerstone of society. This is because of the important role it plays in the development of individuals and in maintaining social order. The family is said to carry out the **primary socialisation** of children. This means that it teaches children the 'lessons' that will prepare them for their adult roles. Socialisation begins at birth and continues throughout life. The family has a vital role to play in protecting, providing for, and supporting members at various stages of their development.

FIGURE 2.9: The role of the family

Providing	Informal education of children so that they learn attitudes, values and the rules of social behaviour.
	Physical resources needed for growth, intellectual development, such as food, housing, toys and other stimulation.
Supporting	The emotional development of the person from infancy through to adulthood. Family relationships are a source of stability, security and a setting where emotions can be experienced and expressed.
	Members of the family are supported financially at points in their lives where they cannot support themselves.
Protecting	Family members play an important role as informal carers in protecting the health and well-being of other members at all stages of the life cycle.
	The family protects the interests of children and young people through the giving of advice and guidance, particularly about education, relationships and personal safety.
	Family relationships are said to be 'primary' relationships because the people involved generally know each other very well, their ways of relating to each other are informal and one person in the relationship cannot simply be replaced by a new person. Within a family there are a number of different possible relationships between the various members. Relationships are formed:

- ✪ between parents

- ✪ between parents and children

- ✪ between children

- ✪ with other relatives.

☼ ACTIVITY

Individuals may live in different types of family or household. From the point of view of a child, a teenager and an elderly person, identify both the positive and negative effects of living in

- ⊗ a nuclear family

- ⊗ a lone-parent family.

WORK RELATIONSHIPS

Work relationships are usually with people who are not members of our biological family and whose connection with us is more short-term. Work relationships are said to be **secondary relationships** because:

- ⊗ **interaction between people is limited to work situations**

- ⊗ **there are clear rules about how to relate (for example with your boss or supervisor)**

- ⊗ **they are expressed through clearly defined social roles.**

Relationships at work can be formal or informal. **Formal relationships** are those in which the connections are purely work-related and there is an element of authority. For example, individual workers have a formal relationship with the senior management of the organisation that employs them.

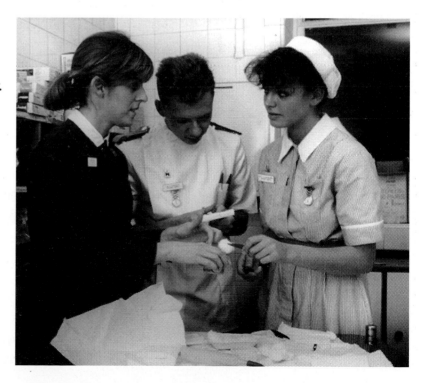

Where there is a contract of employment that states the terms and conditions of employment and the duties and responsibilities of each party, the relationship would legally and formally be described as an employer/employee relationship. **Informal relationships** are also formed in the work context between colleagues. While the main reason for people initially establishing a relationship with others at work is that they need to cooperate and work together to complete work-related tasks, colleagues often form friendships and emotional bonds that result in more informal behaviours and ways of relating to each other.

SOCIAL RELATIONSHIPS

Social relationships are those that we choose to establish with other people because we share interests or because there is a mutual liking. Friendships are important **informal** social relationships. There is an emotional connection between friends, though perhaps not one that is as deeply rooted as in family relationships.

Individuals also have more superficial social relationships with acquaintances who they would not class as friends. These social relationships tend to be formal because there are rules about inter-action and behaviour and they are expressed through clearly defined roles. For example, you may have a 'social' connection (relationship) with the person who regularly serves you at your local shop. The relationship may be friendly but is acted out through 'customer' and 'shop assistant' roles. Both parties probably expect to talk only about superficial every-day topics (the weather) rather than anything to do with their personal or emotional life which they might discuss with closer friends.

CAUSES OF CHANGE IN RELATIONSHIPS

Throughout our lives, the relationships that we develop with other people change and evolve. For example, as a young child a person's relationship with his or her parents is likely to have been one of dependence from a practical and emotional point of view. As individuals move into adolescence and then young adulthood, the person's relationship changes. They become more independent and able to care for themselves and find other sources of emotional support.

This type of change is caused by maturation and the experience of transition from one life stage to another. The relationships that we have in childhood, adolescence, adulthood, mid-life and old age tend to be founded on different 'connections' or grounds. A relationship may be strong at one particular stage in life, because the parties have a clear connection that is important to them. It may weaken or end because the connection does not survive the transition into the next stage.

ACTIVITY

1 **List your childhood friends (at primary school and in your local area).**

Tick all of those who were, or are, still a friend at secondary school.

Add to your list friends made at secondary school.

2 **Which of your current friends, school or college colleagues and other people do you expect to be an important part of your life in ten years' time ? Explain why, identifying the connection that will persist over the next ten years.**

MAJOR LIFE EVENTS

Predictable and unexpected life events alter people's relationships. This happens because life events affect our roles, abilities and behaviour. For example, a parent who suddenly acquires a disability, such as loss of sight, will need additional support and assistance from other family members and may not be able to carry out his or her usual work or domestic role until new coping skills are learned.

THE EFFECTS OF BREAKDOWN IN RELATIONSHIPS

Relationships change and evolve as people experience life transitions and life events. Change and development can be positive and is important to allow people to develop and adapt. For example, young people may form a romantic, affectionate relationship that changes over time to reflect their deeper love and attachment to each other. Sometimes the changes that occur in relationships cause them to break down. For example, marital or other intimate relationships may break down when people no longer love each other and would prefer to be divorced. The consequences, or effects, of relationship breakdown for the individual can be seen in a number of areas of life.

Effects on emotional life

The ending of an important relationship can cause people to feel sadness, loneliness, anger, and unsettled and negative about themselves. It is not unusual for people to feel rejected and unwanted when their personal relationships are unsuccessful. The unhappiness and stress that is felt when relationships break down often leads to interrupted sleep patterns, with individuals finding it difficult to go to sleep and waking early. Some people use food, eating either too much or too little, as a source of comfort. For most people these feelings and behaviours are temporary and are replaced with more positive feelings and behaviours when the person has come to terms with the severing of the connection.

Effects on social life

Relationship breakdown can lead to individuals withdrawing and reducing their social contact with others. For example, where social activities revolved around meeting others with their partner, a divorce or separation may lead to the loss of social life. The consequences of divorce may be more time spent at home and social isolation, especially where one partner is left with young children to support and care for.

Effects on intellectual activity

Relationship breakdown is emotionally upsetting and sometimes traumatic. People who are experiencing strong emotions, particularly negative ones about themselves, find it difficult to concentrate on other matters. They can become preoccupied with their feelings and the problems resulting from the ending of their relationship. Many people find it difficult to study and to concentrate on work in such circumstances.

Physical effects

Relationship breakdown can also have physical effects. People may feel that they have no appetite or they may over-eat to comfort themselves. They may neglect their physical appearance and hygiene, or find it hard to maintain their usual exercise routine through lack of motivation. The stress that people feel when their relationships break down can also be expressed in the form of different physical symptoms. Illnesses such as headaches, pain and tiredness often reflect underlying emotional distress.

QUICK response

Have any of your formal or informal relationships ever broken down?
Think about the effects that they had on you.

ACTIVITY

Relationships are very important to people. As we meet others, undergo different life experiences and simply grow older, our relationships change and sometimes break down. Read the following letters to the problem page where you are the columnist. Think about each one and write an appropriate reply.

Letter 1

Dear Columnist,

I am 15 years old and recently started seeing someone. He is also 15 and lives near to where I live. My parents don't want me to see him. They say that I'm too young. This has led us to row about him. I think that my dad just doesn't understand me anymore. My mum says he's only protecting me and that I should concentrate on my homework, not on boyfriends. I've decided that I will ignore what they say and go out and see him when I get home before my dad gets in. What do you think about this? How do you think it might affect my relationship with my parents?

    Yours, Rachel B.

Letter 3

Dear Columnist,

I work with two other people in an office. We all get along very well normally. Recently one of my colleagues began putting pressure on me to go for a drink with him. I've tried telling him that I like him as a workmate but that I don't want to go out with him but he won't take no for an answer. This is causing me a lot of stress and I feel that I must tell somebody and get some advice on what to do. Should I tell my other work colleague about it? I thought that I should but that it might affect the atmosphere in the office. I would be grateful for your thoughts on what the effect of this might be.

    Yours sincerely,
    Julia Jones

Letter 2

Dear Columnist,

My son Stephen is 19 years old. Recently his behaviour has been out of character. He has started spending nearly all of his time in his room, rarely says much and eats junk food and takeaways that he buys at night from the local shops. He's stopped going out with most of his friends, something he used to love doing. When I try to talk to him about how he's feeling or when I tell him to tidy up and start looking after himself again, he either gets angry and tells me to stop picking on him or tells me that there's nothing wrong and that I should leave him alone.

I've heard from the mother of one of his friends that Stephen has recently split up with his girlfriend. He won't talk to me about this. Could you tell me whether this could be the reason for his changed behaviour and explain why it has affected him so badly ?

    I look forward to your reply.
    Malcolm Higginbotham

Letter 4

Dear Columnist,

I am a single mother of two teenage children. My relationship with my current partner, who lives with us, has all but broken down. We both feel that it is over but have kept it from the twins as they are studying for their GCSE exams. My partner has told me that he has met someone else and is going to leave at the end of the month. This is in the middle of the twins' exams. How do you think this will affect them? How can I help them to cope with this? I would be grateful for your advice.

    Yours sincerely,
    Marina F.

ACTIVITY

Make short notes on the following terms. If you are unsure of any, look back at the chapter.

- Relationship

- Nuclear family

- Reconstituted family

- Socialisation

- Formal relationship

- Informal relationship

- Life event

PORTFOLIO ASSIGNMENT

EXPERIENCES OF FAMILY LIFE

INTRODUCTION
There are many different types of 'family' in Britain today. This assignment gives you the opportunity to investigate and explain the role of the family in the development of two individuals.

TASK 1
Your own experience of family life is a starting point from which you can develop your investigation. Divide your life span into the following four stages:

- early childhood (0–5)

- later childhood (5–11)

- early adolescence (12–14)

- late adolescence (15–18).

Using your own memories and information from others within your family, identify the main events, relationships and your changing role and behaviour within the family during each stage. You might like to make a table to record and present this.

TASK 2
Interview another person who is around the same age as you about his or her experiences of family life in each of the above stages. You will need to prepare questions and conduct your interview carefully to get the type of information that you require. You should ask the interviewee to describe:

- the type of family that he or she grew up in

- the ways the person's family influenced the person as he or she grew up

- who the influential people in the family were

- what role he or she feels the family performed at different times and stages of the person's life.

Remember to conduct your interview sensitively and avoid pressurising your volunteer to reveal things that he or she would rather not. Keep any questionnaires, lists of questions, or letters and notes about setting up your interview as these may be added to your portfolio.

TASK 3
Produce a case study called Experiences of Family Life that describes and explains the role of the family in the development of your interviewee. To preserve confidentiality you should not use the real name of your interviewee unless he or she wishes you to. Do not disclose things that the person does not wish to be made public. You should cover all of the stages that you wrote about in Task 2.

EXPLORE THE INTERACTION OF INDIVIDUALS AND HOW THEY MAY INFLUENCE HEALTH AND WELL-BEING

SOCIETY AND SOCIAL ROLES

In the last part of the chapter we will be considering how people as individuals interact within society through the social roles that they perform. We will look at how the experiences and circumstances of people's lives affect their health and well-being. We will explore how individual choices are influenced by these characteristics and then affect health.

"To all intents and purposes a new-born human baby is helpless. Not only is it physically dependent on older members of the species but it also lacks the behaviour patterns necessary for living in human society … In order to survive, it must learn the skills, knowledge and accepted ways of behaving of the society into which it was born … It must learn the culture of its society."
(M Haralambos and M Holborn, *Sociology: Themes and Perspectives*, HarperCollins, 1995)

The quote above makes the point that individuals live and work together in social groups and that in order to do so successfully they must develop and share a culture, or way of life. Culture is important because it gives people shared guidelines by which they can live their lives cooperatively with others. Without a shared culture people would not be able to communicate and cooperate.

SOCIAL NORMS

The guidelines that people share are known as **norms**. A norm is a specific guide to action which defines acceptable and appropriate behaviour in particular situations. For example, there are norms governing dress in British society. Men and women dress in different ways because there are social norms guiding their choice of clothes.

Norms are enforced by positive rewards, such as approving smiles and compliments, and negative sanctions, such as hostile looks and critical comments. For example, there are norms relating to how doctors are supposed to dress and behave. A doctor who saw patients while dressed in leather trousers, T-shirt and cowboy boots and who was very informal would probably attract negative sanctions from his patients and fellow health workers. A person dressed in this way could attract positve reactions if he were performing the role of a youth television interviewer or comedian as the norms for behaviour in these roles make their appearance and behaviour acceptable.

Some norms are formalised and made into laws. These are enforced by official punishments such as fines and imprisonment. For example, there is a norm that only people who are legitimately employed as police officers are allowed to wear the uniforms and insignia of the police service. It is an imprisonable offence for anyone else to wear a police uniform and 'impersonate a police officer'. The norm is specific because it applies particularly to police uniforms. People commonly wear other uniforms, such as replica versions of their favourite football and rugby teams but are not breaking any laws by doing so.

SOCIALISATION

Members of a society usually take their culture for granted. The process by which we have all learnt the culture of our society is known as **socialisation**. As we have seen, important early socialisation takes place in the family. By responding to approval and disapproval and through copying the behaviour of adults within the family, children learn the language and behaviour patterns of their culture. Socialisation does not end in childhood. **Secondary socialisation** continues in work and community settings. The learner nurse, social worker and care assistant all have to learn their occupational roles and the ways of behaving and interacting that are expected of them.

SOCIAL ROLES

All members of society have a number of different **statuses**. For example, we may have personal statuses as brother, sister, mother, father, girlfriend, or boyfriend. We also have occupational statuses, such as nurse, social worker, dentist, electrician. Finally, we have other statuses that are based on our biological make-up, such as white, black, male or female.

Each status that we have is accompanied by a number of norms that define how we are expected to act. A group of norms is known as a **social role**. For example, the **status** of a dentist is accompanied by a group of **norms** associated with the **role** of a dentist. Playing or performing social roles involves social relationships. People play their own roles in relation to other people's roles. For example, the role of a dental nurse is played in relation to that of a dentist and patients. There are expectations about how each person should act and how they ought to interact with each other. Individuals therefore interact in terms of roles. When a dental nurse is at work he or she interacts with the individuals who are dentists in terms of their work roles.

Social roles are important because they enable us to regulate and organise behaviour. They help us to know what is expected of us and allow us to predict how others will relate to us. For example, in a dental consultation both dentist and patient know what to expect, what to do and how to behave, by interacting on the basis of their expected roles.

> **QUICK** response
>
> **Which health and social care roles have the highest status?**

ROLES PEOPLE PLAY IN DIFFERENT SOCIAL SETTINGS

We all play a number of different social roles. On any particular day we may play several roles at different times, or even at the same time. This situation occurs because we all move between different social settings. For example, a person may wake up at home as a sister and daughter, then go to work where she becomes a colleague and employee. At the same time she may have the status, and role, of being a neighbour, taxpayer, and voter. The roles that we play depend on the social setting that we are in and the roles of others in these settings. The main social settings that we move through are outlined below.

Roles in the family

The family is a social setting in which people play a number of different social roles. In a nuclear family setting an adult may play the roles of husband or wife and parent. Children play the roles of brother or sister to each other and of child to their parents. Each of these roles is played in relation to the other roles in the family. Each member of the family is expected to act and interact according to his or her role and the norms that are attached to it.

ACTIVITY

Make a list of the different roles that exist in your own family. What are the norms that are attached to each role? Write these alongside your list.

Roles in the workplace

Within the workplace, roles are often very clearly defined in terms of who is responsible to whom and who is in charge. There is also a formal distinction between the roles of the employer and the employee. This means that the law sets out the duties and responsibilities of the employer and the employee. The Health and Safety at Work Act (1974), for example, makes it a duty of employers to ensure 'the health, safety and welfare at work of employees' and makes it their legal responsibility to provide and display a written health and safety policy. Employees have a duty to 'take reasonable care for the health and safety of themselves and others'. They have a responsibility not to behave in a way that may put others at risk. The Health and Safety at Work Act (1974) can be used to enforce employer and employee roles and punish behaviours that break the boundaries of these roles.

Recreational roles

The two obvious 'leisure roles' are those of participant and organiser. As an organiser of a charity sports day an individual would be expected to be well organised, to make decisions and to be able to sort out any problems or difficulties that arose.

These norms would not apply to a participant in the sports activity. Participant roles would involve joining in events, wearing appropriate sports clothes and following the rules and regulations set down by the organisers. The role and interactions of an organiser would be played out in relation to the roles of the participants and spectators. Each would have certain expectations of the other and would be able to predict and interpret their behaviour as a result of knowing the other's role.

Roles in the wider community

As citizens of Britain we all have roles that we play in relation to the government and other people who live in our community. If you are an employed person earning money you play the role of taxpayer to the government's role of income tax collector and the local authority's role of council tax collector. People who are aged 18 or over and who are registered with the local authority as occupants of a dwelling in a particular area play the role of voter when there are local or national elections. The role of voter is played in relation to that of the candidates seeking election. These roles are formally defined in laws and rules which set down the conditions of eligibility to vote and pay taxes. One role that we play in the wider community which is not affected by law but which is governed by social convention is that of neighbour.

ACTIVITY

Make a list of the expectations you have of the following roles and the behaviour that you associate with them. You should write down words and phrases that express your ideas about each of the following.

- ⊗ **A good employee.**
- ⊗ **A good neighbour.**
- ⊗ **A good husband/wife.**
- ⊗ **A sporting opponent.**

STATUS AND SOCIAL CHARACTERISTICS

The different roles that we play each have a **social status** attached to them. Social status is the sense of esteem, prestige or value that is given to a social characteristic and is an indication of a person's position in a group or in wider society. There are basically two different types of social status.

⊗ **Ascribed status refers to the status that we are born with.**

⊗ **Achieved status refers to the status that we earn or acquire at some time in our life.**

The social experiences that we have and the circumstances in which we live determine the status that we have in society and the position that we occupy in society.

ACTIVITY

Rate the following social characteristics in terms of the level of prestige that you feel is generally attached to each. You should score your choices as follows.

1 High social status.

2 Medium social status.

3 Low social status.

Housing status	Home owner	Council tenant	Homeless
Environment status	Urban, town area	Inner city area	Rural, country area
Education status	University graduate	No qualifications	NVQ qualified
Employment status	Unemployed	Temporary employee	Permanent employee
Financial status	Bankrupt	Wealthy	Overdrawn

Think carefully about the range of different social characteristics (such as ethnic identity, gender, religion, nationality) that you possess. Without using your name or describing yourself physically, write a paragraph about yourself under the heading 'Who I am...'. The paragraph should describe the roles and social characteristics that you have which give you your social identity.

You will need to consider:

⊗ the different roles that you take in different group settings

⊗ the different social characteristics that describe you.

CLASSIFICATION SYSTEMS

Systems for grouping people according to their social characteristics are known as **classification systems**. Many classification systems are based around people's **socio-economic characteristics**. These include people's occupation, the amount of income they earn, and the wealth and material possessions that they own. Classification systems enable us to understand the way in which society is structured, or made up, of people with differing socio-economic characteristics. They are used by government and commercial organisations to put people into different social groups.

SOCIAL CLASS

One of the most important classification systems is known as the **Registrar General's social class scale**. The Registrar General is the government official who is responsible for collecting data on births, marriages and deaths. A **census** is conducted every ten years which contributes data to the Registrar General's scale. Some of the information that is collected is used to produce a social class scale. In this scale the status, or 'general standing within the community', of a person's occupation, or job, is used as the basis on which to allocate them to one of six social classes.

The different class groupings are shown in Figure 2.10.

FIGURE 2.10: The Registrar General's social class scale

Category of Occupation	Class	Examples
Professional and higher administrative occupations	A	Accountant, lawyer
Intermediate occupations	B	Manager, teacher
Skilled occupations (non-manual)	C1	Clerical worker, secretary
Skilled occupations (manual)	C2	Bus driver, carpenter
Partly skilled occupations	D	Bus conductor, postman/woman
Unskilled occupations	E	Labourer, cleaner.

ACTIVITY

Where would you place the following jobs in the Registrar General's classification system?

Hospital workers	Community workers
Clinic receptionist	Home help
Chef	Qualified social worker
Porter	Unemployed volunteer
Registered nurse	Nursery nurse
Pharmacist	Optician
Domestic cleaner	General Practitioner (GP)
Care assistant	Health visitor
Hospital consultant	Youth club leader
Hospital manager	Driver (meals on wheels van)

Working alone allocate each of the jobs to one of the social classes in the Registrar General's scale. Remember that the jobs should be classed according to their 'standing in the community'. The highest status jobs will be in the higher classes and the lower status ones in the lower classes.

Discuss your decisions with other members of the group. What do you agree on? Are there any areas of difference? Which jobs are the most difficult to classify?

PROBLEMS OF CLASSIFICATION

The Registrar General's scale is the official government classification system. It is often used in surveys of health and social well-being. Although it is based on the status attached to jobs, this is not the only way of defining social class. This way has problems because it misses out many of the other factors that help to define a person's social class. The Registrar General's classification system tries to use 'objective' or factual criteria to put people into clearly defined classes. Problems occur for three main reasons.

1 Individuals' occupation does not always reveal enough reliable information about their other social characteristics and their background. For example, a person may now be a Member of Parliament but have an occupational background as a coal miner. He may have been brought up in a family that had little income and have received only a basic education. He may still define himself as working class, rather than the higher class that his occupation suggests.

2 The status attached to jobs at times when there is a lot of social and industrial change is not always clear. For example the social status of the occupation of printing has fallen as craft skills have been replaced by machines.

3 New occupations are being introduced all the time. It is often not clear for several years what their 'general standing in the community' is.

Old job
Internal Mail Supervisor
Doris Roberts, 54, has worked in the postroom of a large psychiatric hospital for twenty-six years. For the last five years she has been a supervisor.

Salary: Just under £13,000

Typical day: Start at 8 am Pouches of mail are opened and sorted for delivery. From 9 am it is taken around the hospital to wards and offices. There are six hourly mail-rounds each day. Outward mail is picked up as deliveries are made. A supervisor and mail workers each walk about five miles per day around the hospital. They wear a uniform and are given four pairs of shoes a year.

New job
E-Mail System Manager
Vikram Robben, aged 25, has worked for a large pharmaceutical company for two years. He has been e-mail systems manager since joining. All 200 staff have an e-mail address and access to a computer to post e-mail messages to each other. This cuts out paper memos and other internal post.

Salary: £ 22,000

Typical day: Start at 9 am. Check that the system is running smoothly. Deal with any overnight problems. Speak to the Help Desk staff and support technicians about the system and e-mail files. The manager spends most of the day on the phone or at a computer dealing with queries and keeping the files tidy and preserving the integrity of the system.

ACTIVITY

1 **What effect has technology had on the job of 'mail management' described above?**

2 **Has the 'occupational status' attached to 'mail management' changed as a result?**

3 **Which social classes do you feel that Doris and Vikram each belong to ? Explain the reasons for your decisions.**

Occupation is a useful starting point from which to classify individuals. It is not the only way of doing this and is problematic because society is changing and classification systems are always imprecise. Compared to other possible socio-economic indicators it is the best predictor of a person's other social characteristics.

INDIVIDUAL CHOICE AND HEALTH AND SOCIAL CARE OUTCOMES

Researchers who study health and social care have found that different social groups tend to have different patterns of health behaviour and to use care services in different ways. The individuals who make up social groups have some things in common, such as similar levels of income, similar types of job and similar standards of education. They are also likely to share a similar outlook on life. To some extent these shared characteristics influence health choices. Social groups are, however, made up of people able to make their own, personal decisions. The question that this raises is whether people can make decisions that will influence their health and well-being positively.

Some researchers, politicians and health workers feel that people are restricted by their position in society and by the financial and social pressures that they experience. The other side of the argument is that people are free to make choices about aspects of their health behaviour. This might include choices about whether or not they should smoke, how much alcohol they consume and whether they eat a balanced diet.

⚙ ACTIVITY

Look at the following list of factors which influence health and well-being. Produce a list of some of the choices that people could make about each. The choices that you come up with should have a clear influence on health and well-being.

Individual choice	Possible choice	Effect on health and well-being
Use of care services	To go to the dentist	Possible tooth decay and mouth problems if not checked regularly
Nutrition	Whether to ...	
Alcohol consumption		
Smoking habits		
Personal hygiene		
Exercise		
Attitude to education		
Maintenance of housing		
Use of available income		

The lists produced by several different people will show that there are a wide range of health choices that can be made in each of these areas. Researchers who have studied the choices that people make have found that similar choices are made by people within the same social class group.

PATTERNS OF HEALTH AND WELL-BEING

FIGURE 2.11: Social class and death rates in men and married women aged 15–64

Social surveys conducted by government and academic researchers have found that there are some clear differences in the health and well-being experienced by different social groups. Many of these studies look at the health and illness differences between the social classes using the Registrar-General's classification. Some of the findings are outlined in Figure 2.11.

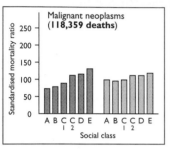

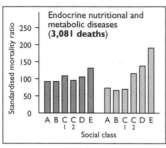

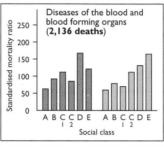

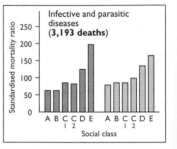

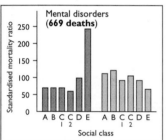

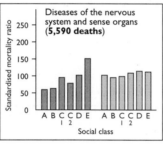

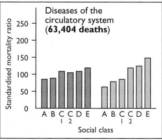

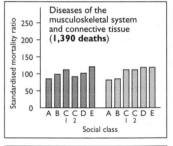

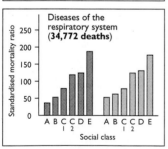

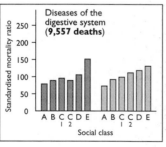

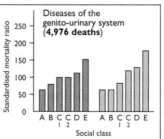

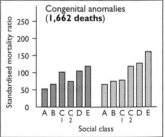

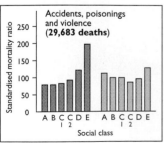

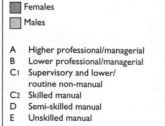

Females
Males

A   Higher professional/managerial
B   Lower professional/managerial
C1   Supervisory and lower/
     routine non-manual
C2   Skilled manual
D   Semi-skilled manual
E   Unskilled manual

QUICK response

What pattern of health is revealed by these statistics on cause of death in different social classes?

Source: Department of Health, 1980

USE OF CARE SERVICES

Health and social care services in the statutory sector are supposed to be available equally to all people regardless of their social characteristics or ability to pay. Research has regularly shown that some social groups use care services more often than other groups. For example, women use GP services more frequently than men. People in social classes A and B use GP services more often and have longer consultations than people in social classes C2, D and E, even though people in the lower groups experience higher levels of illness and ill-health.

NUTRITION

Children from social classes C2, D and E have twice as many decayed teeth as their counterparts in classes A, B and C1. Tooth decay, like many other diseases, is more likely to occur because a person has a certain type of diet. There are also social class links between diet and disease levels. For example, men are more likely to suffer from coronary heart disease (which is strongly linked to the level of saturated fat in the diet). Men in social classes D and E are more likely than men in other social classes to die as a result of these diseases.

SMOKING HABITS

People in social classes D and E are more likely to smoke cigarettes than people in the other social classes. The pattern of deaths due to diseases such as lung cancer and respiratory disorders reflects this higher level of smoking by people in the lower social classes.

ALCOHOL CONSUMPTION

Alcohol is a socially accepted drug. It causes illnesses such as cirrhosis of the liver, as well as many accidents and injuries from fights.

ACTIVITY

Answer the following questions.

⊗ **What does Figure 2.12 tell us about the general trend in smoking behaviour?**

FIGURE 2.12: Changes in smoking patterns by social class, 1960 and 80

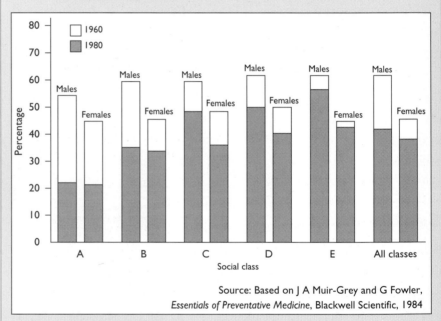

Source: Based on J A Muir-Grey and G Fowler,
Essentials of Preventative Medicine, Blackwell Scientific, 1984

⊗ **In which social class were people most likely to be smokers in 1960?**

⊗ **In which social class were women least likely to be smokers in 1980?**

⊗ **In which social class were women most likely to be smokers in 1980?**

⊗ **How has the ratio of men:women smokers changed over the period of the graph?**

⊗ **What factors do you think may have contributed to this last change?**

HOUSING

Housing provides people with the material, or physical, conditions in which they will spend much of their time. The type and standard of housing that peole live in is related to the income that they have. People on low incomes are less able to afford a good standard of housing or to be able to maintain it and heat it adequately. Damp, overcrowded and neglected properties provide the kind of conditions for respiratory disorders and infectious diseases such as tuberculosis and bronchitis to develop.

Families with very low incomes who are unable to afford to rent or own their own homes are now increasingly likely to experience even lower standards of housing in bed and breakfast hotels. People who are homeless and who sleep rough are very prone to poor physical and mental health. They live in a very harsh physical environment and face difficulties in getting the financial and emotional support that they need.

	Owned home outright	Owned home with mortgage	Rented home
Professional	11	75	14
Employers and managers	13	74	13
Intermediate non-manual	11	68	21
Junior non-manual	12	57	31
Skilled manual	14	60	26
Semi-skilled manual	12	42	46
Unskilled manual	11	32	57
Economically inactive	45	11	44
All socio-economic groups	25	42	33

Note: Excludes members of the Armed Forces, economically active full-time students and those who were unemployed and had never worked.

Source: *Social Trends 26*, 1996

FIGURE 2.13: Socio-economic group of head of household in Great Britain, 1994–5

PORTFOLIO ASSIGNMENT

ROLES THAT PEOPLE PLAY

INTRODUCTION

This assignment gives you the opportunity to investigate and compare the roles of two different people and to describe how laws, rules, and conventions affect them.

TASK 1

Recruit two volunteers willing to be interviewed by you about the various roles that they play. You should try to find two adults who have different social roles as this will give you a better contrast.

Keep any letters or notes about recruiting your volunteers that you produce, as these can be used in your portfolio.

TASK 2

Develop a list of questions to ask your interviewees. You will need to find out about:

- the different roles that they take in their family, through their work, in their recreation time, and as a result of being a member of the wider community

- the laws, rules and conventions that influence their behaviour in some of their roles.

You will need to think about how you are going to record the information they give you. For any tape recording you must have the prior agreement of the interviewee.

TASK 3

After you have carried out your interviews write up your findings as a case study. Your study should do the following things.

1 Briefly describe how you recruited your volunteers and conducted the interviews.

2 Give examples and compare the roles of each person in their family, through their work, in their recreation time, and as a result of being a member of the wider community.

3 Outline the similarities and differences in the roles of your volunteers.

PORTFOLIO ASSIGNMENT

INDICATORS OF SOCIAL CLASS

INTRODUCTION

Classification systems such as the Registrar General's scale, group people together according to their socio-economic characteristics. The main indicator of social class is seen to be a person's occupation. This assignment gives you the opportunity to explore and compare other characteristics that people may have in common.

TASK 1

What do you think the main indicators are that determine people's social class apart from the job they do? Think of a list of indicators, giving examples that are important in telling you which social class individuals belong to. The following headings might be used to help you with this task.

- Housing status.

- Environment in which they live.

- Educational background.

- Employment status.

- Financial status.

TASK 2

Use newspapers, magazines and books to find evidence to support and illustrate the contrasts you've made between the characteristics of people in different social classes. Produce a poster or other display that compares the various characteristics of different socio-economic groups.

PORTFOLIO ASSIGNMENT

MAKING HEALTH CHOICES

INTRODUCTION

At the beginning of the twentieth century health problems were mainly linked to poverty and poor environmental conditions. As we approach the end of the twentieth century health problems are mainly linked to poor diet, lack of exercise and the effects of tobacco, alcohol and drugs. For most people these are things that they have some choice and control over in their lives.

This assignment gives you the opportunity to investigate and describe how people's health choices affect their health and well-being.

TASK 1

We are able to make a number of choices that may affect our health. These include:

- the types and quantities of food that we eat

- whether and how we exercise

- whether we consume alcohol and in what quantity

- whether we smoke and how many cigarettes we consume

- whether we take drugs and which drugs we use

- whether we make use of health and social care services

- how we use our money

- whether and how we look after our housing.

Conduct a survey of ten people.

- What are their views on how any five of the above may affect health and well-being?

- What choices have they made in relation to the five items chosen?

- What effects have their choices had on their health and well-being?

Keep any letters or notes or lists of questions that you produce relating to your survey as these can be used in your portfolio.

TASK 2

After you have carried out your survey present your findings as a survey report. Your report should:

- briefly describe how you recruited your participants and conducted the survey

- include a copy of the survey questions that you used

- give a graphical display of your findings

- include a brief written summary of your findings, explaining how people's choices may affect their health and well-being.

✔ MULTIPLE CHOICE QUESTIONS

These questions are designed to test your knowledge and understanding of chapter 2. There is only one correct answer (A, B, C or D) to each question. You can check your choices with the answers given at the back of the book.

1 The growth spurt that occurs during puberty is controlled largely by hormones being released into the body by a person's:

A organs   C soft tissues

B glands   D arteries

2 The way in which we see ourselves and interpret other people's views of us determine our:

A self-confidence   C personality

B self-concept   D social class

3 The extent to which we value ourselves and our own qualities and abilities is an indication of our:

A personal culture   C social status

B age   D self-esteem

4 Which of the following are socio-economic factors that have an influence on health and well-being?

A wealth and income

B genetic inheritance

C ethnic background

D all of the above

5 The process in early emotional development where a link develops between a baby and a parent is known as:

A responding   C bonding

B belonging   D nurturing

6 Certain physical and intellectual abilities, such as walking and abstract thinking, inevitably occur as a result of:

A maturity   C chance

B learning   D socialisation

7 The change in physical mass/size that occurs, especially between infancy and adulthood, is known as:

A development   C childhood

B ageing   D growth

8 The biological term used to refer to the physical changes that occur during the teenage years is:

A the menopause   C puberty

B adolescence   D attachment

9 Which of the following is a predictable life-event?

A winning the National Lottery

B leaving school

C having a car accident

D getting divorced

10 What does the term 'life cycle' mean?

A We inherit chromosomes from parents.

B The length of time between a person's birth and death.

C We all pass through a number of life stages between infancy and old age.

D Our abilities deteriorate as we grow older and more frail.

✔ MULTIPLE CHOICE QUESTIONS

11 Which of the following factors does the Registrar General's scale **NOT** take into account when determining an individual's social class?

A age

B educational background

C housing status

D all the above

12 The shared way of life that is followed by a group of people is referred to as their:

A culture

B social role

C status

D social class

13 In which period of their lives are people who are 60 years old?

A adulthood

B old age

C adolescence

D mid-life

14 The expected patterns of behaviour that we associate with different personal statuses are known as:

A roles

B rules

C norms

D lifestyles

15 A family that is made up of children, their parents and two of their grandparents and who are all living together is:

A an extended family

B a nuclear family

C a reconstituted family

D lone parent family

16 The onset of a severe, disabling condition, such as multiple sclerosis, at any point in a person's life could be described as:

A a predictable life event

B an inevitable life event

C an unexpected life event

D an accident

17 The social class that individuals are allocated using the Registrar General's scale is determined by their:

A educational background

B occupation

C housing status

D personal wealth

18 Which of the following is an example of a 'formal relationship'?

A relationships at work between employer and employee

B relationships between friends

C relationships between family members

D relationships between colleagues at work

19 Social conventions, such as being polite to other people, affect how we behave. Breaking them can result in which of the following reactions:

A arrest by the police

B negative social sanctions from other people

C a final written warning from an employer

D positive social sanctions from other people

20 Which of the following is an intellectual characteristic that develops rapidly during childhood and adolescence?

A feelings

B strength

C thinking

D friendships

Health and Social Care Services

CONTENTS

OUTLINE

This chapter will help you to develop your knowledge and understanding of the services and facilities provided by the health and social care services in the United Kingdom.

The first part – covering element 3.1 – describes the scope, coverage and funding of national and local services and facilities provided by informal carers, the statutory sector and the non-statutory and independent sectors.

The second part – covering element 3.2 – focuses on the needs of different client groups in terms of the use of health and social care services and facilities, and how they can best gain access to the services.

The final part – covering element 3.3 – gives you the opportunity to investigate the roles of people who work in health and social care by considering the broad functions which they perform. You will also look at the career paths and qualifications of a range of people who work in these services.

After working through this chapter you will be able to:

- ⊗ **investigate the provision of health and social care services**

- ⊗ **describe how the different needs of clients are met by health and social care services**

- ⊗ **investigate jobs in health and social care.**

The chapter looks at health and social care organisations, the services that they provide to different groups of people and the roles of the different health and social care workers who work within them. It is written in a way that tries to give you opportunities to apply the information that you have just read through. It is advisable to spend time working on the various activities, quick response questions and the case studies as they come up.

INVESTIGATE THE PROVISION OF HEALTH AND SOCIAL CARE SERVICES

THE MAIN SECTORS OF CARE ORGANISATION IN THE UNITED KINGDOM

Health and social care services in the UK can be grouped into a number of different care **sectors** which have developed over the last 100 years. Today there are four main sectors, or sources, of care provision. These are outlined in Figure 3.1.

Each of the four care sectors makes an important contribution to the overall provision of health and social care for the wide variety of patients and clients who need care. There are a variety of important differences between the different sectors but at the same time there are areas in which they collaborate and work together to provide their services. These differences and the areas of overlap are discussed and explained in more detail later in the chapter.

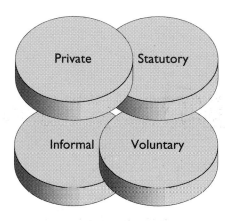

FIGURE 3.1: Sectors of care provision

The majority of health and social care services that we are familiar with have their origins in the creation of a nationalised care system designed to provide care for all people free of charge. This **statutory**, or government-funded, system, which includes the National Health Service (NHS) and the welfare benefit system, began in 1945 following the Second World War.

While most of us are familiar with the statutory sector, there are also other important services in the independent sector. The independent sector includes voluntary and privately funded organisations and, together with the statutory sector, makes up a more complex network of care organisations.

THE INTERNAL MARKET IN CARE

One of the most important recent changes in the statutory health and social care sector has been the development of a **purchaser-provider** relationship and the internal market in care.

The internal market is based on the principle of **provider** organisations offering to sell care services to potential '**purchasers**'. When all provider organisations do this, and there are many purchasers shopping around, a market in care services is created.

THE HEALTH CARE MARKET

In health care the providers are mainly NHS Trust Hospitals and general practitioners (GPs). Voluntary and private-sector organisations and independent practitioners also offer their health care services to purchasers but on a smaller scale.

The main purchasers of health care services are District Health Authorities and fund-holding GPs. Private individuals and voluntary and private-sector organisations purchase care on a smaller scale.

THE SOCIAL CARE MARKET

In social care the main service providers are local authority social services departments, voluntary and private-sector organisations. Voluntary organisations, private individuals and the local authority social services department's own 'purchasing' section make up the main group of social care purchasers. Social services departments employ **care managers** to purchase social care for clients who live in the area covered by the local authority.

The funding of statutory care is a sensitive, political issue. There is some disagreement over whether the government can afford to meet all of the demand for care, and indeed, whether it should be obliged to do so. When the NHS began in 1948, one of the main principles on which it was based was that services would be 'free at the point of delivery'. This principle has been challenged by the continuing high level of demand for care and the limited amount of money to pay for it.

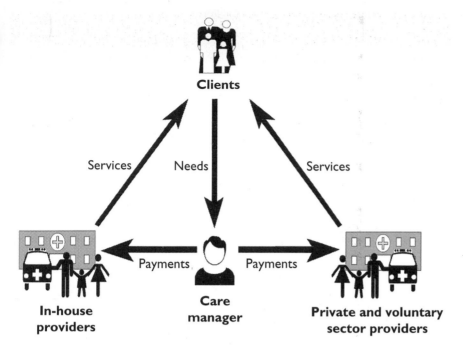

Clients

Services   Needs   Services

Payments   Payments

In-house providers   **Care manager**   **Private and voluntary sector providers**

Source: Based on P Sharkey, *Introducing Community Care*, HarperCollins, 1995

FIGURE 3.2: Purchasers and providers in the social care market

ACTIVITY

Health and social care has to be funded by one means or another. The issue of who should pay for care and education for pre-school children is particularly difficult and sensitive. Think about the following funding options.

- ⊗ Everyone who works should pay more tax from their income to pay for publicly funded child care.

- ⊗ People who use child care services should pay the full cost.

- ⊗ Child care should be provided by charities who raise money through donations.

- ⊗ Parents should look after their children at home.

a If you were a parent, which of the above options would you support and why?

b In a small group discuss the advantages and disadvantages of the different options. Your discussion should raise some of the different perspectives about how child care could and should be paid for.

c Feedback the main points of your discussion on each option to the class.

d As a class, vote on the issue of how to fund care and education for pre-school children.

STATUTORY HEALTH AND SOCIAL CARE SERVICES

The structure and organisation of statutory care services in the UK can be understood by looking at the different levels – **tiers** – of the system and by making a distinction between health care and social care service organisation.

THE GOVERNMENT LEVEL

Statutory services are those which are funded by government and which have to be provided by law. For example, old age pensions and schooling up to the age of sixteen are statutory services that must legally be provided by government-funded bodies.

Central government has been the main provider of finance for health and social care services for many years. This money is used to employ hundreds of thousands of people in a wide variety of jobs and provides the funds that are needed to run most hospitals, social service departments, primary and secondary schools and the welfare benefits system, among other services.

The Department of Health is responsible for care at the top level, or tier, of the statutory system. It does not provide care services directly. At this level politicians and civil servants make decisions about, and work on policies that affect how health or social care services are organised and paid for throughout the country. The politicians who have responsibility for health and social care provision are the Secretary of State for Health and his or her ministers. They are assisted in this work by civil servants.

QUICK response

What is the name of the current Secretary of State for Health?

STRUCTURE OF THE STATUTORY HEALTH CARE SYSTEM

THE REGIONAL LEVEL

The next tier in the health care structure is the regional level. England is divided into eight **Regional Health Authorities (RHAs)** – see Figure 3.3.

FIGURE 3.3: Regional Health Authorities in England

The role of the RHAs is to:

⊗ **develop health care services within their boundaries**

⊗ **allocate funds received from the Department of Health to other organisations within their region**

⊗ **oversee the work of the District Health Authorities (see below) and the Family Health Service Authorities (see below)**

⊗ **sort out disputes between the different organisations who buy care on behalf of patients and those who provide care.**

THE DISTRICT LEVEL

Below the Regional Health Authorities are the **District Health Authorities (DHAs)**, now known as Purchasing, or Commissioning Agencies. The Commissioning Agency is responsible for:

- ⊗ **assessing the health care needs of those people who live within its area**

- ⊗ **making contracts with NHS Trust Hospitals and other organisations that provide care, so that the care needs of its population are met.**

The **Family Health Service Authority (FHSA)** is also responsible at district level for purchasing the primary, or community, health services for a local population. It is at this level that the 'internal market' in care operates. The terms 'primary' and 'secondary' care are explained in more detail later in the chapter.

THE LOCAL AREA LEVEL

It is at the local level that health care is actually provided. NHS Trusts and directly managed services provide hospital and community-based services for a wide range of clients in a particular area. The range and nature of these services is explained later in the chapter.

Figure 3.4 shows how the different parts of the statutory health system would typically affect a local area.

FIGURE **3.4**: The statutory health system

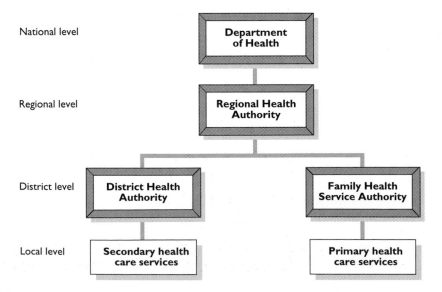

ACTIVITY

Find out the following using resources such as *Yellow Pages*, local service directories, the Community Health Council and your local library.

a   What is the name of your Regional Health Authority?

b   Where are the headquarters of your Regional Health Authority?

c   What is the name of your District Health Authority?

d   Where are the offices of your District Health Authority?

e   Where is your nearest NHS Trust Hospital?

f   Where are the offices of your local Family Health Service Authority?

STRUCTURE OF THE STATUTORY SOCIAL CARE SYSTEM

There are two main levels of organisation in the statutory social care system.

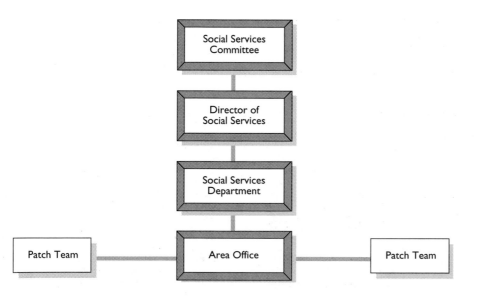

FIGURE 3.5: The social care system

THE CENTRAL GOVERNMENT LEVEL

The top tier is the central government level. This is where the Secretary of State for Health and the Department of Health operate making policy and providing funds for social care services.

THE LOCAL AREA LEVEL

It is at the local level, through local authorities, that social care services are provided. Local authorities with responsibility for providing social care are also known as councils.

In rural areas, where the population is relatively low in number, a county council is responsible for providing social services. In more populated urban areas district councils are responsible for provision.

All local authorities must have a social services committee, which is made up of local councillors. This committee is responsible for monitoring social services in its area and appoints a director of social services to run the social services department. It is through this department that social care services are provided to the public.

Many social service departments are organised into area offices and 'patch teams'. A patch team is a group of social workers who provide social work services to people in a particular 'patch' or area of a town, city or rural location.

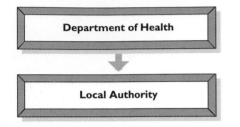

FIGURE 3.6: Local authority social services

⚡ QUICK response

Do you know where your social services department and patch team are based? How could you find out?

FUNDING STATUTORY SERVICES

Statutory services are those provided by central or local government. Regional Health Authorities and local authorities pay for care services from taxes collected by the Inland Revenue. Health and social care costs the British taxpayer £40bn every year. The amounts spent on different aspects of care are shown in Figures 3.7 and 3.8.

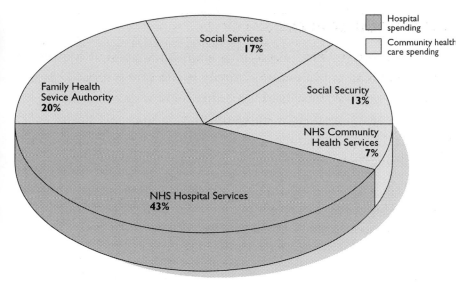

Hospital spending

Community health care spending

FIGURE 3.7: Health and social care spending, 1989–90

Source: Based on R Baggott, *Health and Health Care in Britain,* Macmillan, 1994

Social Services
17%

Family Health
Sevice Authority
20%

Social Security
13%

NHS Community
Health Services
7%

NHS Hospital Services
43%

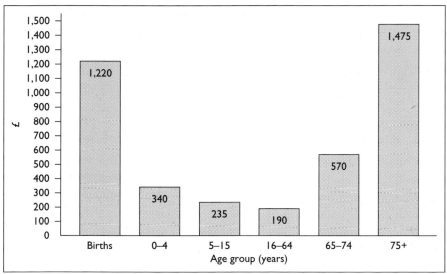

FIGURE 3.8: Health and social care costs by age group

Source: HM Treasury

QUICK response

What does Figure 3.8 tell you about care costs of different age groups?

TYPES OF SERVICE IN THE STATUTORY SECTOR

The NHS is the biggest provider of health care in the UK. Within the NHS there are different types of care provision. The three main types of care offered to patients in the statutory system are:

- ⊗ **primary health care**

- ⊗ **secondary health care**

- ⊗ **tertiary health care.**

PRIMARY HEALTH CARE

This term refers to those services that are the first point of contact for people who require health care. Primary health care is carried out in community settings, such as health centres, and is provided by a number of health workers working together as a **primary health care team (PHCT)**. The general practitioner (GP) is a key member of the team. Other primary health care workers include district nurses, community psychiatric nurses and health visitors.

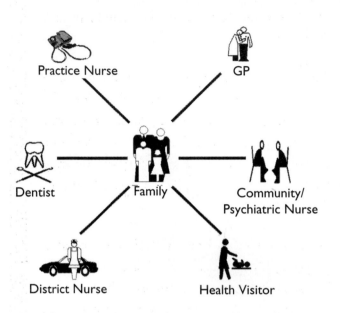

FIGURE 3.9: The primary health care team

Practice Nurse

GP

Dentist

Family

Community/
Psychiatric Nurse

District Nurse

Health Visitor

Primary health care workers provide direct care services for a local population and may visit patients in their own homes if they cannot get to the local surgery or health centre. Team members meet regularly to discuss the patients they have in common in order to coordinate their work and make sure that the patient receives the best possible treatment. It is often the GP who has the responsibility of being the team leader or coordinator.

The PHCT is often involved in providing care in cases of minor illness or injury and in monitoring individuals' health to prevent them from becoming ill or to prevent their condition worsening. PHCT workers often provide a range of check-ups, clinics and classes aimed at health improvement and illness prevention. These are usually publicised in leaflets and posters at the health centre or surgery. Examples include weight-loss clinics and smoking- and stress-reduction classes.

In many health centres the GP or practice nurse will see people who come in feeling unwell and who want a diagnosis of their illness and some treatment to help cure it. Many of these visits are for common complaints like colds, flu, cuts and bruises and psychological problems such as feeling depressed and anxious. If a patient requires an operation or has a more serious illness, a member of the PHCT will refer them to local secondary level services, such as the local hospital.

The PHCT works with the full range of client groups in a particular local area. Team members see babies and young children, teenagers and adults and the elderly and infirm. Most PHCTs run special clinics to meet the varying needs of these groups. The following case study gives you some idea of the range of services that are provided.

 CASE STUDY

Working at the health centre

Waverton Health Centre is situated in the centre of Waverton town and is one of three health centres that provide primary health care for the local population.

The day at the health centre starts at 7.30 am, with an early morning clinic for people who are unable to come during their working hours. The two **GPs** at the centre, Dr Jane Cassidy and Dr Richard Kirk, take it in turns to run the early clinic. They see people who are suffering from common, minor complaints, such as colds, flu, sports injuries and illnesses that affect their ability to go to work.

Most of the other staff arrive at 8.30 am to prepare for a 9 o'clock start.

Arlene Thomas is employed by Dr Cassidy and Dr Kirk as the **practice nurse**. She sees patients for health checks, gives inoculations, carries out cervical smears and is available to see any patient who would rather see a nurse than a GP.

Mrs Muriel Jones has worked as **receptionist** for the last five years.

Caroline Evans is the **health visitor** attached to the centre. She sees mothers and babies by appointment at their homes and also runs some health education classes and ante-natal clinics at the centre.

Raj Ramana is the **community psychiatric nurse** attached to the practice. He sees some clients for counselling and gives medication to people who need to have a regular injection. He also visits patients in their own homes if they are mentally distressed and cannot or do not wish to come to the health centre.

The other members of the PHCT who are based at the health centre are Priti Shah and Yvonne Black, who are **district nurses**. They usually visit people in their own homes to provide care and advise on treatment. Their main area of work is with the elderly and physically infirm patients of the health centre.

All of the members of the primary health care team meet each day at 8.30 am to discuss new referrals and patients that they have in common and to plan the work of the day. On some occasions they will decide to work together with a particular patient, but most of the time they see patients alone and refer to each other when they need the specialist help that another team member can offer. The team tries to meet all of the primary health care needs of the patients registered with the Waverton Health Centre.

How much do you know about your own health centre and PHCT? If you think that you already know a lot, try answering the following questions straight away. If you need to find out the answers to some or all of the questions, arrange to make a visit to the health centre to do this. It is advisable to contact the receptionist at the centre in advance to make sure that a team member will be able to help you and that your visit is not too disruptive to its busy appointments system.

a   Where is your local health centre?

b   Who is employed to provide care?

c   How many GPs work at the health centre or surgery?

d   What does the practice nurse do?

e   What sort of special services are provided for mothers and babies?

f   How do patients make appointments?

g   What kinds of preventive health checks and screening services are provided for women?

h   Are there any district nurses or health visitors based at the health centre?

SECONDARY HEALTH CARE

Hospitals generally provide a secondary level of health care – they become involved when the patient has already been diagnosed as having an illness, disease or other condition (such as pregnancy) that requires medical, nursing or other therapeutic help. Most patients who go into hospital have been referred to the secondary services of a medical team or other specialist by their GP or another member of the PHCT.

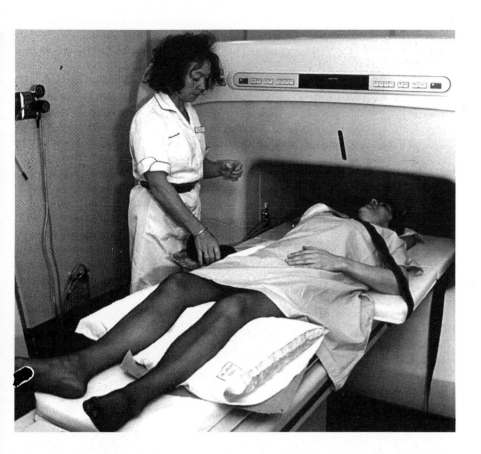

Most secondary hospital care is provided by NHS Trusts. There are different kinds of hospital.

- **District General Hospitals** provide a wide range of health care services for all of the population of a local area. They provide services for people who are acutely ill and who need an operation or treatment that involves contact with specially trained doctors and nurses.

- **Local Community Hospitals** usually provide a more limited range of treatments for smaller populations of people in a local area. They often have facilities for people to be seen on an out-patient basis and smaller in-patient facilities than the District General Hospital.

- **National Teaching Hospitals and specialist units** provide highly specialist medical, surgical and psychiatric treatments to patients who may be referred to them from anywhere in the country. Their expertise is available to both in-patients and out-patients. Two examples are Great Ormond Street Hospital for Sick Children in London and the Royal National Orthopaedic Hospital at Stanmore in Middlesex.

TERTIARY HEALTH CARE

Tertiary health care refers to long-term and rehabilitative care that is concerned with helping people to adapt and come to terms with either illness or disability that they will often have for the rest of their lives.

Some tertiary health care, such as long-term physiotherapy, may result in improved functioning and well-being for a patient depending on the problems that he or she has. Other forms of tertiary care, such as the care offered by hospices, are focused on maintaining people's comfort and dignity when their condition is terminal and will result in death.

Tertiary care is usually specialist and requires a referral from secondary care providers. The number of people receiving tertiary care is relatively small compared to those receiving primary and secondary care.

ACTIVITY

This activity is designed to test your understanding of the different forms of care that you have just read about. After reading through each case study, try to identify the form of health care that each person provides. You should refer back to the information at the beginning of the section and the explanations above to help you with this activity.

Sister Jennifer Kyriacou has worked in three different hospitals since she qualified as a nurse five years ago. She now works in a health centre as a practice nurse. She is often the first person to see and treat patients who come in with a wide range of minor conditions and injuries. She sometimes refers patients with more complicated and serious problems to hospital.

Mr Routledge is a specialist paediatric surgeon. He receives referrals from GPs and other doctors from around the country who wish to send children to the hospital where he works for specialist operations.

David Wood is an occupational therapist. He carries out assessments of the needs of people who have long-term mental health problems. Most of the patients who are seen by David are over the worst effects of their conditions but will always require some care and support. He aims to help them to regain the skills and abilities that have been affected by their conditions.

STATUTORY SOCIAL CARE

Local authority social services departments provide a range of personal social services to meet the needs of clients in their area. Personal social services are mainly provided for clients within the community and, where possible, in their own homes. Social care workers try to enable their clients to function more independently and offer care which enables them to avoid entry into permanent residential care. There are four main areas of social care provision.

- **Residential care – care provided in residential homes and units with staff to support residents.**

- **Domiciliary care – care provided in the client's own home.**

- **Day care – care provided at special centres in the community.**

- **Fieldwork – care provided by social workers allocated to individual clients.**

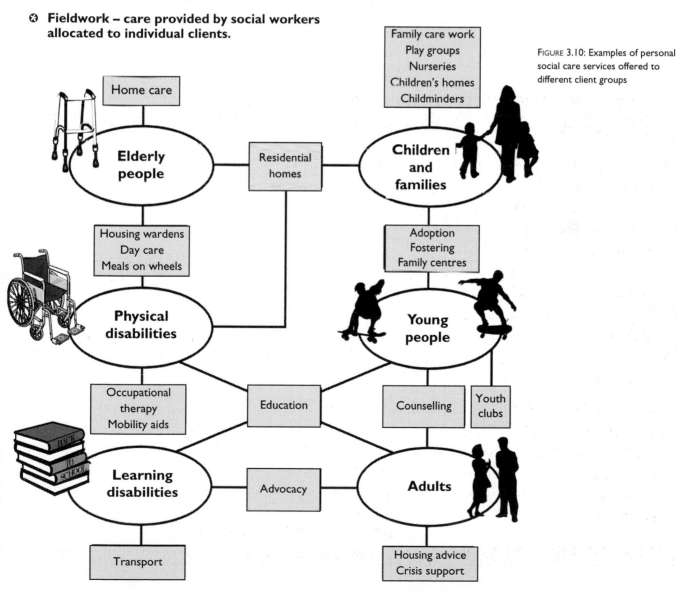

FIGURE 3.10: Examples of personal social care services offered to different client groups

Social care services are aimed at meeting the needs of a variety of **client groups**. A client group is a group of people who have similar characteristics such as age group or disability and whose individual needs can be met by similar forms of care. Figure 3.10 outlines some of the social care services that may typically be offered through a local authority social services department to the range of client groups who they care for.

THE NON-STATUTORY AND INDEPENDENT SECTORS

The non-statutory and independent sectors consist of health and social care organisations and some individual practitioners whose services are not funded by central government. There are three main categories of service provider in these sectors.

- ⊗ **Voluntary organisations.**

- ⊗ **Private, commercial organisations.**

- ⊗ **Self-employed carers.**

VOLUNTARY ORGANISATIONS

The voluntary care sector has its origins in the nineteenth century when there were very few statutory services for ordinary people and when most private services were beyond the financial reach of all but the rich. Charities and voluntary organisations grew out of the donations of a few rich benefactors and the campaigns of philanthropists such as Joseph Rowntree who wished to help their local communities and reduce the deprivations and suffering that they saw around them.

The voluntary sector includes organisations such as MENCAP, which campaigns for people with severe learning difficulties, Age Concern and the National Society for the Prevention of Cruelty to Children (NSPCC). Like most voluntary organisations these groups are also registered charities. This means that they finance their services and the running of their organisation through fund-raising, and may also receive grants from central or local government, but put all their income back into running their services.

Voluntary organisations are staffed by care workers – paid employees – who provide care and support services and by unpaid volunteers who provide their time and skills for free.

Voluntary groups tend to focus on a specific issue or client group and target their services accordingly. For example, the NSPCC works for children while Age Concern works for elderly people and their carers; the Terrance Higgins Trust is concerned with sexual health, and Shelter is concerned with housing.

FIGURE 3.11: Characteristics of voluntary groups

Source of funding	Fund-raising Donations Some government grants
Type of work	Provide advice and care services Run health education campaigns Produce information for a range of client groups
Who runs them?	Generally employ health and social care workers Use a lot of volunteers
Other characteristics	Usually charities and non-profit making Often concerned with narrow range of issues or single client group More likely to be involved in providing social care than health care

 ACTIVITY

Individually, or in a small group, investigate voluntary health and social care organisations that provide services for one type of client such as the elderly, people with learning disabilities or children.

Some organisations operate nationally and have local branches, others are smaller and may only exist in your area. Use your general knowledge, local directories and voluntary services directories (look for these in the reference section of your local library) to obtain the addresses of several different organisations. Write to them to obtain information about their work. Summarise the information you obtain in a chart like the one below.

Name of voluntary group	Client group(s) focus	Main areas of work
MENCAP	**Learning disabilities – children and adults**	**Raising public awareness**
		Providing housing and social care
		Campaigning
		Fund-raising

When you write a letter to any voluntary organisation requesting information about its work, you should always include an A4 stamped self-addressed envelope to help it to cover the costs of helping you.

THE PRIVATE SECTOR

Private companies and independent practitioners have a long tradition of providing both health and social care to people who want, and are able, to pay for their services. The companies that run care services charge clients fees in order to make a profit for their shareholders. Independent practitioners charge fees in order to make a living for themselves.

The private sector offers a narrower range of services and has fewer organisations and clients than either the statutory or voluntary sectors. Private-sector clients often pay the costs of their care by claiming on health insurance that they have taken out as a precaution against illness and the need for care at different times of their lives.

Fee-paying residential homes for the elderly and the disabled, private hospitals and clinics, and fee-paying nursery schools and playgroups are all services that operate in the private sector.

QUICK response

What is your attitude to private health care? Is it a good thing? Would you choose it nor not?

Source of funding	Fees charged to individuals and insurance companies
Type of work	Provide advice and care services for a range of client groups
Who runs them?	Generally employ health and social care workers Managed by directors and business managers
Other characteristics	Must be profit making to survive Often concerned with a narrow range of conditions or problems Target their services at people who can afford to pay for them

FIGURE 3.12: Characteristics of private organisations

ACTIVITY

What 'private-sector' services are there in your area. Using headings such as Residential Care, Nursing Homes, Childminders, Nurseries and Private Hospital, look through local telephone and trade directories for examples of services in your area. Make a note of any that you find or are already aware of. You may like to contact them to build up information on services available in your area.

Remember that private-sector organisations are companies or independent practitioners who charge fees and aim to make a profit out of providing care. Be careful not to choose voluntary organisations, which are charities and do not seek to make a profit for shareholders or themselves.

SELF-EMPLOYED CARERS

There are opportunities for individuals who are properly qualified to provide care to set up their own service or small business and to become a self-employed carer. The area in which this is most common is child care. People who work as registered childminders, foster parents and those who run their own nurseries are often self-employed.

There are also a growing number of paramedical workers, such as physiotherapists, chiropodists, chiropractors and counsellors now working in their own practices as self-employed carers. Such people have generally gained qualifications, expertise and experience through a period of working for others. When they become self-employed they tend to set up small-scale services where they charge their customers/users directly for the care that they provide. Self-employed carers are also a part of the private sector.

FIGURE 3.13: Private-sector services

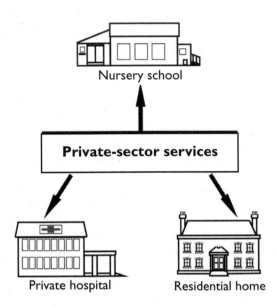

INFORMAL SUPPORT AND CARE

QUICK response

Do you know of any informal support groups in your area?

Most of the health and social care that is provided for sick and vulnerable people in the UK is carried out by non-professional carers outside of care organisations. Individuals' family, friends and neighbours offer a wide range of care and support interventions either without the aid of care professionals or with some assistance from them.

Children, the elderly and the long-term sick are the main client groups who benefit from such informal care. The pattern of people caring for their elderly relatives and children at home is well established.

CHILDREN AS CARERS

Children suffer as they care for disabled parents

CHILDREN as young as nine are neglecting school work and friends to look after disabled parents at home, according to a study published today.

Young carers tend not to draw official attention to their own needs out of fear that disclosure would mean they are taken into local authority care and the family broken up. Their contributions go largely unrecognised and their problems remain invisible until family problems develop into a crisis, the report says.

Sandra Billsborrow, who carried out the research for the Barnardo's children's charity and the Carers' National Association, concludes that a fundamental assessment of the role of young carers is required to fill the present policy vacuum.

Her study combined research over the last decade with interviews on Merseyside with 11 young carers and 45 professionals – mainly doctors, social workers and community nurses.

The young people mainly females aged between nine and twenty-one, were caring for relatives with disabilities ranging from multiple sclerosis and arthritis to quadriplegia and after-effects of strokes.

They were asked about their responsibilities, how these affected school and social life, and about their knowledge of parental illness or disability. For some it was the first time they had spoken about looking after the parent.

Most felt they could leave the dependent relative for at least a few hours but all said they were concerned about accidents to them while they were away.

Some, particularly those who had cared for several years, reported feelings of powerlessness about changing the situation. One 15-year-old said: 'It gets you down and it wears you down. You grow up fast, as well. Sometimes you just want to go out and have a laugh. You can't say, "Right, I've done that for my mum, and she'll be all right tonight." You always have to do something for her. You've never finished the job.'

Most of those sampled had taken days off school because of their domestic responsibilities. Those duties took their toll on friendships, through lack of time for social life.

Interviews with professionals suggested the young carers were rarely regarded as recipients of social services – more an essential link in the chain of support provided to the parent.

In one case, a home help service was withdrawn from a disabled adult when the sole carer, a teenaged child, was deemed able to cope alone. 'In a climate of limited resources, services are prioritised and, for this reason, the young carer was seen by the home help service as a resource rather than as "in need".'

Yet intervention by officials threatened the child with exclusion from decisions about the family's future. 'There is a risk for a young carer who actively seeks assistance from service providers. The statutory powers of the local authority may be more damaging than the status quo.'

Judy Jones,
The Independent, May 1992

The article about child carers refers to a number of different forms of care provided by children when acting as informal carers.

- ✪ Informal *nursing care* involves children giving direct help and practical support to help their relative to meet his or her physical needs. This might include aspects of personal care, such as washing and dressing a parent, or helping them to move around when they have a mobility problem.

- ✪ There are also a wide variety of tasks that children, and informal carers generally, undertake to provide *help in the home*. Cleaning the house, washing clothes, doing the shopping and cooking are all aspects of informal care that may be a part of a carer's regular routine.

- ✪ The third aspect of informal care – *companionship* – is possibly the most valued but least obvious one. Many people who have a disability or illness that limits their ability to care for themselves and to get out to meet others value the company and friendship of their carers as much as the practical help they receive.

INFORMAL SUPPORT GROUPS

There are many thousands of local, informal support groups operating throughout the UK. They are set up and run by carers and people who have particular health and social care needs. The groups may be small and short term or may have become well established and provide regular, ongoing support to an individual or a group of clients.

The purpose of informal support groups is to provide practical and emotional support to informal carers and the people they care for. They may consist of a group of neighbours who share child care arrangements, people in a local area who all look after a relative at home alone and meet regularly to talk and support each other or a group of people who have got together to raise money to help an individual who requires money to finance their medical or social care needs.

 # CASE STUDY

Informal care for an elderly person

A lot of care for elderly people is now provided on an informal basis by relatives, friends and neighbours. For some people this is a positive development and enables them to avoid entering permanent residential care. Read the following brief case example and then answer the questions.

Alice Bell is 79 years old and lives alone. She has some memory impairment and forgets what time of the day it is, whether she has eaten, and also the names of all but her closest relatives and her neighbour, Mrs Gott. Alice is unable to walk any distance due to her arthritis, very rarely goes out alone, and feels frightened of using her bath as she has difficulty getting in and out of it.

a What forms of informal care would Alice benefit from?

b Identify who might provide each form of care for her.

ACTIVITY

1 Have you ever received 'informal care' when you were unwell or had personal problems? Write a short paragraph describing the situation, who provided the care and the form of care you received.

2 Over the last fifteen years many long-stay psychiatric and geriatric hospitals and homes for people with long-term disabilities have closed. There has also been a reduction in the number of hospital beds to which people may be admitted generally. Informal care provides a large part of the overall provision of care in the UK.

In a small group, discuss the advantages and disadvantages of this development for:

a informal carers?

b people who need care?

Present the main points of your discussion to the class. You should make notes on the range of points made in the class and small group discussions.

METHODS OF FUNDING NON-STATUTORY HEALTH AND SOCIAL CARE SERVICES

The non-statutory health and social care sector includes voluntary and private care organisations and independent care practitioners. Non-statutory care organisations and independent practitioners can receive the money that they need to provide their services through a variety of sources, including:

- ✪ **donations** – from individuals, collections, flag days, wills and business firms

- ✪ **government grants** – these can be from central or local government and might be given as regular or one-off payments

- ✪ **contracts** – these are made with service purchasers

- ✪ **fee payment** – from clients receiving services or from other charities using services

- ✪ **health insurance** – firms such as **BUPA, Private Patients Plan** and **Norwich Union Health Care** offer insurance schemes to individuals which can fund care provided in the non-statutory sector.

The method of funding used depends on the nature of the service offered and the needs of the patients and clients who use it. The following three case studies outline the sources of funding for three different care providers working in the non-statutory sector.

CASE STUDY

Terrance Higgins Trust receives funding for the services it provides in the field of HIV and sexual health from the following sources.

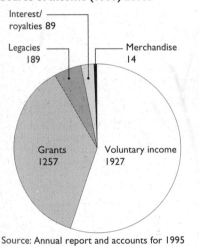

Source of income (1995) £000s

Interest/royalties 89

Legacies 189

Merchandise 14

Grants 1257

Voluntary income 1927

Source: Annual report and accounts for 1995

QUICK response

Describe in words how the care provider in each case study funds its services.

CASE STUDY

Waverton Home Care is a private domiciliary care agency. It operates to make a profit and receives income – funding – from the following sources.

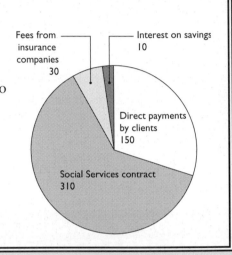

Source of income £000s

Fees from insurance companies 30

Interest on savings 10

Direct payments by clients 150

Social Services contract 310

CASE STUDY

Darren Samuels is a self-employed physiotherapist who runs his own practice. He receives income from the following sources.

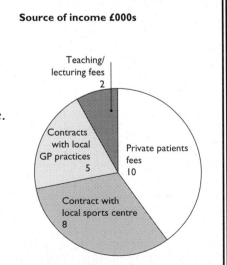

Source of income £000s

Teaching/lecturing fees 2

Contracts with local GP practices 5

Private patients fees 10

Contract with local sports centre 8

PORTFOLIO ASSIGNMENT

INVESTIGATING LOCAL CARE SERVICES

INTRODUCTION

People who want to use health and social care services need information about their local organisations. They need to know:

- where these organisations are located

- what these organisations can offer

- how they can gain access to the services that are offered.

In this assignment you are asked to carry out an investigation of local health and social care organisations. You must produce a report and could make a presentation of your findings to meet some of the core skills criteria for communication. This assignment will give you the opportunity to investigate the provision of health and social care in your area and develop some of the skills needed for independent research.

TASK 1

Identify six examples of local or national care organisations, two each from the following categories.

- Private service providers

- Voluntary service providers

- Self-employed providers

There are a number of different sources of information that may help you to find examples of these organisations, for example, *Yellow Pages*, your local health centre/clinic, local library, local newspapers and magazines, the Community Health Council office, local directories and people who use or work in local health and social care organisations.

Make a note of how you went about finding your organisations and list the six that you have chosen to investigate further. Try to select organisations that offer services to different client groups such as children, adults and elderly people.

TASK 2

Investigate each of your chosen organisations further. You may need to arrange to visit them to collect information on the following.

- Who are their services aimed at?

- What services do they offer potential users?

- How can people gain access to their services?

- How do they help people to understand and make the best use of their services?

- What are the main jobs within the organisation?

Keep a record of how you went about obtaining your information as well as collecting the information itself.

PORTFOLIO ASSIGNMENT

TASK 3

Once you have investigated each of the organisations, produce a report on 'Local Health and Social Care Services' with a section allocated to each of your chosen organisations. You might like to include pictures, photographs, maps and graphical information to illustrate your work.

TASK 4

Present the main points and findings of your investigation to the other members of your group. When making your presentation, encourage and respond to questions about your report. Make notes of the points and findings covered by other students that were not included in your own report. Both the report and your notes will be added to your portfolio as evidence of your work in this unit.

TASK 5

You may wish to use information technology to prepare and present your report. If you do so, you should keep evidence, for example, disks, printouts, notes, of your work.

DESCRIBE HOW THE NEEDS OF DIFFERENT CLIENTS ARE MET BY HEALTH AND SOCIAL CARE SERVICES

The organisations that provide health and social care aim to deliver services that meet the needs of their client groups. In the second part of the chapter we look at:

- **individual needs**

- **the range of needs associated with the different client groups**

- **the services that are provided to meet patients' and clients' needs**

- **the different methods of gaining access to services**

- **the forms of support that are available to help clients make best use of services.**

ASSESSING HEALTH AND SOCIAL CARE NEEDS FOR A LOCAL AREA

HEALTH CARE

District Health Authorities (DHAs) are responsible for assessing the health care needs of their local population. Each area has its own District Health Authority which carries out an annual survey of need in the local population. Once the DHA has information on the social and health characteristics of the population, it can work out which services it needs to buy from different health care organisations. For example, an area with many young families will need more ante-natal and child care whereas an area populated with retired people will need to provide health care for their particular needs.

Health care workers in health centres and hospitals carry out **individual needs'** assessments on all patients whom they come into contact with. The aspects that they focus on are outlined below.

PERSONAL SOCIAL SERVICES

Local authorities are responsible for assessing the social care needs of the people who live in their area. As a result of the NHS and Community Care Act (1990), local authorities have a duty to make and produce a plan of community care services in their area and to assess the needs of those who may require community care services.

An individual's social care needs may be assessed by one or more social care workers, such as a social worker, a housing worker or an occupational therapist. The overall assessment is coordinated by a care manager, who is usually a local authority social worker.

INDIVIDUAL NEEDS

People have a range of health and care needs that must be met if they are to function effectively and maintain an acceptable quality of life or level of social independence. A need is something that individuals must have if they are to experience health and well-being.

Physical needs

One of the key aspects of our 'health' is the physical condition that we are in. Physical needs are the basic foundations of our health. The following can be said to contribute to physical health and well-being:

PHYSICAL FITNESS...

ABSENCE OF DISEASE OR INJURY...

ADEQUATE HOUSING...

ADEQUATE CLOTHING...

ADEQUATE FOOD AND WATER...

- ☺ physical fitness

- ☺ absence of disease or injury

- ☺ adequate housing

- ☺ adequate clothing

- ☺ adequate food and water.

Our physical needs change as we get older. Physical health for an 82-year-old will be different to that for an 18-year-old. As we age, our physical abilities and needs change. At different times of life people may be unable to meet their needs. Illness, injury, disability and personal or social problems can all affect a person's ability to meet their physical needs and may result in them having 'additional' and unmet needs. These can result from:

- ☺ *acute*, short-term conditions of sudden onset – breaking a bone or contracting influenza are examples of acute physical illnesses

- ☺ *chronic*, long-term, continuous, disabling conditions or problems – arthritis and multiple sclerosis are examples of chronic physical illnesses.

⚡ QUICK response
Write down four differences between the physical needs of an 82-year-old woman and an 18-year-old woman.

💡 ACTIVITY

Using the above definitions as guidelines, brainstorm a list of illnesses, injuries and disabilities, under the two headings of 'Acute' and 'Chronic', that would result in 'unmet or additional physical needs' for either a child, an adult or an elderly person.

Emotional needs

People experience a range of emotions in their daily lives. Love and hate, anger and elation, happiness and sadness, frustration and despair are all feelings that you have probably experienced. Our mood, or emotional state is affected by the events that we experience. For example, when children begin primary school and young people finish secondary school, they often experience strong emotions because of the change involved. Many people have emotional needs, for comfort, affection and a sense of security, following the death of a person whom they care about.

1 What kinds of situation could lead to psychological and emotional 'loss' in a person's life?

2 What were, or are likely to be, your emotional needs at these points in your life?

3 How were your emotional needs met at this time?

Can you think of examples of times when your own emotional needs have been greater than usual?

Mental health needs

People's experience of illness, injury and traumatic life-events often causes major disruption in their lives and can have a profound impact on them. At such times people can feel vulnerable and insecure. Where people's problems involve difficulties with their thinking or perception, their mental health may be disrupted at a deep level. For example, depression is a deeper, more complicated problem than feeling unhappy or a bit down.

There are a number of conditions, such as schizophrenia and manic depression, that can lead to people experiencing mental distress and severe problems. Helping people with such mental health needs requires specialist skills and training. There are a range of mental health workers, including specialist nurses, social workers, counsellors, psychotherapists and psychiatrists who can offer help and support to people who have such needs.

1 What kinds of situation could lead to an experience of 'loss' for those affected?

2 Brainstorm a list of possible situations and add a list of possible emotions that you might expect people to experience as a result.

Social needs

Being with other people, having relationships with family, friends and more intimate partners and engaging in leisure activities are all ways of meeting our needs for 'social' contact, expression and development.

People are 'social' in the sense that they tend to prefer the stimulation and company of others rather than being on their own for long periods. While we all experience times when we would prefer to be left alone, contact with others is important at all stages in our lives.

⬤ ACTIVITY

Explain why 'social contact' may be important in the lives of the following people:

a   a baby of 3 months old

b   an only child of 7 years of age

c   a teenager, aged 15

d   a young woman at university

e   a family who has recently emigrated from Britain to France

f   a woman of 67 who has recently been widowed.

Work, leisure and play are all important ways through which we meet our social needs at various points in our lives. For people who are experiencing illness, injury or disability the opportunity to participate in social activities may be temporarily restricted. People who experience long-term financial hardship, who have language or communication problems or who are isolated because of immobility, infirmity or because they have spent many years living in institutions may also find that they are unable to meet their social needs without the help of carers who come into contact with them and identify this as a problem.

CASE STUDY

Identifying individual needs

Caroline lives in a flat on an inner-city housing estate with her 4-year-old son Darren and 2-year-old daughter Natasha. She had been on the council waiting list for a flat for eighteen months and moved in just after Natasha was born.

Caroline came to London five years ago when she was 16. She originally lived with her parents in Devon. She moved when her mother died following a long illness. She didn't get on with her step-father and decided to leave home to start a new life.

When she first arrived in London she lived in a hostel for homeless young people. This is where she met Damien, now aged 25, the father of her two children. They never married but lived together until three months ago. Damien worked for a mini-cab firm, driving mainly at night. He gave Caroline money to decorate the flat and to buy things for the children. Damien lost his driving licence six months ago. He has not been able to find work since then. Their relationship got steadily worse after he lost his job. They started to row and decided to split up for a while.

Caroline still sees Damien. He visits every week to see the kids and enjoys playing with them. If he has any money, he gives it to Caroline for the children but this is quite a rare occurrence. Caroline is still faced with the same level of bills for food, electricity, gas and everyday expenses that she had when Damien was earning better money. She is now in debt and is finding it very difficult to cope on her income support and child benefit. Both of the children need new coats and shoes but she can't afford them.

CLIENT GROUP NEEDS

In this section we look in more detail at the needs of the following client groups:

- ⊗ **babies**
- ⊗ **children**
- ⊗ **young people**
- ⊗ **adults**
- ⊗ **elderly people**
- ⊗ **families.**

The needs of babies and children

Babies and pre-school children are more or less dependent on adults, usually their parents, to protect them and meet their physical, emotional and social needs in a caring way. As children grow older they gain more self-care abilities but, until late adolescence, are still dependent to some extent on other people to look after them.

Darren and Natasha are both very lively and demanding children. Darren's behaviour has been causing problems recently. He has developed a bad temper and refuses to do what she tells him. He often wants to go out to play in the local park, which he can see from their fourth-floor window, but Caroline has other things to do around the flat or feels too tired.

Caroline feels that she is doing her best to bring up her children. She complains that she has no money, is often too tired to cook and clean as much as she would like to and that she has no support or help. She says that she misses Damien and wishes she could get out away from the children now and again.

1 What do you think Caroline's main problems are? Make a list of these and, next to each, suggest possible ways of dealing with them.

2 Who could help Caroline? If Caroline and the children lived in your local area, where could she get help from? Identify local services and find out what they offer and how Caroline could go about getting help from them. Present your findings in a short report.

3 Caroline is trying to cope with her situation alone at present. She would rather struggle to look after the children than let Damien join in and make decisions about them when he feels like it. What do you think Damien's rights and responsibilities are in this situation? In a small group, discuss the situation from the points of view of Caroline, Damien and the children. Try to come to some decision about what the best arrangement might be.

ACTIVITY

Look at the pictures of the 6-month-old baby and the 7-year-old boy. Brainstorm examples of the physical, emotional and social needs that each would have. You might like to use books on child development for reference as well as your own ideas and experience to complete this task.

The needs of young people

As children grow and develop their needs change. Adolescence – the teenage years – is a period of rapid physical growth and development and deep emotional change. While it is exciting for young people to have new experiences and broaden their lives, it can also be a confusing and uncomfortable time. As well as experiencing physical change, young people start to think and feel differently during adolescence. Their social and emotional needs change and begin to involve more people outside of the family.

One major area of importance for many young people is establishing some independence from parents. Expressing a sense of personal identity may involve dressing and behaving in ways that parents don't agree with, spending more time with friends than family members, and forming and expressing views and opinions that are different to those of parents.

QUICK response

How do you think parents can best cope with their adolescent children's desire for greater independence?

ACTIVITY

Brainstorm a list of needs, under the headings physical, emotional and social, that may result from changes experienced during adolescence.

The needs of families

There are many types of family in Britain today. Single-parent families, families where partners have lived in other families before and may have children from earlier relationships or marriages, and families where grandparents, parents, dependent children and other relatives all live together are as common as the 'typical' family of parents and 2.4 children.

Social changes, such as the changing roles of men and women, the decline in the size of the family and the increase in the number of people who live into old age have put greater pressure on the family and challenged its 'caring' role. Families may have a variety of care needs depending on their particular situation. Children and elders, especially those who are frail, may require more care than their family is able to offer. Informal carers in the family may need practical help and support to enable them to cope with the responsibility and stress of providing care.

Type of household	% of households 1981	% of people 1981	% of people 1992
One person	22	8	11.1
Married couple	26	20	23.4
Married couple with dependent children	32	49	39.9
Married couple with independent children	8	10	10.9
Lone parent with dependent children	4	5	10.1
Other	9	8	4.6

Adapted from *Social Trends* 13 and 24

FIGURE 3.14: Households and people in households in Great Britain, 1981 and 1992

QUICK response

What does Figure 3.14 tell you about changes in patterns of family organisation between 1981 and 1992?

Financial problems are also a major area of concern for many families on low incomes or those in receipt of welfare benefits.

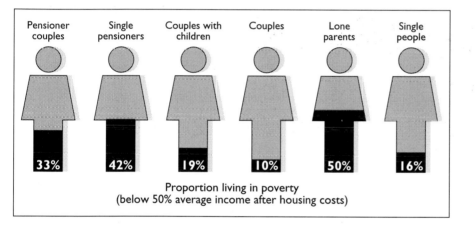

Proportion living in poverty
(below 50% average income after housing costs)

FIGURE 3.15: Risk of poverty by family status

Source: C Oppenheim, *Poverty: the Facts*, Child Poverty Action Group, 1993

The needs of people with disabilities

Disabilities at any age may result from impairments caused by illness, injury, an inherited condition but particularly affect the elderly. There are many different types of impairment and the disabling effects that they have vary considerably between people who experience them. Impairments can have various disabling consequences as shown in Figure 3.16.

People may have additional needs as a result of their individual experience of disability. For example, a person with multiple sclerosis may experience muscle wastage and develop mobility and dexterity problems, and depression and social isolation in some cases. They would then have additional needs for help in these areas.

FIGURE 3.16: Disabling consequences of impairments

Impairment	Disabling consequences
Physical	Mobility problem, dexterity/coordination problem
Sensory	Degrees of sight and hearing loss
Mental	Degrees of thought disorder and lower ability to cope with stress
Learning	Limited learning and intellectual ability

ACTIVITY

Using a medical dictionary or CD-ROM program, find out about each of the following impairments. Copy and complete the chart below.

Impairment/ condition	Medical details	How might it result in 'additional needs'?
Cerebral palsy		
Glaucoma		
Down's syndrome		
Arthritis		
Alzheimer's disease		
Deafness		

Needs of the elderly

Statistics show that more people are living into their seventies, eighties and nineties than ever before. As people age their needs change. Many older people make very positive contributions to their families and their local communities and adapt their lifestyle to cater for their changing physical, social and emotional needs.

Physical ageing is a natural process and results in a diminishing physical ability. Eyesight and hearing may be less sensitive, strength and stamina are reduced and older people may develop disabling physical problems such as arthritis or cataracts. Reduction and loss of abilities may lead to some older people requiring assistance with activities that they once performed independently, such as walking or bathing themselves.

As people grow older their relationships with partners, friends and family members change. People who live into their seventies and eighties are likely to experience the death of partners and friends, and some may become lonely and isolated. Many older people make considerable efforts to live active lives and maintain their relationships in order to meet their continued but changing needs.

FIGURE 3.17: The elderly population, Great Britain 1901–2025 (in 000s)

Historical trends 1901–81

	65+	%	75+	%	85+	%
1901	1,734	4.7	507	1.4	57	0.15
1931	3,316	7.4	920	2.1	108	0.24
1951	5,332	10.9	1,731	3.5	218	0.45
1961	6,046	11.8	2,167	4.2	329	0.64
1971	7,140	13.2	2,536	4.7	462	0.86
1981	7,985	15.0	3,053	5.7	552	1.03

Projections (1985 based)

	65+	%	75+	%	85+	%
1985	8,371	15.2	3,544	6.4	671	1.22
1991	8,847	15.8	3,925	7.0	865	1.55
2001	8,995	15.7	4,320	7.5	1,146	2.00
2011	9,404	16.3	4,374	7.6	1,301	2.30
2021	10,562	18.2	4,678	8.0	1,300	2.23
2025	11,013	18.9	5,177	8.9	1,331	2.28

Source: 1901–81 Census data OPCS; Population projections by the Government

(HMSO, 1988)

QUICK response

What do the projected estimates in Figure 3.17 tell you about the changes that are expected to occur in the elderly population over the next thirty years?

BAINBRIDGE PENSIONERS' CLUB *Summer Season Events*

TUESDAY 10 JULY

10.30 am — Talk by Penelope Slade: 'Vegetarian cookery for one'

12.00 pm — Jumble sale in the Club House.

2.30 pm — Bus leaves Club House for trip to the Bainbridge Country Farm. Walk commences at 3.00 pm. Bring sturdy shoes!

FRIDAY 13 JULY

10.30 am — Talk by Patrick Ologu: 'How to claim all of your welfare benefits'

11.30 am — Swimming and aerobics classes at Bainbridge Sports Centre

2.30 pm — Tea dance in the Old Hall

ACTIVITY

Read the entertainments notice of Bainbridge Pensioners' Club and answer the following questions.

a How might each of the activities meet the needs of the club's members?

b What kind of activities could be organised to enable members to meet their emotional needs?

WAYS OF PROVIDING SERVICES

arlier in the chapter we looked at the different types of care organisation in Britain. There are a number of these in your local area, and the area where you live will be covered by an NHS Trust Hospital and a local authority social services department.

The care organisations that exist in your area provide services that aim to meet people's physical, social, emotional and mental health needs. Care organisations target their services at particular groups who have specific needs. Community mental health care, for example, is aimed at people who have recently been discharged from hospital or who need support to avoid admission to hospital for mental health problems.

While the District Health Authority in your area usually purchases NHS hospital and local GP services to meet the health care needs of the local population, it will not necessarily be able to pay the full cost of all of the care and treatment that people require. This is also the case for social care. There are a number of other ways in which care services can still be provided.

Services 'free at the point of delivery'

Many services are provided because the law requires health authorities or local authorities to provide them. They are 'free at the point of delivery' because people do not pay for receiving them.

Services for which a basic fee may need to be paid

The prescription that your GP writes for you and which you present to the pharmacist in return for medicine is an example of this kind of service. You are likely to incur a prescription charge unless you are in an exemption category.

Services where ability to pay is taken into account

This means that all people in need can receive the service but that those with low incomes or who receive welfare benefits have their care subsidised. For example, local authorities do not have to provide home care services for elderly people but often subsidise this type of social care for elderly clients who can afford to pay some but not all the cost involved.

QUICK response

Make a list of the categories of people who you think are exempt from prescription charges. How might you check if your list is correct?

Services run on a charitable basis

There are sometimes situations where people have no means by which to contribute to the cost of a service. In such circumstances groups that operate as registered charities provide free services. For example, there are a number of groups working with the homeless and people in poverty to provide services such as temporary housing or emergency food and clothing to clients who have no means to pay.

Services for which the individual pays the full cost

People who choose to receive care as private patients pay the full cost of the services that they receive to the care provider. For example, following private dental treatment, the client receives a bill payable to the dental practice.

FINDING OUT ABOUT LOCAL HEALTH AND SOCIAL CARE SERVICES

There are a number of sources of information to help you to find out about the way in which services are offered in your local area. *Yellow Pages* contains addresses and telephone numbers, the Community Health Council will be able to tell you about health services and local authority offices often have an information centre that will provide you with information and leaflets about social care services in your area. Other sources of local information include the notice boards at your college, health centre, GP practice or dentist and local news-papers.

QUICK response

Where are the noticeboards containing this type of information located in your school or college?

ACTIVITY

Look at the chart showing ways of funding and providing services. Match the type of provision to an example of a local health or social care service and an identified client group by producing and filling in a chart like the one below.

Method of providing and funding service	Example of a local service	Client group at whom the service is targeted
Services that are free at the point of delivery		
Services for which a basic fee may need to be paid		
Services where ability to pay will be taken into account		
Services run on a charitable basis		
Services for which the individual pays the full cost		

GAINING ACCESS TO HEALTH AND SOCIAL CARE SERVICES

People with health and social care needs can gain access to services offered by the various care organisations in a particular area by finding out about and following the appropriate **method of referral.** This means that they must have some knowledge about services and then be able to follow the correct procedure for making contact with the service. This is often not an easy process for people who are sick or vulnerable and are unable to care for themselves. As a result, many care organisations have made the referral process as easy to follow and use as they can or take referrals from other care professionals. It is possible to identify four common referral patterns.

SELF-REFERRAL

Many health and social care services try to be as open and accessible to the public as possible. They encourage potential clients to make use of their services by offering self-referral or 'walk-in' facilities. This means that where a person can identify their own need for care or treatment, they can then get help by directly approaching a service that they know about. Many of us do this when we make an appointment at the GP or dentist in response to illness or toothache, or when we go to a Citizens Advice Bureau for help, advice or information.

PROFESSIONAL REFERRAL

This is where one health or social care professional refers a patient or client to another professional or service with more appropriate skills or facilities. Often people's problems and care needs are complex and cannot be easily resolved by one person. For example, it is very common for a GP to act as referer to other health and social care workers when a patient is pregnant and needs ongoing care throughout pregnancy and following the birth. The GP will refer the patient to the appropriate hospital consultant, midwifery service, social work department or health visitor in order to ensure that her needs are best met.

REFERRAL BY OTHERS

There are situations where people who are in need of health or social care do not realise that they have this need or are unable to identify where they can get help from, and also are not in contact with care professionals who can make an appropriate professional referral. In such circumstances individuals are sometimes referred to care organisations by friends, relatives or neighbours who care for them or are concerned about their need for help.

Referral by others, as this method is known, is not unusual and is a means by which people who have a knowledge of the caring services but who are not themselves professional carers can use it to help others. In most of these referral situations the non-professional referrer should gain the consent of the person whom they feel needs help before they make any referral.

REFERRAL BY EMERGENCY SERVICES

All the previous methods of referral are likely to be used in circumstances where the client has a health or social care need that could be met with professional help but which is not life-threatening or requiring immediate attention. The emergency services, particularly the Ambulance Service, attend many accidents and incidents where people suffer physical injuries that need immediate attention. In such circumstances, and where people suffer acute mental health and psychiatric problems, or where children are at risk, referrals are made by members of the emergency services to health and social care workers who can offer an immediate response to the client's physical, mental or social care need.

✦ ACTIVITY

RECEIVING REFERRALS

For each of the following case studies identify:

- ⊗ which client groups are involved
- ⊗ the different types of referral that have been made in each situation
- ⊗ what you feel the main needs of the clients are in each situation.

a **Mrs Arkwright** is 78 years old and is rather frail. She has a weekly visit from **Mr Peters**, a local authority home carer, who carries out domestic tasks. On one of his visits, **Mr Peters** notices that **Mrs Arkwright** is very unwell. With her permission he rings her GP asking for an urgent home visit. The GP asks the district nurse to go with him that afternoon.

b **The Smarts**, in their mid-twenties, have three children under 5 years old. Both parents have full-time jobs. **Rosie Abdi** is a social worker for the under-fives. She has received a letter from the **Smarts'** GP expressing concern about the amount of time that the children are left alone and the effect that this is having on their behaviour. **Rosie** has alerted the social services' child care team of this situation. They plan to visit the **Smarts'** home tomorrow.

c **Mr Ghupta**, aged 35, has a long-term mental illness that prevents him from working. He has lived alone since his wife divorced him six months ago. This evening his neighbour, **Kate**, reported a fire at **Mr Ghupta's** house to the emergency services. When they arrived they found **Mr Ghupta** lying unconscious in his smoke-filled bedroom.

An ambulance took him to the accident and emergency department where a psychiatrist saw him and admitted him to a psychiatric ward for mental health care.

MAKING REFERRALS

For each of the following case examples decide:

- ⊗ what sort of help is required in each case
- ⊗ who could refer the person needing help
- ⊗ who the most appropriate carers or services are to provide the help needed.

a **John** is 12 years old and has been brought before the courts for repeated minor offences relating to vandalism and petty theft. His parents have been finding him very difficult to cope with as they have two other children under 7 and have had financial problems since **John's** father was made redundant six months ago.

b **Ellisha** is 5 months pregnant and is 18 years old. She has broken off the relationship with the father of her baby after he was violent towards her. She is determined to have the baby. After a row with her parents over this, she is found wandering the streets at 1 am in a distressed state. Her parents say that they do not want her back.

c **Mrs Rowe** is 73 years old and is due to be discharged from hospital following treatment for a stroke. She lives alone and has no close friends or relatives to help her. The hospital occupational therapist and social worker feel that she will not be able to care for herself unaided at home.

It is not unusual for both health and social care services to be jointly involved in providing care to the same client. This may occur after one service identifies a need that they cannot meet and refers their patient or client to a service or practitioner who can offer help.

HELPING AND SUPPORTING CLIENTS TO USE CARE SERVICES

Health and social care organisations can be confusing and daunting places for many people who are unfamiliar with how they work, how to find their way around inside a hospital or other care building, or whom they should talk to when they arrive. Hospitals, dental surgeries and clinics can also be sources of fear and trigger unhappy memories for people who have to use their services.

As a multiethnic society Britain has many citizens whose first language is not English and who may find English difficult to understand. Many native speakers of English also find the long complicated medical words on hospital signs difficult to understand and follow. In order to overcome these, and other, problems that prevent patients and clients from using care services most effectively, care organisations generally offer information and language support services that simplify access to and knowledge about the care services offered.

> **⚡QUICK** response
>
> What are the images that 'hospital', 'dentist', 'operation' and 'doctor' conjure up in your mind?

TYPES OF HELP AND SUPPORT SERVICES

Leaflets and poster displays

At the entrance to the premises of most care services there are a range of leaflets, sometimes in the various languages of the local population, and often poster displays that give health advice and information about opening times, making referrals, getting help and advice and the cost of services.

GP surgeries, hospital wards and social service departments also produce leaflets outlining the services that they offer and clients' rights concerning what they are entitled to receive and how they will be treated.

Information desks

In some larger organisations there are help and information desks staffed by advisers who can give directions, provide information about opening times or making appointments or who will give information about patients' and clients' rights within a service.

Translation services

Where there are a variety of languages spoken in a community or where a person who is being cared for cannot speak sufficient English to understand their care workers or get the most out of a service, a care organisation may provide a translation service or a multilingual care worker who can act as interpreter for them.

In hospitals and social services departments that cater for a multilingual community the direction signs and information boards are often written in the different languages of the service users.

Advocacy services

An advocate is someone who speaks on another person's behalf. In some care settings patients and clients may find it difficult to explain their own opinions and views. Other people are unable to express themselves fully when faced by professionals or relatives.

There are also circumstances where by law a person must have an advocate to represent them. For example when an individual under the age of 16 is held at a police station, a 'responsible adult', usually a parent or social worker, must be present to protect the young person's interests before being interviewed by the police. In such circumstances advocacy will involve working with the young person to find out and express his or her wishes and views and to protect and promote his or her rights.

ACTIVITY

Health and social care services need to be 'user friendly' if potential clients are to make the best use of them. Information about services should be freely available, there should be easy access to the building where the services are located and health care staff should put clients at their ease.

Look at the pictures of the health centre. Dr Halford and Dr Thandy have asked your advice on how to make their new health centre 'user friendly'. The main users of the health centre are mothers with babies, a large group of elderly people and many members of the local Asian community.

b Arrange to visit a local health centre or GP's surgery. Evaluate the use of support strategies – provision of information, ease of access, language support/signs in different languages – to help clients make the most of the services available.

- ⊗ What are the good points?

- ⊗ What areas could be improved?

- ⊗ How would you suggest improving these areas?

Produce a short report on your visit and your findings.

a Review each part of the health centre. How can it be made user friendly? Make suggestions about how the environment, the provision of information and the personal approach of the staff could be adapted to support the clients who use the health centre.

PORTFOLIO ASSIGNMENT

HEALTH AND SOCIAL CARE NEEDS

INTRODUCTION

This assignment will give you the opportunity to survey the needs of people in three client groups and to identify and describe the local services that are available to meet these needs.

TASK 1

Identify three people who may be willing to talk to you about their health or social care needs and the services that they use. You should choose people who fall into the different client groups covered in the unit. These groups include babies, children, young people, adults, elderly people and families. One of the people you choose should use services provided by the NHS and at least one of the others should require the use of other care services.

Keep copies of any letters you write or notes about telephone calls or conversations that you have as a way of getting your three volunteers.

TASK 2

Plan and carry out an interview with each person or, in the case of the baby or child, with their carer. You will need to obtain information about physical, emotional and social needs.

You will need to think about how you will record the things that they tell you. Possible methods include writing notes, tape recording or giving them a questionnaire that you have produced. You will need to get the permission of your interviewee before you do any of these things and to explain clearly to them who will read or hear the things that they tell you. It is important that they only give you information that they are happy about you disclosing to others involved with your course.

Again keep copies of your questions, questionnaires or tapes that you make.

PORTFOLIO ASSIGNMENT

TASK 3

When you have collected your information, compile a brief case study about each person. You may change their names and omit addresses from your case studies but make sure that you give information about their:

- age

- gender

- cultural background

- physical needs

- emotional needs

- social needs

- who their main relationships are with

- who their main carers are

- which local services they use.

TASK 4

Are there any services available locally that are designed to meet the needs of the people you have interviewed but that they are not using at present? Produce a brief list of local services that may be useful to your interviewees. Your list should include:

- the name and address of the organisation

- the service that it offers

- the methods of being referred to the service.

INVESTIGATE JOBS IN HEALTH AND SOCIAL CARE

The NHS is the largest employer in Europe. Within the statutory, health and social care sectors in the UK it is estimated that there are more than 1 million people in paid employment. In the third part of this chapter we look at the range of jobs in health and social care, identify the main job types and look at what is actually involved in training and working as a health or social care worker.

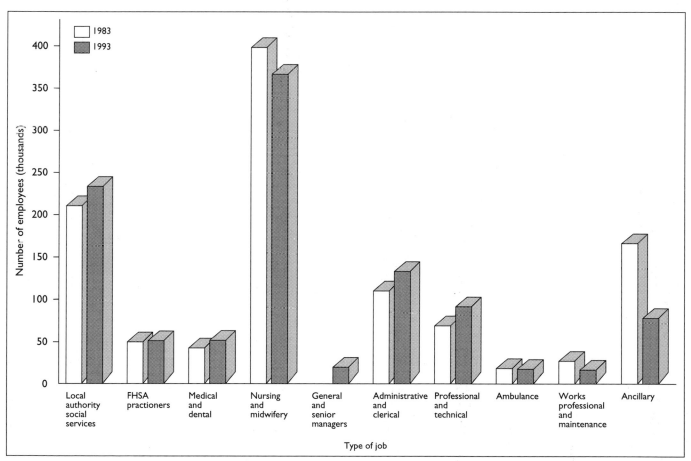

Source: *Health and Personal Social Service Statistics for England* HMSO, 1995

FIGURE 3.18: NHS employees

THE RANGE OF JOBS IN THE CARE SECTOR

There are a large number of different jobs and specialist roles in health and social care workplaces. Many of these are complementary to each other as care workers often work in teams and coordinate their efforts to help patients and clients.

In order to simplify the range of care roles it is useful to consider the differences between:

- ⊗ **health care and social care**

- ⊗ **direct care workers and support service workers.**

Health care and social care

People who are employed as health workers usually deal with patients and clients who have physical, medical-related problems such as a disease, injury or acute illness. People who work in social care usually deal with clients who have a personal, social/emotional or financial problem or difficulty but which does not have a physical/medical component to it.

Many clients have problems that have both health and social care aspects to them. There are, of course, care roles where a person who is predominantly a health worker also has a significant amount of social care to provide as part of their job. A community psychiatric nurse is one such role.

FIGURE 3.19: Behind the scenes in a hospital

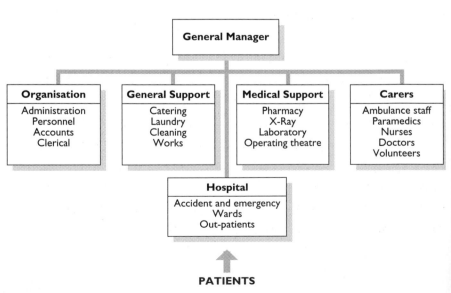

ACTIVITY

Look at the following list of health and social care jobs.
Reorganise them into three lists headed 'Health jobs', 'Social
care jobs' and 'Mixed roles'. You should also write a sentence
that briefly describes what you feel is involved in each job.

District nurse	Health visitor
Community psychiatric nurse	Psychologist
Residential social worker	Gynaecologist
Social worker	Occupational therapist
Hospital manager	Chiropodist
Psychotherapist	Hostel manager
Nursery nurse	Surgeon
Housing advice worker	

You could use careers booklets and computer databases to find
out about occupational roles such as these.

Direct care workers and support service workers

In hospitals, social services departments, nurseries, schools and health
centres some workers care directly for patients and clients while others
run the organisation and support the direct carers.

As a patient or client of the care services the people that we are likely
to come into contact with, other than reception staff, are direct care
workers such as doctors, nurses or social workers. Behind the scenes in
any care organisation there are also a range of support workers who
ensure that the organisation works efficiently and effectively. Buildings
are cleaned, paper work is completed and the maintenance of equipment and general facilities are carried out in all care organisations
without most patients or clients noticing. Figure 3.19 describes the
way in which this might operate in a hospital.

ACTIVITY

1 Allocate each of the following roles to a job type (direct care or support role) and a setting (hospital or community based), then copy and complete the chart below.

2 Produce your own list of jobs. You should try to add at least ten new jobs to the list. Indicate whether they are direct care or support roles, and whether they are hospital or community based.

	Job type		Setting	
	Direct care	Support role	Hospital	Community
Anaesthetist				
Business manager				
Counsellor				
Doctor (GP)				
Educational psychologist				
Foster parent				
Gardener				
Housing advice worker				
Interpreter				
Junior doctor (hospital)				
Kitchen assistant				
Laundry worker				
Mental health nurse				
Nutritionist				
Occupational therapist				
Psychiatrist				
Quality standards adviser				
Receptionist				
Social worker				
Telephonist				
Ultrasound technician				
Venesectionist				
Ward sister				
X-ray technician				
Youth worker				
Zimmer frame designer				

OCCUPATIONAL AREAS IN HEALTH AND SOCIAL CARE

So far we have identified the differences between health care and social care jobs (with some overlaps) and direct care and support roles. Jobs in health and social care can also be grouped into occupational areas. Some of the more familiar occupational areas are:

- ☻ **medicine**

- ☻ **nursing**

- ☻ **social work**

- ☻ **social care**

- ☻ **child care**

- ☻ **professions allied to medicine (PAMS)**

- ☻ **administration and support work.**

Within each of these occupational areas there are many specialist roles that develop after a 'core' occupational training. For example, within child care a person could begin their career as a nursery assistant, later work as a nursery nurse and, with further experience and training, go on to become a classroom teacher in primary education, or a nursery manager for the local authority. Care workers tend to undertake a general training in one of the occupational areas to gain their basic qualification and then gradually specialise in a particular area of that occupation.

PREPARING FOR WORK IN HEALTH AND SOCIAL CARE

Most students who choose a GNVQ Intermediate Health and Social Care course have made a decision that they would like to work in an area of the care services. Some students make decisions early on about which specific roles and areas of work they are interested in while others take longer to decide.

If you are in either of these groups, there are three main areas to research and think through before you arrive at a final decision. Careful thinking and preparation at the early stage of your career in care work will help you to achieve what you want later on.

QUICK response

What are your current thoughts and ideas about this?

PERSONAL QUALITIES AND EXPERIENCE

Care work is all about working with other people, often at times of their lives when they are vulnerable and distressed. To be able to do this care workers must have a strong sense of wanting to help others and the ability to like and work with a wide variety of people. Many students choosing courses such as GNVQ Intermediate Health and Social Care feel that they have 'a caring personality' and that they possess the right qualities needed to care for others.

ACTIVITY

1   Brainstorm a list of qualities that you associate with a 'good carer'.

2   Swap ideas with a partner and try to explain to them the importance of each item in your list.

3   Discuss which of these qualities you currently possess and which you feel you need to develop further.

In order to gain entry to jobs and training courses in care work it is often necessary to show that you are able to use your 'caring qualities' in practical ways. Education and training are very important in developing effective skills and the values needed to work in all areas of health and social care. Gaining experience of care work is important to test out for yourself whether the practical aspects of care jobs match up to your expectations of them and is an important way of demonstrating to employers and course tutors that you are suitable and committed to a career in this area.

As a part of your GNVQ Intermediate Health and Social Care course you may gain basic experience of care work through work placements. You may also have, or be able to gain, experience through providing informal care to relatives, friends or neighbours. Experience gained through part-time, full-time and temporary work is valuable in supporting your learning in college and will help you to progress further.

QUALIFICATION REQUIREMENTS

There are currently three different qualification routes into care work for young people and adults. These are shown in Figure 3.20.

FIGURE 3.20: Qualification routes into care work

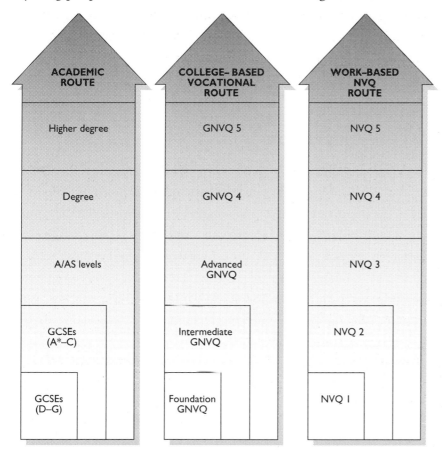

Some areas of care work, particularly medicine, require students to follow the **academic route** into higher education. People who choose this route have to achieve a degree level qualification. There are a wide range of courses available but only a relatively small number of people take this route compared to the GNVQ and NVQ routes.

GNVQ Health and Social Care qualifications provide a college-based **vocational route** that can also lead to higher education or can enable students to progress to employment. They are particularly aimed at 16–19-year-old students with little experience in care work who wish to have both employment and further study options open to them. GNVQ Health and Social Care courses give students a broad under-pinning knowledge of the care area and help them to improve their core communication, application of number and information technology skills. Students can progress from GNVQ courses into a variety of support worker level posts.

NVQs are qualifications gained 'on the job' by health and social care workers. The **work-based NVQ route** is used to improve skills and career prospects by people who wish to have a practical role in a health and social care service. People usually begin NVQ courses by either getting a paid job with a care organisation or a training place with their local Training and Enterprise Council (TEC) or college of further education. NVQs cover a variety of areas of adult and child care work and enable students to establish and improve practical skills.

CAREER PROGRESSION

Within each occupational area of care work it is possible to progress in a number of different ways. Gaining basic qualifications and experience is the important first step in a career in care work. Finding out about the different ways in which your career may be able to develop later as you gain experience is important when thinking about which area of care to enter. People like to progress in their careers and having a good idea of the different possibilities at the beginning makes career planning easier and gives many people an incentive to develop their skills in particular areas. Most care workers progress by gaining further qualifications and experience in specialist areas of their field.

CAREER ROUTES AND TRAINING

In this section you will look at the career routes that people may follow to get into and develop careers in each of the different occupational areas, compare the popular image – **stereotype** – of the role with the reality and look at the work patterns and conditions they experience.

MEDICINE

To qualify as a doctor it is necessary to attend a university medical school for five years to gain the basic academic knowledge and practical experience to pass the first stage of medical training, which is to get a degree in medicine. To gain entry to medical school an applicant needs at least five GCSEs and three A levels with high grades.

When a person qualifies from university, they must then work for at

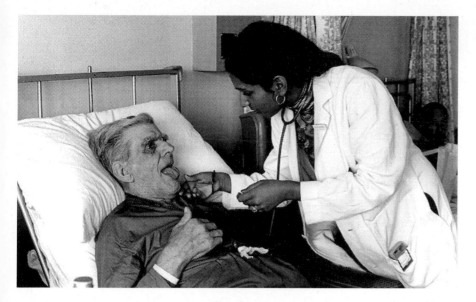

least a year as a junior house officer in a hospital setting. Here they rapidly gain experience of a range of diseases, illnesses and medical problems. Following this, junior doctors undertake further professional examinations to become a specialist in an area of medical practice, such as surgery, general practice or psychiatry.

Doctors must continually update their knowledge through reading specialist journals that cover the latest research and by attending courses to develop and improve their skills. Hospital doctors gradually work their way up the career ladder from house officer to registrar, then to senior registrar and finally consultant. GPs take a specialist training course after gaining basic hospital experience.

Doctors often work long hours and may work at weekends, in the evenings and at night to deal with the very large caseloads of patients who they see and treat. It can take doctors many years to progress up the career ladder and they are required to continue studying and working while they do this.

FIGURE 3.21: Career progression for doctors

CONSULTANT	£41,760–53,900
SENIOR REGISTRAR	£23,685–29,960
REGISTRAR	£20,550–24,940
SENIOR HOUSE OFFICER	£18,395–23,335
HOUSE OFFICER	£14,740–16,640

CASE STUDY

Dr Sandra Saunders has worked as an **anaesthetist** at St Joseph's Hospital for the last three years. She works a 'shift rotation' system, which means that, together with her six colleagues in the anaesthetics department, she works shifts to cover the 24-hour needs of the hospital and its patients. She works in the accident and emergency department and in the hospital's operating theatres. Her job is to anaesthetise patients and then to manage their airway and respiratory system safely while they are being treated or operated on. Dr Saunders works closely with other doctors and nursing staff as part of the on-call team. As a senior anaesthetist, she attends regular meetings with hospital managers to represent her colleagues and department at the Hospital Management Committee.

CASE STUDY

Dr Natasha Olabogun works as a **GP** in an inner-city health centre with three other GPs. After medical school and her two years as a hospital doctor she took a specialist GP training course. She now has a large and varied list of patients and sees them by appointment and at drop-in clinics between 8.30 am and 6 pm each weekday. Dr Olabogun diagnoses and treats most of the illnesses that her patients come to her with. She refers more complicated and serious cases to the local hospital. Dr Olabogun and her colleagues take it in turns to be on call to see patients one weekend in every four.

NURSING

Nurses make up the largest group of care staff in the UK. There are approximately 345,000 qualified nurses working in a range of areas of health care. There are important differences in the type of training and work that professionally qualified nurses and vocationally qualified health care support workers, also known as nursing assistants undertake.

Registered nurse

To become a professionally qualified nurse a person must undertake an approved nurse training programme that lasts for three years which results in a Registered Nurse qualification. The minimum entry qualifications are passes in five GCSEs or equivalent. Since the introduction of the Project 2000 training programme all applicants undertake an 18-month Common Foundation course in basic physical and social sciences and nursing studies and can then choose to specialise in adult, mental health, learning disabilities or children's nursing in the final 18 months of their course.

When qualified, a registered nurse generally works as a 'staff nurse' to gain experience and improve his or her practical skills. Nurses work a variety of shift patterns, including days, nights and sometimes weekends. Many nurses then choose to undertake further specialist courses to progress in their careers.

Nurses must update their knowledge and skills continuously through attendance at courses and through personal study and reading about the latest research and practice in professional magazines and journals. Nursing is often a physically and emotionally tiring job. Caring for people who are sick and dependent can involve carrying out tasks that are unpleasant and physically demanding, such as changing and remaking soiled beds. As well as carrying out their care role, nurses have to complete administrative work relating to patients and often have a role in training student nurses.

SENIOR NURSE MANAGER (I GRADE)	£22,020–24,950
CLINICAL NURSE SPECIALIST (H GRADE)	£19,890–22,745
SISTER/WARD MANAGER (G GRADE)	£17,800–20,595
SISTER/CHARGE NURSE (F GRADE)	£15,095–18,490
STAFF NURSE (E GRADE)	£13,605–15,760
STAFF NURSE (D GRADE)	£11,895–13,605

FIGURE 3.22: Career progression for nurses and midwives

CASE STUDY

Marjorie Manzoma qualified as a registered general nurse ten years ago. After gaining some experience as a staff nurse in a hospital medical ward, she undertook further training in psychiatric nursing. Marjorie now combines her general and mental health nursing experience by working in a unit for elderly frail people who experience confusion and memory problems. Marjorie would like to continue working with this group and plans to increase her skills and experience through working in a day care centre and then as a community psychiatric nurse.

CASE STUDY

Kitty Seymour is unit manager for a children's surgical unit in a major teaching hospital. After qualifying as a registered general nurse fifteen years ago, she worked her way up to becoming ward sister of a surgical ward. She has also worked in operating theatres and gained her BSc degree in nursing five years ago. Kitty developed an interest in management and took some short courses to support her practical skills in this area. Two years ago she became unit manager for the surgical unit where she worked as a sister. Kitty would like to spend more time as a manager and intends to undertake a teaching course so that she can pass on her skills and experience to others.

HEALTH CARE SUPPORT WORKER

The other way in which people can gain some vocational training and experience in nursing is as a health care support worker. Most health care support workers follow the NVQ route and gain their training and experience under the supervision of registered nurses. Health care support workers are increasingly trained and qualified to NVQ level 2 or 3 and may be found working in all areas of health care. They often have a great deal of direct patient contact, assisting registered nurses and other care staff in providing care.

The role of health care support workers is different from that of a nurse in a number of important ways.

- ⊗ **They carry out most of the domestic tasks in a care setting such as making beds.**

- ⊗ **The physical care that they provide relates to routine procedures such as lifting, bathing and dressing patients.**

- ⊗ **They carry out care planned by registered nurses.**

Like nurses, health care support workers work both day and night shift patterns and may also work weekends.

CASE STUDY

Health Care Support Worker
37.5 hours per week,
£10,034 per annum
Ref: HCSW 101

We are looking for motivated, enthusiastic people interested in working with elderly people. As a Health Care Support Worker you will work in a team of health care staff, have good communication skills and be well-motivated. Care qualifications and previous experience desirable but not essential as training will be given to NVQ level 3.

Our aim is to provide a high standard of assessment and respite to patients who use our service.

For an application form and job description, please contact the Recruitment Office quoting the reference number for the post.

Stephen Walkes, aged 22, has worked as a health care support worker in a learning disabilities unit for the last five years. He works day and night shifts and provides direct care and support to the ten residents of the bungalow where he works. He helps the residents in different ways depending on their individual needs. Some people need help with personal care, such as going to the toilet, washing and dressing, others need assistance when travelling to college or on social outings, and all of the residents benefit from the relationships that they have developed with Stephen. He is currently taking an NVQ level 2 in direct care and plans to go on to develop his care and managerial skills. He hopes to work in day centres and progress to social work training later in his career.

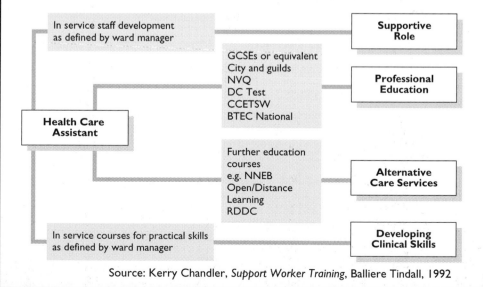

Source: Kerry Chandler, *Support Worker Training*, Balliere Tindall, 1992

FIGURE 3.23: Qualifications for health care workers

SOCIAL WORK

A social worker is a person who has gained a professional social work qualification, normally a Diploma in Social Work, and who has experience of working with clients with social, financial and emotional problems. The Diploma in Social Work is a two-year course of study and practical placements. Courses are run in further and higher education institutions and require a minimum of A level/GNVQ Advanced level qualifications and some social care experience. Mature students over the age of 21 may win a place on the basis of experience and other qualifications. Because of the difficult and stressful nature of the work, and the need for some maturity and life experience, most social work courses have a minimum entry age of 21.

Most professionally qualified social workers are employed as 'field' social workers. This means that they have a caseload of people who they work with in community and institutional settings. Some social workers specialise in working with particular types of clients, such as child protection work or psychiatric social work, whereas others operate as 'generic' social workers and will see people with various problems who are referred to them.

Within social work there is a grading structure through which people progress as they gain experience and demonstrate their ability. Career opportunities can arise for social workers to become team leaders or go into management and become care managers and ultimately, director of social services.

Social Worker (Children and Families Team)

£17,154 to £23,568 p.a. inclusive depending on experience

Full time or job share

Required to join our team of enthusiastic social workers providing a service to children and their families in the city. Your role will include liaison with schools, health authority professionals and voluntary agencies.

You must be:
- DipSW or equivalent qualified
- have experience of working with families with children with disabilities and behavioural problems
- have experience of child protection work
- have a good understanding of anti-discriminatory practice.

Please quote reference SW96/children

CASE STUDY

Kimberley Taylor is a psychiatric social worker working in the accident and emergency department of a hospital. She starts work at 9 am every weekday morning. Her day can be unpredictable as she is never sure who will come in or how they might need her help. People arrive with a variety of psychological problems. Kimberley receives referrals from the duty doctor and nurses in the department and interviews all of the people referred to her to assess their mental health needs and social problems. Following each assessment she organises social care and support in hospital or at home and liaises with other care workers to ensure that care can be provided. Kimberley attends several meetings with colleagues during the week to discuss the patients she has seen and the running of the department.

CASE STUDY

Jenny Gilberto is a social worker employed by social services to work with children and families. She works a 9–5 day, with some evenings on call each month. She tries to provide a link between social care services and families when they are in need of help and support. Each morning Jenny sees new referrals at the local family centre or at their home to assess their social needs. She tries to sort out any immediate financial or personal problems that they have and puts them in touch with other services, such as the Department of Social Security which can give financial help. Each week she organises and runs case conferences for those clients who are to be discharged. At these meetings all the care workers involved with a particular client meet with the client and their informal carers to discuss what care needs to be provided and who will offer it after the client has left hospital. As a placement tutor, Jenny often has a student social worker with her and gives teaching sessions and support where necessary.

SOCIAL CARE

There is a range of vocationally qualified and non-qualified people who also work in social care settings in a support capacity. Like the health care support worker, social care workers now tend to have NVQ training gained through experience and work under the supervision of qualified social workers, often providing much practical help and support for clients and having much client contact.

Social care jobs are advertised by local authorities and voluntary and private-sector organisations in local and national papers. For some posts previous experience and specific qualifications are required, while for others a relevant vocational qualification, such as GNVQ Intermediate Health and Social Care, and an aptitude for care work are requested.

Social care jobs fall into three main areas:

- **domiciliary care**
- **residential care**
- **day care.**

Social care workers may work a variety of different shift patterns. Day care workers tend to work 9–5, Monday to Friday, domiciliary care workers may work at any time of the day from early morning to late evening, while residential social care workers may work day and night shifts and weekends.

 CASE STUDY

Bhupinder Mann is employed as a home carer by a local authority. She works a shift system that includes days, nights and weekend work. She has undertaken NVQ level 2 training and has been on lifting and handling, and food hygiene courses. She visits up to six different elderly clients in their homes each day. She helps them to wash and dress and prepares breakfast or an evening drink for them. Bhupinder enjoys the practical side of her job and feels that it is important to be well organised and understanding to do her job well.

CASE STUDY

Daniel McClaren is a residential social worker in a private children's home. He works shifts on a rota system, which means that he works two weekends per month, three months of nights each year, and day shifts in between. After gaining his GNVQ Intermediate in Health and Social Care, he began an NVQ level 2 in child care with his local TEC. His placement experience at the children's home led to a full-time post. He is part of a care team that looks after six children when they are not at school. Daniel has special responsibility for organising the recreational and sports activities for the weekends and school holidays.

CHILD CARE AND EDUCATION

Child care and early years education are areas in which there are a wide range of care roles and career opportunities, both in health care and social care. Child care workers may have one or more of a range of qualifications or may gain work because of their own experience of bringing up children. NVQs in Child Care and Education are specifically designed to develop and assess skills gained by child care workers in the workplace. Many nursery, playgroup and classroom assistants now undertake NVQ training.

FIGURE 3.24: Child care and education jobs

Nursery nursing

A qualified nursery nurse has achieved a qualification such as an NNEB or BTEC Diploma in Nursery Nursing. Nursery nurses are employed in private and local authority nurseries, usually providing direct care and education for children under five.

Playgroup work

People who work as assistants in playgroups and nurseries may work under the supervision of a nursery nurse or another experienced playgroup worker. Many carers take NVQ qualifications to improve their knowledge and skills.

Play specialist

Play specialists work with children in hospital. Their role is to use play as a means of developing children's practical and communication skills at a time in their lives when ordinary school life and opportunities to play with other children are limited by their illnesses or disabilities. Play specialists can undertake specialist courses to improve their knowledge and skills.

Early childhood teaching

Nursery and infant teachers work in state and private primary schools and have to achieve a degree qualification to obtain a post as a teacher. They work with groups of children, planning and assessing learning activities for them, often using play to do this. Early years teachers work school hours and often work at home to prepare and mark work and do their record keeping.

Classroom assistant

Classroom assistants are not qualified teachers. They assist the teacher with practical activities, such as setting up the classroom and supervising children on outings, and help children with basic care tasks, such as changing their clothes and going to the toilet where they are unable to do so for themselves. Classroom assistants can take specialist courses and NVQs to improve their skills. They work school hours during week days.

Registered childminder

Childminders work in their own home looking after one or more children, usually in office or other working hours when the children's parents are working. Childminders must be registered with their local authority and must be able to offer the facilities and experience needed to provide a good standard of care.

PROFESSIONS ALLIED TO MEDICINE

Besides medicine and nursing, there are a number of other care roles within the health care occupational area. When grouped together these are referred to as professions allied to medicine (PAMS). Practitioners in these areas generally work in multidisciplinary teams with medical, nursing and social work staff in both hospital and community settings. People who train and work in the professions allied to medicine generally have a degree level qualification. Entrants to training courses require A level /GNVQ Advanced level qualifications and some care experience. Mature students over the age of 21 may be able to gain a place on the basis of their prior care experience and educational ability. There are also some opportunities to work as 'assistants' to professionally qualified practitioners. These are advertised in professional magazines and local newspapers by NHS Trusts and social services departments.

CASE STUDY

Darren Samuels is a self-employed physiotherapist. After gaining his degree in physiotherapy, he acquired experience as a basic grade and then senior physiotherapist in a District General Hospital. Darren's role was to plan and carry out exercise, movement and massage programmes for patients who required rehabilitation following injuries and illnesses that affected their physical abilities. As a hospital-based physiotherapist Darren worked week days, 9–5, seeing patients by referral from other professionals. Darren became self-employed, running his own practice, two years ago. He now sees patients by referral from other professionals and people who refer themselves. He works longer hours, including some evenings and Saturdays to fit in with his clients' lifestyles.

SUPERINTENDENT I	£23,850–26,270
SUPERINTENDENT II	£21,850–23,850
SUPERINTENDENT III	£19,880–21,850
SENIOR I	£17,355–19,880
SENIOR II	£14,605–17,355
BASIC GRADE	£12,635–14,605

FIGURE 3.25: Career progression for physiotherapists

CASE STUDY

Rikki Starr works as a senior occupational therapist at the Highgrove Mental Health Centre. She assesses patients' social, psychological and physical needs and abilities and offers them programmes of activity and therapy designed to enable them to develop or reacquire practical skills and personal attributes, such as self-esteem and confidence, that increase their independence. Rikki undertook a degree course to gain her basic qualification and has since taken several short courses to improve her skills in management, counselling and artwork.

HEAD I	**£23,850–26,270**
HEAD II	**£21,580–23,850**
HEAD III	**£19,880–21,580**
SENIOR I	**£17,355–19,880**
SENIOR II	**£14,605–17,355**
BASIC GRADE	**£12,635–14,605**

FIGURE 3.26: Career progression for occupational therapists

CASE STUDY

Jenny Field has recently qualified as a radiographer. She is now a junior diagnostic radiographer at St Joseph's Hospital. Her job involves her taking X-rays of patients with fractures, internal problems and ultra-sound scans of pregnant women. Jenny works shifts, including nights and weekends, at the hospital. To qualify Jenny took a three-year diploma course in radiography at the hospital.

SUPERINTENDENT I	**£23,850–26,270**
SUPERINTENDENT II	**£21,850–23,850**
SUPERINTENDENT III	**£19,880–21,850**
SENIOR I	**£17,355–19,880**
SENIOR II	**£14,605–17,355**
BASIC GRADE	**£12,635–14,605**

FIGURE 3.27: Career progression for radiographers

ADMINISTRATION, MANAGEMENT AND ANCILLARY JOBS

Health and social care organisations are staffed by a wide range of support staff who carry out the administration, management and ancillary jobs that are essential for all organisations and direct care workers to work efficiently.

Administrative work covers secretarial and clerical jobs such as typing, filing, record-keeping and wages' calculations. Information technology, accountancy, typing and customer care courses are all available as NVQ courses through colleges and many training departments within care organisations.

Management work involves taking responsibility for the effective and efficient running of various aspects of a care organisation. People who work as managers may have specialist qualifications in the area in which they are working, such as medical laboratory science, and an additional management qualification and experience gained through working in various posts. Managers have more power and responsibility than administrative staff and are usually responsible for a group of staff and a department. Managers usually work office hours, Monday to Friday. They have a variety of qualifications including NVQs, degrees and diplomas in different areas of management.

Ancillary work covers areas needed to keep the care organisation running effectively such as catering, cleaning and maintenance. People who work as ancillary workers may have vocational qualifications appropriate to the area in which they work, such as catering or electrical work, or may obtain their jobs because of prior experience and the practical skills that they have. Ancillary workers work a variety of shift patterns with some working office hours while others work at night and at weekends to keep the care services operating.

CASE STUDY

Angela Bee is the facilities manager at St Joseph's Hospital. She is responsible for the safe and efficient running of the catering, laundry, portering, maintenance and gardening services that operate behind the scenes at St Joseph's. Angela works with the staff in each of the areas mentioned, holds daily meetings to discuss staffing and operational issues, and liaises with other managers responsible for the direct care and financial aspects of running the hospital. Her job is mainly a 9–5 one, but she can be contacted to sort out problems that occur outside of office hours.

CASE STUDY

Eric Allman is an accounting technician working in the local authority finance department. He is responsible for monitoring and producing financial records of spending by the social services department through the contracts that they make with various social care organisations. He works office hours, mainly in the finance office. He has undertaken an NVQ level 2 in Accountancy and is currently studying for an NVQ level 3 in Information Technology. He works office hours, Monday to Friday and is part of a team of workers in the finance section.

CASE STUDY

Anthea Bytheway works as a domestic cleaner in the dermatology out-patients clinic attached to the hospitals burns unit. She works five days a week, 6 pm–9 am. She is responsible for cleaning the floors, desks and other surfaces, and generally tidies the department each morning before other people arrive. Anthea is currently taking an NVQ level 2 in Cleaning.

ACTIVITY

Many people wish to work in health and social care jobs. When making decisions about which specialist area to enter, individuals need advice based on good research and up-to-date information. Sources of such information include the national bodies of the different caring professions.

This activity puts you in the position of a careers advice worker who receives letters from those interested in care work. After you have read each letter, write a reply based on research on the area that the writer is interested in.

1

Dear Sir/Madam
I am 15 years of age and want to work in the health and social care area. I am taking six GCSEs and help out at a local nursery in the school holidays. I would like to be a children's nurse or something similar. I don't know very much about the work that children's nurses do so I would be grateful for any details you could provide. I would also be grateful for information on the types of qualifications that are needed to enter training and what the training involves.
I look forward to your reply.
    Yours faithfully
    Savita Khan

2

Dear Sir/Madam
I would like to join the Ambulance Service and become a paramedic. Could you tell me how to do this? I am 21 years old, have a GNVQ Advanced in Health and Social Care and five GCSEs. I am willing to work hard to train and be successful. I would be grateful for further details about entry requirements, training and what is involved in the work of a paramedic.
    Yours faithfully
    Daniel Tavernier

3

Dear Sir/Madam
I am currently taking a GNVQ Intermediate in Science. I would like to become a health visitor. What else do I have to do after my GNVQ to qualify and work as a health visitor? I would also be grateful for any information on the type of work that health visitors do as I would like to learn as much as possible about the job.
    Yours faithfully
    Suzanne Humphries

4

Dear Sir/Madam
I work as a volunteer in a home for the elderly. I really enjoy working with the people who live there and would like to develop a career working with them. Please could you tell me what jobs I could train for that would enable me to work with the elderly. I already have an NVQ level 2 in Direct Care.
I look forward to your reply.
    Yours faithfully
    Jon Torrence

5

Dear Sir/Madam
I recently completed a computer questionnaire that said my ideal career would be in 'social work'. Could you please advise me on the qualifications and experience I would need to do this. I don't know very much about social work at the moment so any information on what is available would be useful. I don't have any qualifications at present and would prefer to have practical on-the-job training.
I look forward to your reply.
    Yours faithfully
    Erica Oakley

USEFUL ADDRESSES

A range of national organisations provide information about careers, terms and conditions of employment and qualifications needed to work in particular occupational areas. It is advisable to be clear about what information you require when you write to them. Remember to enclose an A4-size stamped self-addressed envelope.

Social care and social work

Central Council for Education and Training in Social Work, Derbyshire House, St Chad's Street, London WC1H 8AD
National Council for Vocational Qualifications, 222 Euston Road, London NW1 2BZ

Child care and education

Business and Technology Education Council, Head Office, Central House, Upper Woburn Place, London WC1H 0HH
Nursery Nurse Examination Board, Argyle House, 29–31 Euston Road, London NW1 2SD

Nursing

English National Board for Nursing and Midwifery, Victory House, 170 Tottenham Court Road, London W1A 0HA
National Board for Scotland, 22 Queen Street, Edinburgh EH2 1JX
Northern Ireland National Board, RAC House, 79 Chichester Street, Belfast BT1 4JE
Nurses and Midwives Central Clearing House, English National Board, PO Box 346, Bristol BS99 7FB
Welsh National Board, Floor 13, Pearl Assurance House, Greyfriars Road, Cardiff CF1 3AG

Professions allied to medicine

British College of Occupational Therapy, Marshalsea Road, London SE1 1HL
The Chartered Society of Physiotherapy, 14 Bedford Row, London WC1R 4ER
College of Radiographers, 14 Upper Wimpole Street, London W1M 8BN

LOCAL SOURCES OF INFORMATION

Your local Training and Education Council (TEC) and college of further education may offer advice, information and details about NVQ Health and Social Care and Child Care and education training placements in your area.

PORTFOLIO ASSIGNMENT

WORKING IN HEALTH AND SOCIAL CARE

INTRODUCTION

There is a wide range of different jobs in the health and social care area. People who work in health and social care must have a good understanding of people and be able to respond to their needs in an effective, supportive way. Most experienced health and social care workers are very skilled at doing this. As a newcomer to the health and social care field, you could learn a lot by observing and talking to experienced care workers.

This assignment gives you the opportunity to plan and carry out a work experience placement in which you investigate aspects of the care worker's role in working with clients in health and social care.

social care role. If any one of these roles is missing within your placement, arrange to speak to someone connected with the placement, either directly or indirectly, who performs such a role. The aspects of the job that you need to investigate through your interview are:

- the career route of the person who is in the post
- possible alternative career routes for people who may wish to do the job in future
- the sort of work pattern that is associated with this job
- what the stereotype of the role is
- how this differs from the actual day-to-day work.

TASK 1

Identify the roles of the people whom you work with in your care placement. Give their job title and a brief outline of what their day-to-day work involves. It is important to distinguish between whether they provide care or are part of the service that supports those who provide care in some way.

TASK 2

Choose three of the jobs to investigate more closely. The jobs that you choose should cover a support service role, a health/medical role and a

TASK 3

Produce a 'job profile' for each person describing:

a the nature of the job (stereotype and actual role)

b the patterns of work involved

c possible career routes

d your impressions of how this role contributes to the work of the placement organisation.

Your profile should be based on the interview and the observations that you made during your work placement.

✔ MULTIPLE CHOICE QUESTIONS

These questions are designed to test your knowledge and understanding of chapter 3. Answers are given at the back of the book.

1 **Health and social care services provided by government-funded organisations are known as:**

   A voluntary services

   B statutory services

   C informal services

   D private services

2 **Social services in England and Wales are provided by the:**

   A Department of Health

   B local authorities

   C Community Health Council

   D Department of Social Security

3 **What is likely to be the most important source of funding for a hospital in the private sector?**

   A government grants

   B public donations

   C insurance fees

   D European Parliament grants

4 **Secondary health care services are provided at:**

   A national government level

   B local area level

   C regional level

   D European level

5 **Which type of care sector covers the family, relatives and friends?**

   A statutory

   B private

   C informal

   D independent

6 **Which of the following is an example of statutory primary care provision?**

   A hospital operating theatre

   B regional burns unit

   C GP service at a local health centre

   D transport service for physically frail adults

7 **Which one of the following is likely to lead the primary health care team?**

   A GP

   B dentist

   C practice nurse

   D receptionist

✔ MULTIPLE CHOICE QUESTIONS

8 Which one of the following is a 'provider' of health care services?

A Family Health Service Authority

B District Health Authority

C private patient

D NHS Trust Hospital

9 Secondary health care is provided through which of the following?

A health centres and GP surgeries

B hospitals

C social services departments

D nurseries

10 The local authority social services department provides which one of the following?

A emergency surgery

B eye tests

C nursing homes

D home helps

11 Domiciliary social care is provided in which one of the following settings?

A at a special clinic

B in the home

C in the hospital

D at day centres

12 Voluntary organisations are different from both private and statutory organisations because they:

A are usually registered charities

B only employ volunteers

C never receive government funding

D provide free services

13 Private health care services can be used by:

A all people who are unwell

B people who live in the local area

C people who pay the fees charged

D wealthy people

14 Which one of the following is an example of informal care?

A accident and emergency department at a general hospital

B a home care service

C neighbours doing occasional baby-sitting for each other

D a nursing home for the elderly

15 One task that an informal carer may carry out to meet the needs of a client is:

A removing his or her stitches

B doing his or her shopping

C taking a blood sample

D taking an ultrasound scan

✔ MULTIPLE CHOICE QUESTIONS

16 Which of the following is a professional referral?

A a friend calling an ambulance for a person involved in an accident

B a person with stomach pains going to a GP

C a district nurse referring an older person to a day centre

D a social worker offering a client another appointment

17 Which of the following is a social need?

A books to read

B contact with other people

C love from parents

D food to eat

18 Which of the following might meet both social and physical needs for an elderly person?

A playing cards at a pensioners club

B attending an aerobics class with other people

C listening to the radio alone at home

D going for a long walk alone

19 Emergency care at an accident and emergency department is an example of care that is provided:

A free at the point of delivery

B for which the person pays the full cost

C on a charitable basis

D where ability to pay is taken into account

20 Which one of the following provides a health care service to children?

A gynaecologist

B psychiatrist

C paediatrician

D geriatrician

Communication and Interpersonal Relationships in Health and Social Care

CONTENTS

OUTLINE

This chapter will help you to understand the importance of effective communication and good interpersonal relationships in health and social care.

The first part – covering element 4.1 – focuses on developing your own communication skills in familiar interpersonal situations with peers and with people of different status such as teachers.

The second part – covering element 4.2 – looks at a key factor that adversely affects the quality of interpersonal relationships – the influence of unfair and unjust discrimination.

The final part – covering element 4.3 – brings these two aspects together in investigating issues related to interpersonal relationships in health and social care. It considers the nature of the caring relationship and issues of confidentiality.

After working through this chapter you will be able to:

develop your communication skills

explore how interpersonal relationships may be affected by discriminatory behaviour

investigate aspects of working with clients in health and social care.

The essential skills that health and social care workers need to develop, and practise in their work with patients and clients, are their communication skills. Being able to support, respond, and especially to listen to those we care for are key features of good care practice. The communication skills that care workers try to use in their work with clients can be developed and used in our everyday relationships and the interactions that we all have with people we know and meet.

This chapter describes, and gives you the chance to practise, skills that will help you to communicate effectively with others. It highlights the factors that are obstacles to good communication, such as discriminatory behaviour, and also considers how communication skills are used by care workers in their interactions with patients and clients in health and social care settings.

DEVELOP COMMUNICATION SKILLS

THE COMMUNICATION PROCESS

WHAT HAPPENS WHEN WE COMMUNICATE?

Communication is something that occurs between people. When a person communicates they pass on a message to another person or group of people in a language that the person or group understands.

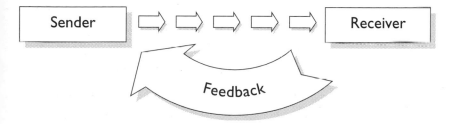

FIGURE 4.1: The communication cycle

Figure 4.1 describes the communication cycle. There are three basic parts to this cycle.

- ⊗ **We send messages mainly by verbal and non-verbal language.**

- ⊗ **We receive messages through sight, touch and hearing.**

- ⊗ **The receiver of the message usually responds, or gives feedback, to the sender.**

Where a message is deliberately passed and consciously received with some response by the second person, there is said to be an **inter-personal interaction**.

WHY IS COMMUNICATION IMPORTANT?

If you were unable to communicate with other people, life would be very difficult. You would face considerable problems in meeting your basic physical, psychological and social needs.

Similarly, if you were a care worker and communicated in a way that others failed to understand, or if you were unable to understand the communication of your patients or clients, you would not be able to identify and meet *their* needs.

The skills needed for effective communication in care work are known as **interpersonal skills**, that is, they are the behaviours that enable and encourage people to share their thoughts and feelings and to pass on information about themselves and their environment.

ACTIVITY

This activity asks you to concentrate on the use of your senses. If you role play it with other students in a classroom, move the chairs and tables to make the area safe before you begin. You will find that it helps to 'block' some of your senses and communication 'tools' by putting cotton wool in your ears, closing or blindfolding your eyes and not speaking or touching while you do the following.

Imagine that you are unable to speak, see or feel anything. There is nobody to guide or help you. You are in a place with some other people. They are also unable to speak, see hear or feel anything. You are all left alone.

- ⊗ What problems might you, as an individual, face if this situation occurred now?

- ⊗ If the situation were prolonged, would any type of 'relationship' be possible with the others?

- ⊗ If you could have one of your senses back to help you to cope and communicate, which one would you choose? Explain your reasons.

REASONS FOR COMMUNICATION

People use different methods to achieve different communication objectives. Some of the reasons why we communicate are:

To obtain and give information

If you wish to obtain or give information, you might use oral communication to ask questions or give orders, or you might write words in the form of a letter to request what you want or reveal something to another person. Our ability to think and express ideas and feelings develops during childhood and on into adulthood. For example, in adolescence and then as adults, we use our communication skills to find out about, explore and express beliefs and preferences about religion and politics.

To express how we feel

People need to communicate their feelings to each other. We use verbal and non-verbal communication to express our emotions about how we feel about ourselves, about what is happening to us and about how we feel about each other. A baby, for example, may cry to attract its mother's attention and express its discomfort. A child or an adult may learn to say how they are feeling or may develop behaviours, such as sulking or biting their nails, to express the things that they are feeling.

To learn about the world

People need to communicate with each other to find out about and make sense of the world in which they live. Young children learn how to behave, the difference between right and wrong, how to be safe and how to get along with others through the communications that they have with their parents, carers and other children at an early stage in their lives.

To form and maintain relationships

Communication skills are an important part of all of our relationships. Family, friendship and personal relationships are all established and nurtured by verbal and non-verbal communication skills. For example, many people use gossip and informal chats to enjoy and develop their friendships.

THE IMPORTANCE OF COMMUNICATION IN SOCIALISATION

During early childhood and adolescence we learn about ourselves, other people and the world we live in. The process by which we learn and develop is known as **socialisation**. In most societies the family is responsible for early – **primary** – socialisation.

ACTIVITY

DEVELOPING COMMUNICATIONS SKILLS THROUGH SOCIALISATION

During socialisation we develop and learn about values, beliefs and ways of behaving, thinking and feeling in relation to others. The following questions can be used as prompts to identify what you have learned and how your communication skills have developed as a result of different socialisation influences.

When you have read through the questions write your responses to each set in note form. Discuss your own ideas with a partner or in a small group.

- ✪ **What beliefs and values have you learned from your parents?**

- ✪ **How did they teach you these things?**

- ✪ **What communication skills did you develop?**

- ✪ **What did you learn about behaviour towards others from your primary school years?**

- ✪ **How were you taught these things?**

- ✪ **What new communication skills did you develop?**

- ✪ **What beliefs and values have you learned from your friends?**

- ✪ **How did they teach you these things?**

- ✪ **What new communication skills did you develop or improve?**

- ✪ **What have you learned about behaviour from being part of a college group?**

- ✪ **How were you taught these things?**

- ✪ **What new communication skills did you develop?**

REASONS FOR COMMUNICATION

The family is the primary agency of socialisation. Friends, or peers, are also a very important secondary source. Why is it important that we learn to communicate with others in these settings?

Write a short paragraph outlining your ideas on the importance of learning to communicate with family and friends. You will need to consider:

- ✪ **How we develop ourselves through communication with each group.**

- ✪ **How we learn about, develop and express our personal beliefs and preferences in each setting.**

- ✪ **How we use communication to form and maintain social groups.**

As we grow older and move into other areas of social life, we come into contact with schools, friendship groups, the media and work, among other influences. These are all sources of **secondary socialisation**. Our successful socialisation and development into adults is dependent on us being able to develop and use communication skills at the different stages of socialisation.

METHODS OF COMMUNICATION

You can already communicate. You possess a wide range of communication skills and can use them in a variety of ways. You need to use your communication skills many times every day but are probably not aware of how much you use them or depend on them to form and maintain relationships with other people.

In health and social care settings people communicate with specific purposes in mind. Sometimes they use the language and jargon of care workers to do this in a kind of shorthand. Doctors, for example, sometimes talk to each other in medical jargon that is difficult for others to follow. When communicating with patients, clients or colleagues, care workers should always try to ensure that the person they are communicating with fully understands the point or piece of information that they are trying to get across.

People use a number of methods to communicate in health and social care settings. The methods outlined in Figure 4.2 can be divided into **verbal** and **non-verbal** forms of communication.

VERBAL COMMUNICATION

This is the form that most people associate with 'communication'. We communicate orally when we use our voices to speak or sing. Verbal communication involves using words and other

FIGURE 4.2: How we communicate

Posture

Gesture

Touch

Proximity

Written

Graphic/Symbol

Non-verbal communication

Talking

Singing

Verbal communication

sounds to convey messages. Our ability to communicate verbally develops in childhood and is generally very sophisticated by the time we reach adulthood.

Spoken languages, such as English, Urdu, Patois or French, are made up of words and a series of rules about how to use and put these words together. Verbal communication involves more than just saying words in a language that is understandable to others. Our voices are also used to show how we feel, to put emphasis on words or phrases that give the message a particular meaning, and say something about our regional origins, our social class and often our ethnic origin through our accents.

Effective verbal communication involves speaking and listening to others. To be effective in care settings messages should be conveyed clearly in ways that are supportive to clients and respect their rights and personal values.

ACTIVITY

- In small groups take it in turns to say the following sentence. Each person should emphasise – put the stress on – a different word to try to change the meaning of the sentence from that of the previous person.

    'I am going to play tennis today.'

- How else could you change the meaning of the communication with your voice? Think about, and perhaps try experimenting with, how speed, loudness/quietness and the pitch of your voice affect the message that other people hear.

QUICK response
Is there such a thing as 'talking properly'? What do you think about this?

NON-VERBAL COMMUNICATION

People often use aspects of their behaviour to express themselves and communicate with others. Our appearance, gestures, the way that we use eye-contact, our posture, physical closeness to others and the way that we use facial expressions are all non-verbal, behavioural means by which we communicate what we think and feel.

As with verbal communication we are all skilled to some degree at 'listening' to other people's non-verbal communication. It is, in fact, often essential to 'listen' to the non-verbal cues that people give us to fully understand their message. The following are all means by which people use their bodies to communicate without using words and are pointers that we use to 'listen' to what they are saying.

Eye-contact

People look at each other to collect information. In conversation people have eye-contact for 25–75 per cent of the time. It occurs more in the listener than in the talker. Eye-contact shows interest in the other person and tends to start off the communication process. It occurs more when people are comfortable with each other, though excessive eye-contact can make someone feel uncomfortable.

Facial expression

People look at the eyes more than any other part of the face. Eye-contact and facial expression both communicate emotions and attitudes. Facial expressions occur through movements of the mouth, eyebrows and nose. The main expressions are those that indicate happiness, sadness, anger, surprise, fear, disgust and interest. In some care settings patients are unable to communicate effectively by facial expression because of neurological disorders such as multiple sclerosis, parkinsonism and strokes.

Gesture

Gestures are performed with the head, hands and feet. Head nods are typically used to indicate agreement and rapid head nods may indicate that the listener wishes to speak. Care workers should be watchful for gestures, particularly in clients who have impaired verbal communication skills or find it difficult to express themselves in words. It is important to remember that a gesture may have different meanings in different cultures and that people from some cultures may not find a particular gesture meaningful.

Posture

Even though you may not be able to see an individual's face, the person's mood and emotions may be expressed and may be understood through his or her body posture. For example, leaning backwards in a relaxed way can indicate a dominant attitude. Postural echo, or copying someone else's posture, tends to indicate agreement and friendliness.

Touch

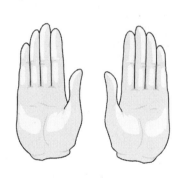

Carers tend to be given special privileges to touch their patients and clients. In situations where patients or clients require intimate physical care, the usual social rule that people do not touch each other unless they have an intimate relationship is suspended. For example, nurses can use touch to show liking or sympathy or to carry out personal care for a patient. Certain areas are normally taboo to touch but by careful explanation and reading of the patient's non-verbal signals this taboo can be overcome in care settings. A client or patient may decide how caring you are on the basis of the way in which you touch and handle them.

Barrier signals

A patient or client who is uncomfortable or anxious will tend to use 'barriers' to protect themselves. A common example of this is the body-cross where the arms or legs are crossed either partially or completely across the body. Another example is the leg-cross away from the person you are communicating with. This tends to indicate a reluctance to continue with the communication. While some body-crossing may indicate dislike, it is better interpreted as a signal of mild anxiety.

Physical distance

How close do you allow others to get to you when they are communicating with you? The acceptable distance varies with culture. A distance of about 46 centimetres is comfortable for most people in western societies. Being too far away, over 1.22 metres, gives an impression of an impersonal relationship. Care workers who carry out interviews with patients and clients need to be aware of the physical distance that they place between themselves and their interviewees when doing so. Being too close can intimidate the client and being too far away can make the carer appear cold and uninterested.

How is non-verbal communication used in care settings?

Non-verbal communication is very important in enabling care workers to build and maintain their relationships with patients and clients. Most first impressions are gained from non-verbal communication. The clothes, appearance, posture, tone of voice and amount of eye-contact that we use all say something about us to people when we meet for the first time.

Clients and patients, like everybody else, are continually monitoring their interactions with care staff for the non-verbal communication of feelings, preferences and confirmation of verbal messages. Carers need to use their non-verbal behaviours carefully to establish and maintain positive relationships with their patients or clients. Often non-verbal signals are the more powerful means of communicating messages than verbal means.

When non-verbal messages are at odds with the things that people say, the listener is more likely to believe the non-verbal message that they receive. If care workers form a negative impression of a patient or client, for example as a 'difficult' or dislikeable person, this may be expressed in their non-verbal behaviour rather than through what they say to the individual. Disapproving facial expressions or avoiding being close to the person would tell the patient or client that he or she is not liked by the care worker.

ACTIVITY

Care workers need to use a variety of communication methods with patients and clients. The primary aim of all caring is to meet the needs of those being cared for. Communication methods are chosen because they best meet the needs that clients present.

Read the following case studies. For each of them you need to explain briefly what communication methods could be used to best help the person.

⊗ Salvo is a patient in the medical ward of a large District General Hospital. His diabetes has progressively worsened and he has now lost his sight. He finds this very distressing and tends to stay close to his bed for fear of getting lost in the ward. He asks you if you will take him to the toilet. He stretches out his hand and gently moves to the edge of his bed. He tells you that he's sorry to ask but he's worried about getting there in time on his own.

⊗ Edith is 56 years old and has recently suffered a stroke. This has left her with paralysis down her right-hand side and limited speech. She cannot put her thoughts into words or understand words that are written down but can understand some of what is said to her. You have been asked to find out what she would like to choose from next week's menu. You have been given a pre-printed menu which patients would normally fill in themselves.

⊗ Philip has been in a psychiatric hospital for the last ten years. He has recently moved to the group home where you work as a residential worker. Today it is Philip's turn to go to the supermarket to get the weekend shopping for the five residents. He has limited experience of shopping and managing money and asks you, 'What do I have to do?'

⊗ Kamlesh has hardly seen anybody other than her husband and children since the birth of her twin daughters six months ago. Her husband says that she rarely goes out and is becoming depressed because of her lack of contact with other women. You are a volunteer at a local playgroup and have been asked to visit Kamlesh to try and befriend her and persuade her to come along.

⊗ Suman is 7 years old. He goes to a behavioural support unit during the day. His behaviour at home is reckless, aggressive and very unsettled. He was sent to the unit after he climbed on to the roof of his local shopping arcade and began throwing down tiles at passers-by. He does not understand why he has to attend the unit. You have been asked to explain to him without being critical of him personally.

THE BENEFITS OF EFFECTIVE COMMUNICATION

Good communication in care settings helps both carers and clients in their relationships. The following list describes some of the benefits of effective communication from each point of view. You may wish to add others that occur to you or which your experience, as either a carer or client, has highlighted as being important.

For the carers	For the patient or client
1 Good communication enables you to obtain and provide information that is relevant to your clients' care and well-being.	1 Good communication enables clients to feel secure and respected as individuals at times when they are physically and emotionally vulnerable.
2 Good communication enables you to express the important values of acceptance, trust, understanding and support.	2 Cooperation, involvement and partnership in a caring relationship requires open, supportive communication.
3 Through good communication you can enable your clients to make the most of their abilities and personal resources.	3 Effective communication allows the client to express their needs, worries and wishes.
4 Good communication allows you to choose the most effective means of meeting your clients' needs.	4 Clients and patients need to maintain their sense of personal identity while receiving care. This can only be achieved if they are allowed and encouraged to express themselves and be understood by their carers.

DEVELOPING AND IMPROVING LISTENING SKILLS

To be effective in providing care that meets patients' or clients' needs care workers must use a range of interpersonal skills. The most important of these is 'listening'. This section covers a range of basic techniques and skills that need to be learned and practised to enable you to listen more effectively in your everyday interactions and in care settings.

LISTENING

Communication is a two-way process. People give and receive each other's messages. There are many situations in care settings and client/carer interactions where the client wishes to talk or reveal some personal information. Listening is one of the most difficult yet most effective things that you, as a carer, can do to help people.

WHAT DOES LISTENING INVOLVE?

The listener in any interaction must pay attention to the speaker. This is the basis of all listening. Not paying attention leads to poor listening and to poor understanding. It gives the other person a negative impression of you and suggests that you are not interested in them. Good interpersonal communication depends on good understanding between people.

PHYSICAL SIGNS OF PAYING ATTENTION

Paying attention to the patient or client in a physical way shows them that you are listening. Your body has a large part to play in this aspect of listening. The letters SOLER can be used to remind us of the behaviours, or physical tactics, that we can use to ensure that we pay attention physically.

S – face the other person squarely.

O – adopt an open posture.

L – lean toward the other person slightly.

E – maintain good eye contact.

R – try to be relaxed while paying attention.

The SOLER behaviours are non-verbal behaviours that can be used to show that you are paying attention while communicating with others. They are suggestions to help you to improve your listening skills rather than rigid rules. Remember that whatever you do your body is communicating whether you want it to or not. It is better to deliberately use your body to improve the communication process rather than let it give away your lack of interest and failure to pay attention.

LISTENING TO ORAL COMMUNICATION

When we listen to people we pay attention to what they are saying. For most people this means listening to the words and phrases that the person is using and working out what they mean. As well as the words and phrases that people use, there are also other parts of verbal behaviour that are important in helping us to understand what the speaker means.

You will already be skilled at noticing and taking account of many of the things that people do with their voices. The speed at which a sentence is spoken, the volume used and the pitch of the person's voice tends to tell us something about the emotion behind the message and can change the meaning of the words. It can be important to notice how something is said as much as what is said, especially when talking to clients who may wish to reveal more about how they feel rather than what they are thinking.

LISTENING TO NON-VERBAL COMMUNICATION

We have said several times that the body is very communicative. What people say in their non-verbal behaviour can, in fact, be more powerful than the words that they use at the same time. People tend to believe the facial messages and body language of others in preference to their verbal messages. It is important to be able to listen to the non-verbal behaviour of patients and clients. Non verbal behaviour tends to work with verbal behaviour in three different ways.

- ⊗ **Non-verbal behaviour can confirm what is being said when it is saying the same thing as the verbal message.**

- ⊗ **Non-verbal behaviour can deny or confuse what is being said. For example, saying to your friend 'I'm not upset about anything' while tears run down your cheeks tends to make the verbal message sound untrue.**

- ⊗ **Non-verbal behaviour can strengthen the verbal message. For example, saying 'I want to see the doctor now' while pounding your fist on the receptionist's desk tends to emphasise your sense of urgency. Alternatively, throwing your arms around a partner while saying 'I'm so relieved you're all right' emphasises your sense of relief.**

QUICK response

Can you think of examples from your own experience where a person's non-verbal communication told a different story to their verbal message?

☀ ACTIVITY

The following exercises are designed to help you to develop and practise the skills of paying attention and noticing what the speaker is saying and doing during conversation.

EXPERIENCING LISTENING PROBLEMS

Choose a health or social care role in which a worker interacts face to face with a patient or client. Examples might include a health visitor talking to a mother about her baby, a social worker talking to a client about his welfare benefits or a patient talking to a nurse about how she feels. You will take it in turns with your partner to be the worker and the patient or client. In pairs sit opposite each other in chairs of equal height.

- ⊗ Take it in turns to talk to each other on any health subject for up to four minutes. The talker is the patient or client. The 'listener' does not listen but the talker must keep going for the full time and must try to get their partner to listen. The talker must not touch or shout at the listener. The listener must stay seated.

- ⊗ After each person has spoken you should take it in turns to tell each other what you liked/disliked about the activity. Write a short review of the exercise explaining what happened and what it felt like not to be listened to. You should identify the main factors that inhibited the communication process.

EXPERIENCING EFFECTIVE LISTENING SKILLS

Repeat the above role play. You might like to choose a different topic this time. In this role play the patient or client again talks to the health or social care worker. The worker is the listener. The listening behaviours should be changed to make the communication process more effective. In pairs sit opposite each other in chairs of equal height.

- ⊗ Take it in turns to talk to each other on any health topic for up to four minutes. The listener should use the SOLER behaviours.

- ⊗ After each person has spoken you should take it in turns to tell each other what you liked/disliked about the activity. Write a short review of the exercise explaining what happened and what it felt like to be actively listened to.

RECAPPING AND CHECKING LISTENING SKILLS

Now that you have shown your patient or client good non-verbal listening behaviours, you need to show that you are following what the person is saying. Again, using caring roles, work in pairs to practise the skills of checking and recapping. In pairs sit opposite each other in chairs of equal height.

- ⊗ Take it in turns to talk to each other on any subject for up to four minutes. The listener should use the SOLER behaviours. In order to 'recap' the listener should summarise, every so often, in their own words what the speaker has said.

- ⊗ After each person has spoken you should take it in turns to tell each other what you liked/disliked about the activity. Write a short review of the exercise explaining what happened and what it felt like to intervene to recap and to have the listener recap every so often.

ACTIVITY

We communicate 'messages' to others in a variety of non-verbal ways. We use our bodies, the environment, clothes and appearance for example, to say something about who we are, about how we feel about ourselves and others around us. The non-verbal aspects of our behaviour can be as powerful and informative as the things that we say.

a   Identify a place where you could discreetly observe people communicating with each other. This should be a public place, such as a cafe, fast-food restaurant or station, where people interact and communicate openly.

b   Watch for and record, on the checklist below, examples of non-verbal communication over a period of ten minutes.

c   Explain what the people you observed were 'saying' with their non-verbal communication.

Body Language Observation Checklist

Body message	My observations
Approachable	
Relaxed body posture	
Physical openness	
Slight forward lean	
Good use of gaze and eye-contact	
Appropriate facial contact	
Appropriate gestures	
Sensitivity to physical proximity and height	
Appropriate use of touch	
Clothing and grooming	

ASKING QUESTIONS

Health and social care workers use different questioning techniques to help them in various aspects of their work. One way in which they use questioning is to find out information from people. For example, when a person is admitted to hospital a doctor or nurse will take the person's medical history. When social workers meet a new client they have to find out what the client's problems and unmet needs are. In both situations they have to ask questions to get a full picture of the objective facts and also the person's perception of the situation. The value of the information that is provided will depend on the way in which the questions are asked.

Questioning is also a 'responding' skill. When conducting a conversation with a patient or client, care workers need to think about what they say, and how they say it, in response to the other person. The way that a question is used depends on the type of information that the questioner wants to gain. There are a number of different ways of formulating, or asking, a question.

Open questions

When you ask an open question you leave the opportunity to reply as 'open' as possible. For example, if you said 'Can you tell me about yourself?' or 'What do you think about my new flat?' you would be asking open questions. These give the person answering the question the opportunity to choose how to answer. When used with patients or clients open questions encourage the person to express their views, opinions and feelings in the way that they choose.

Closed questions

These are questions that limit the potential response. A 'yes/no' or precise and factual reply results from a closed question. For example, 'Do you want a nursery place?', 'Have you taken your morning medication?', 'Which part of your head hurts?' are all closed questions. There is an expectation that the answer will be short and limited in explanation. The questioner is limiting what can be talked about and is suggesting a particular form of reply.

QUICK response

How would you expect somebody to reply to these questions

QUICK response

How would you expect somebody to reply to the questions in the example?

ACTIVITY

The following list includes both open and closed questions. Spend ten minutes deciding which question is open and which is closed. Give a reason for your decisions. Discuss your decisions as a group.

a How are things?

b How can I help you?

c What made you do that?

d What leisure-time interests do you have?

e How would you cope without cigarettes today?

f Where do you live?

g When can you come here?

h Do you believe that?

i What music do you listen to?

j What do you think of my new hairstyle?

k Do you think that it's safe to hitchhike alone?

l Have you been to the dentist recently?

m What time is it?

n Who's that on the phone?

o Did Sister Watson leave a letter for me?

p Why won't you read this letter to me?

q Is this worry playing on your mind at the moment?

r What is your opinion on workplace creches?

s When is it time to go home?

t What do you think about when you're swimming?

It takes some practice to be able to put together open questions. To allow patients and clients to express their thoughts and feelings fully care workers need to frame their questions as 'openly' as possible. The following activity gives you the opportunity to formulate open questions.

☀ ACTIVITY

Turn the following closed questions into open questions. You should retain the original meaning of the question but allow the respondent the chance to answer more fully.

a Are you enjoying your GNVQ course?

b Are you paying by cash or cheque?

c Did you have lunch?

d Do you think the test results will be good?

e Did you get a lot of visitors today?

f Shouldn't you eat more?

g Do you understand?

h You don't want tea, do you?

i Could your punctuality improve?

j You're worried about your health, are you?

Using open questions will enable you to get the patient or client to express themselves more. When you want them to express their feelings, views or perception of things open questions are essential. In some circumstances you may want a more specific, direct or factual piece of information. In such cases closed questions may give you the more appropriate response.

Open questions can lead to excessive information or to vague responses. Closed questions are easier to put together than open ones. Try the following activity to experience formulating closed questions.

☀ ACTIVITY

Turn the following into closed questions.

a How do you feel about your operation?

b What's on your mind?

c What sort of pain is it?

d Could you explain why you've come here today?

e How has your day been?

f What do you feel about your chances?

g Do I know you from somewhere?

h Will you tell me about your childhood?

i How do you feel about taking medication?

j What can I do for you?

Questions are an important part of oral responding and information-seeking. They are used in different ways depending on the type of information that is sought. Care workers need to be aware of the types of question and how they use them in their interactions as they can fundamentally affect communication with patients and clients.

PARAPHRASING AND SUMMARISING

Questions are only one feature of oral responding. They allow you to obtain information that provides the basic content of a conversation. In addition to obtaining information the care worker must also understand it and communicate this understanding to the patient or client.

The meaning and significance of what someone says cannot always be gauged simply from the words that they use. Messages can become complicated and unclear particularly when people feel vulnerable, stressed or unwell. There are a number of techniques that can be used to both check and communicate understanding of what someone says. These include **paraphrasing** and **summarising**.

Paraphrasing and summarising involve the listener reflecting back the message or feelings that the patient or client expresses. The purpose is to check understanding and to convey interest.

Paraphrasing

This means restating the point that the patient or client makes in order to check that you, as the listener, have understood correctly. When you paraphrase you offer the message back. For example, if a client spoke for the first time about his or her feelings towards a partner whom he or she had separated from, the care worker to whom the client was speaking could use paraphrasing at different points to check understanding and to get the client to enlarge on certain points.

Paraphrasing can be used to help the person you are listening to enlarge on what they are saying or it can be used to end a conversation.

ACTIVITY

Read the following statements and then paraphrase them. Remember that this involves using some, but not all, of the same words to paraphrase meaning.

a 'My back, shoulders and arms ached all night. I couldn't sleep at all. I'm so tired now.'

b 'I heard this breaking sound, like a sharp crack. It happened suddenly. Then my leg hurt.'

c 'I've got to stay here, help me, they'll get me out there. There are people chasing me.'

d 'He said that yesterday, and the day before that. It's frustrating listening to it all again.'

e 'It's first left, straight on, round the corner and straight ahead.'

f 'I rang and rang, nobody answered. I was very worried.'

g 'Do you think it tastes funny, or is it me?'

h 'When will I get the result? I can't relax until I get the result of the tests.'

i 'Nurse, my head hurts and I think I'm going to be sick. I need some help.'

j 'He's my father's brother's son.'

Summarising

A summary is a short restatement of a longer piece of conversation. When summarising care workers need to include the main points made by the patient or client and also to check with the person that their understanding is correct, for example, 'So, you've come to the clinic today because you missed your injection last week, your "voices" have got worse and you want some medication to help. Is that right?' When making a summary you should avoid repeating exactly what the person said as this sounds parrot-like and is irritating to most people. Put the summary in your own words and always end with a question.

ACTIVITY

Read the following statements and then summarise them as though you are responding. Remember to follow the main points of a summary.

a 'I really don't enjoy staying at home all day. When he first became ill I thought I'd have more time to do things if I gave up work. It would be less stress as well. That's what I thought anyway. It's not the way things have turned out. This illness wears me down, it occupies all my time. It's turned into a full-time job and more.'

b 'I woke up…it was very cold…and I looked at the clock. I'm normally a good sleeper, see. Eight hours every night, regular as clockwork. But when I saw it was 5 o'clock I got confused. It was quite dark outside. I wasn't sure what was happening. I'm getting more like this all the time. Sometimes I'm not sure what day it is.'

OBSTACLES TO EFFECTIVE COMMUNICATION

When we communicate, our ability to get our message across effectively to others can be hampered by a number of 'obstacles' There are a number of different types of communication 'obstacle', including those outlined below.

FIGURE 4.3: Communication in a care setting may be affected by the quality of the environment

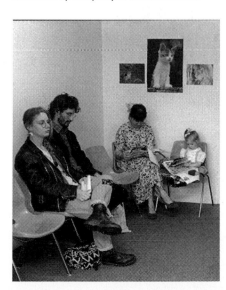

ENVIRONMENTAL OBSTACLES

A physical environment that is noisy, uncomfortable, has poor lighting or which lacks privacy reduces people's ability to communicate with each other. A noisy environment affects our ability to listen and concentrate on what another person is saying. Poor lighting can affect our ability to pick up non-verbal communication, such as facial expressions, and could reduce a hearing-impaired person's ability to lip read.

Offices or clinics that are too cold or too hot, which lack comfortable seating, or which allow other people to see and hear what is going on between a care worker and a patient or client, discourage people from expressing their feelings and problems.

SOCIAL AND CULTURAL OBSTACLES

In Britain there are many different social classes, ethnic groups and age groups in the population. Social and cultural differences within this population can sometimes be an obstacle to effective communication. The social and cultural features in our communication, such as the local slang words that we use, our accents, the expectations that we have about when and where we are allowed to touch another person and how we begin and end an interaction, are taken for granted until we are faced by a situation with which we are unfamiliar or come across a person who does not know or doesn't follow the social and cultural rules of communication that we are used to. At times this can undermine effective communication.

FACTORS LEADING TO COMMUNICATION DIFFICULTIES IN CARE SETTINGS

Health and social care workers should receive training in communication skills in order to help them to work effectively with patients and clients. The organisations that employ care workers are also often aware of the need to provide adequate information to their patients or clients. Communication difficulties still arise despite this general awareness. Some of the problems that can arise are discussed below.

Language differences
Britain is a multicultural nation. Within the mix of different ethnic groups people speak a range of languages. Not everybody speaks or reads English as their first language. If health and social care services only produce and display information, such as signs, notices, posters and instruction leaflets in English and care workers only speak English, some people who need to use services will have difficulty getting the right service.

Sensory impairments
People with a sight or hearing impairment may have difficulty receiving

information and having their specific needs met unless carers are aware of how to overcome their clients' sensory impairment and communicate effectively with them. Groups, such as the Young Deaf Association, which works for people who have sensory impairments, produce guidelines for carers on how to overcome the communication problems that impairments cause.

Environmental problems

Care settings, such as clinics, hospitals and residential homes, are often busy and noisy with many people going about their business carrying out the tasks that are involved in providing care. This can sometimes present a problem for staff and clients who need to talk privately or find themselves intimidated by the hustle and bustle of a busy care setting. The lack of a quiet, comfortable, friendly environment may cause some people problems in their efforts to communicate with each other.

The effects of illness and distress

Illness, injuries and personal problems can cause people to withdraw and feel that they don't wish to see others or talk about how they are. Some conditions and disorders, such as having a 'stroke' or being depressed, may affect people's ability to transmit and receive communication from others as effectively as they might do if they were well.

Lack of time and work stress

Caring is a very busy and stressful job for most care workers. The pressures of having to get many tasks completed and of never having a free moment can result in them feeling that they just don't have enough time to listen and talk to patients and clients as much as they would like.

ACTIVITY

1 Identify and describe three situations where you have tried to communicate with another person, where there was an obstacle that prevented the communication from being effective. The situations that you choose might come from home, school or college, work placement or your social life.

2 How could these obstacles have been overcome? Make suggestions about how communication in the interactions you describe could be made more effective.

EVALUATING YOUR OWN COMMUNICATION SKILLS

The term **interpersonal style** refers to the usual, ordinary, day-to-day ways in which we behave or act when we are with other people (family, friends, colleagues at school/college or work, acquaintances, strangers, people in authority). It includes the skills that you use and the ones that you lack, and your successes and failures in relating to others.

This definition of interpersonal style is quite broad. You would probably say that the way that you relate to others depends on who it is you are relating to and where you are at the time. Complete the following activity in order to expand on this idea.

ACTIVITY

Complete the following statements by saying how you act, what you do, how you think and feel in each situation. For example, 'When I'm with my friends I feel comfortable, I talk easily but I don't like to argue.'

- When I'm with my family I...

- When I'm with my friends I...

- When I'm in school/college I...

- When I meet new people I...

The statements you made will reveal something about your interpersonal style. Care workers need to be aware of how they relate to patients or clients as some features of interpersonal style may inhibit communication with individuals while other features enhance it. When working in care settings we need to consider the various social and behavioural factors that, positively and negatively, influence our ability to communicate with others. This is covered in more detail in the final section of this chapter.

ACTIVITY

We all interact with other people. There are many events and situations each day where we are involved in some form of communication with others. What makes some of these positive and others negative experiences?

1   Think back to the events and situations that you have experienced over the last twenty-four hours. Make a list of five situations in which you interacted with others.

2   For each situation write a sentence explaining the effect that the interaction had on you. Say whether it was positive or negative and why.

3   Think of three people who are 'good for you'? Explain in a brief paragraph how these people have a positive effect on you.

PORTFOLIO ASSIGNMENT

DEMONSTRATING COMMUNICATION SKILLS

This assignment gives you the opportunity to demonstrate and evaluate listening and responding skills in role-play groups of three.

TASK 1

Divide into a group of three. Take it in turns to play the roles of care worker, client and observer. You should each choose a different care worker role, either from the ones suggested opposite, or by developing your own. Decide between yourselves who will act as client and observer in each role play.

Each role play should last about ten minutes. At the end of the role play each person should 'de-role' by disassociating themselves from the role that he or she has just played.

TASK 2

The person playing the client role should decide on a problem/topic that he or she wishes to discuss which is relevant to the role. For example:

- You are worried about your child being safe at the nursery.

- You are concerned about why you get such severe period pain.

- You want to know how you can tell if you are gay.

- You want to know your rights concerning housing or racial harassment.

It may be useful to write down the main points

Client scenarios	Care worker roles
A mother whose child attends a nursery	Nursery nurse
A patient experiencing period pain	GP
A homeless person seeking a hostel place	Social worker
A relative of a mentally ill person	Community pyschiatric nurse
A person with an alcohol problem	Alcohol counsellor
A pregnant woman two weeks before birth	Midwife
An unemployed person	Job centre adviser
A teenager with home problems	College counsellor
A person who has taken an HIV test	HIV counsellor
A teenager concerned about their sexuality	Youth leader
A person who has experienced racial abuse	Advice worker

that you wish to talk about. You should not try to make the situation difficult for the care worker but should develop your role in a way that he or she can listen to and respond to your concerns.

PORTFOLIO ASSIGNMENT

TASK 3

The person playing the care worker should prepare the interview environment. As part of the interview/conversation the care worker should:

- greet the client

- establish the client's reasons for coming to see you

- find out what the client's main concerns are

- find out how the client feels you could help

- suggest the next step that could be taken to help the client

- end the interview appropriately.

As the care worker you should demonstrate listening and responding skills that encourage communication between you and the client.

TASK 4

The observer should use a copy of the Observation Checklist on page 237 to make notes as the role play progresses and should complete the Interaction Appraisal Checklist on page 250 after the role play. You should give a copy of the Appraisal Checklist to the appraisee and discuss your comments constructively with him or her afterwards.

The observer and the role-play participants should all retain a copy of the Appraisal Checklist for their portfolio. They should also write a brief account of their discussion and the suggestions made to the appraisee about their performance.

TASK 5

After the role play the care worker should appraise your own use of communication skills in the role play. What did you do that was effective and which encouraged communication? What aspects of your communication could be improved? What would you change or try in the future to make your communication more effective?

Produce your appraisal in a written or audio/video-recorded form.

PORTFOLIO ASSIGNMENT

TASK 6

In your work experience placement you will be involved in real interactions with patients or clients, other care workers and perhaps relatives and members of the public. Provide your work placement supervisor with a copy of the Interaction Appraisal Checklist and the Observation Guidelines and ask him or her to appraise your use of communication skills in a planned interaction with a group of people. Possible situations might include:

- a social activity involving a group of patients or clients and yourself

- a meeting between staff members, including yourself

- a meeting or social event involving staff and relatives or visitors and yourself.

You should also appraise your own use of communication skills in the situation chosen and indicate in a short review how you could make improvements in future, similar situations.

INTERACTION APPRAISAL CHECKLIST

To what extent was the person:

Listening?

Asking open questions?

Giving attention?

Reflecting back?

Using non-verbal behaviour effectively?

Summarising?

Warm and respecting?

Paraphrasing?

Showing empathy?

General comments on overall use of communication skills

Genuine?

EXPLORE HOW INTERPERSONAL RELATIONSHIPS MAY BE AFFECTED BY DISCRIMINATORY BEHAVIOUR

THE MAIN FEATURES OF DISCRIMINATION

Discrimination happens every day. Some groups of people are more likely to experience discrimination than others. These groups tend to suffer the effects of prejudice and stereotypes being spread through the media and the consequences of political activities of individuals and groups who have the power to enforce unequal treatment. In Britain some of the groups who tend to experience discrimination include:

- the learning and physically disabled

- minority ethnic groups

- minority religious groups

- women

- lesbians and gay men

- older people

- people with mental health problems.

To understand what unfair discrimination is and how it is practised we need to understand what prejudice is and how it is expressed.

PREJUDICE

Prejudice involves experiencing negative or hostile feelings and having negative ideas and hostile attitudes towards other people. Prejudiced feelings, ideas and attitudes have no basis in fact and are not thought through by the person holding them.

When people hold prejudiced views about a group of people they often over-generalise in a negative way about their characteristics. They then apply these generalisations to all people whom they feel belong to the group. When people are prejudiced they are often prejudiced against specific groups of people, such as gays and lesbians or people of different colour. The process of over-generalising and grouping people together in terms of a single dominant characteristic, rather than identifying and appreciating their individual differences, is known as **stereotyping**. People's use of stereotypes express their prejudices and can lead them to act in ways that are discriminatory.

Unequal treatment is the core feature of discrimination. The fact that we view and treat people differently, both as individuals and as social groups, is not always a negative thing. In many ways it is right to acknowledge differences between people and to choose between them. For example, when several people apply for a job, the interviewers must discriminate between them on grounds of qualifications, experience and suitability for the post. The best candidate will be preferred for the post. But what is the difference between negative (unfair) discrimination and positive (fair) discrimination?

Unfair discrimination

This occurs when individuals or groups of people are treated unfairly in comparison to others. The main bases of prejudice and unfair discrimination are:

- ✖ **age**
- ✖ **disability**
- ✖ **gender**
- ✖ **health status**
- ✖ **race**
- ✖ **religion**
- ✖ **sexuality.**

⚡ QUICK response

Do you belong to any groups that are stereotyped by people? What are the groups and the stereotypes?

Unfair discrimination involves a person acting on their prejudices. For example, an employer who refused to interview candidates under the age of twenty-five for a nursery manager post saying 'in my experience, they're not good at accepting responsibility', would be treating this group of people unfairly.

ACTIVITY

Read the following statements and identify:

- how a group of people are being stereotyped

- what the basis of the speaker's prejudice is (for example, age, sexuality).

'I don't want my children to be taught by a lesbian or gay teacher. They could be filling our kids' heads with all sorts.'

'When there is high unemployment I think that women should think more about looking after their families. A man goes for a job because he's the breadwinner. For a woman it's a second income or something to do.'

'If I see a young black man walking towards me I instinctively hold my bag tighter and move out of his way. There's something about him that worries me.'

'I'm impressed when people over 50 apply for jobs in the computer industry but it would be very hard for them. I say "Technology changes so often and so fast, my employees have to learn very quickly all the time. You'd need a young person's mind really."'

'I've got this very quiet Muslim girl in my class. I think she should get more involved but it's probably cultural. They're taught that a woman's role is to be passive.'

'I knew this Down's syndrome boy. He was big but they never grow up really. They always need looking after, can't leave them on their own for a minute.'

'Once they become mentally ill that's it. They're never the same again. Schizophrenics are the worst. They end up being violent.'

Fair discrimination

There are situations where it is fair and reasonable to discriminate between people. For example, it is acceptable to discriminate between interviewees for a nursery manager post on the basis of their experience and qualifications. It is acceptable to discriminate in favour of, or choose, the person who has the best and most suitable background for the job.

ACTIVITY

Look at the cartoons and the job advertisement. Identify whether prejudice and discrimination are, or are not, being expressed.

Somali male member of staff required for residential worker role in group home.
Must speak Somali and have experience of providing intimate personal and physical care for disabled male residents.

In the first cartoon the male visitor expressed negative ideas and feelings about men being carers. There was a suggestion that men who are carers are not 'real men'. This reveals the prejudice – negative ideas and attitudes – that the speaker holds about caring as male work and men who are carers.

In the second cartoon the manager of the nanny agency indicates that she has a number of prejudices and that she acts on them. She doesn't employ men, girls from families she doesn't know, or girls with a background or 'appearance' that she feels is unacceptable. The fact that the manager of the nanny agency puts her prejudices into practice – acts on them – leads her to discriminate against groups of people.

The job advertisement does not reflect prejudice against women or non-Somali people. It is an example of 'positive action' on the part of the employer. This helps the home to recruit a person with the specific characteristics, skills and experience necessary to perform the residential worker job adequately.

DISCRIMINATORY BEHAVIOUR

This occurs where people act on their prejudices. When prejudiced people have the power to enforce their actions, they treat some people unequally and unfairly. While many people have some prejudices, most do not discriminate by acting on them.

One of the core values of care work is that people are treated equally. Care workers need to be aware of their own prejudices. They need to monitor their actions to make sure that they do not start to discriminate in their care practice. Where care workers act on a prejudice in a way that obviously discriminates against someone, they can be said to have practised **direct discrimination**.

Examples of behaviours that indicate direct discrimination are:

- **abusive language**
- **isolating HIV positive clients**
- **racist or sexist jokes**
- **ignoring a person's abilities or qualifications because of a disability.**

There may also be situations where a care worker or care organisation is involved in **indirect discrimination**. This is more subtle and more difficult to explain to the person or organisation whose practice is discriminatory, as they may not have intended this to happen.

Examples of behaviours that indicate indirect discrimination are:

- **hostile or negative tone of voice**
- **body language**
- **avoiding people**
- **imposing conditions that certain groups cannot meet.**

> **QUICK response**
> Are there some groups of people or types of health or social care problems that you would be reluctant to work with? Are your feelings about them underpinned by prejudice?

ACTIVITY

Look back at the first activity on stereotyping. Identify ways in which each speaker might in future show direct and indirect discrimination in their behaviour towards the group they refer to.

ACTIVITY

Look at the cartoons and try to decide:

⊗ whether there is any evidence of discrimination

⊗ who is being discriminated against

⊗ what sort of discrimination it is.

THE EFFECTS OF DISCRIMINATION

Prejudice and discrimination can be damaging and harmful to relationships and to the psychological and social well-being of the person who experiences them. The actual effects of discrimination on individuals vary in the same way that the people who suffer it do.

ACTIVITY

Identify a situation where you felt that you were being discriminated against or where you detected that people were prejudiced against you in some way. You may have experienced discrimination or prejudice because of your age, appearance, ethnicity or gender for example. Describe the incident and how it affected you. Discuss your experience with a partner. Try to identify whether there are any common features to how you were affected by your experiences.

There are some common responses to the experience of discrimination and prejudice. While some people may experience all the following effects, others may experience only some of them and then to differing degrees.

Anger

Unfair discrimination involves being treated unjustly. It may involve being treated with a lack of respect and having rights ignored. The experience of being disrespected, ignored and devalued is likely to provoke feelings of anger in the person discriminated against. These feelings may be short-lived. However, they might stay with the person if he or she is unable to express them or to challenge the discrimination.

Loss of self-esteem and feeling of helplessness

When people with prejudices have the opportunity and power to regularly express and enforce their attitudes, their victims are likely to experience a loss of self-esteem and feelings of helplessness. Persistent, ongoing discrimination, such as bullying at school or work for example, undermines self-esteem. Being treated badly and experiencing threats, criticism and limited opportunities reduces personal confidence. It can lead victims to feel that they deserve to be treated in such a way and that they are powerless to prevent it happening to them.

Lack of motivation

Some individuals and groups become too tired and worn down to challenge discrimination. The enduring stress can lead to resignation about their situation. This is particularly likely where the perpetrator of the discrimination has a lot more power than the victim.

Poor employment prospects

Examples of discrimination at work are often highlighted by newspapers in stories of cases where victims of discrimination have taken their complaints to court. These cases often reveal examples of discriminatory behaviour that has directly affected the victims' opportunities to gain promotion or to develop their careers. For example, there have been many cases where women have taken their employers to court. They argue that sex discrimination at work has meant fewer opportunities and less pay for them than for men with similar qualifications and experience.

EQUAL OPPORTUNITY RIGHTS

We have looked at the ways in which people can be discriminated against and the effects that this can have on their health and well-being. We are now going to look at the idea of equal opportunity rights as this bears on the rights that people in health and social care settings might have.

Over the last decade, care workers and politicians have increasingly stressed the importance of protecting and maintaining clients' rights and ensuring that they are able to make choices and decisions about their own care. If we say that all people have equal rights the question 'what do we mean by "rights"?' needs to be answered.

ACTIVITY

Make a list of some of the things that you feel are important to you and others and which you and other people have a 'right' to. These things might include statements like 'the right to wear what I like' or 'the right to say what I like'. Then explain in a short paragraph why you feel that you have a right to these things.

Many people feel that the things they identify when asked to list their rights are, in fact, the rights that all humans are born with. The difficulty is that, as soon as we talk about 'being entitled' to rights we are faced with the issue of what rights we really do have. It is helpful to distinguish between two different sorts of rights.

⊗ **Universal rights; that is, rights that we have by virtue of being human and which are unchangeable. An example might be the right to think what we like.**

⊗ **Granted rights; that is, rights that depend on other factors and the agreement of other people.**

Most of the things that we assume to be universal rights actually depend on people in positions of power granting them to us. The most common way this happens is through Parliament. Laws are made which establish people's legal rights in particular situations. It is then against the law to discriminate and deny anybody their legal rights.

☀ ACTIVITY

Look again at your list of rights. Think carefully about each item. Which ones depend on other people granting them to you and which do not? Discuss your ideas with a partner.

LEGISLATION AND EQUAL OPPORTUNITY RIGHTS

There are currently eight major pieces of legislation designed to promote equality of opportunity and protect people from discrimination. All of these are of importance to care workers and their patients or clients.

Equality for black and minority ethnic groups

The Race Relations Act, 1976

Outlaws discrimination or segregation on the grounds of colour, race or nationality. People who discriminate against others on racial grounds in employment, education and training, or in the provision of facilities and services can be prosecuted. Racial discrimination might take the form of direct or indirect discrimination.

● Direct discrimination: attacks, harassment, racist comments, segregation on the grounds of race or nationality.

● Indirect discrimination: organisations impose rules or conditions that are not achievable by certain racial groups.

Also makes it an offence to victimise a person who uses the legislation to fight discrimination.

Equality for women

The Sex Discrimination Acts, 1975 and 1986

Make discrimination in education, access to goods, facilities and services, and employment and training, illegal. Also outlaw the victimisation of women who use them to fight discrimination.

The Equal Pay Act, 1983

Makes it unlawful to pay women less than men if they are doing work that is similar or of equal value to the work that men do and which is equally demanding. For example, a woman computer programmer successfully fought against being given less pay than a man on the grounds that 'she would probably take longer to do it'.

The Employment Protection Act, 1975

Gives women the right to maternity pay and to have their job kept for them for a specified period.

Equality for people with disabilities

There is currently no legislation specifically outlawing discrimination against people with disabilities. A campaign is being fought to bring this about. There is, however, some other legislation that affects the rights of people with disabilities.

The Disability Discrimination Act, 1995

Introduces new rights for disabled people in employment, education, public transport, access to goods, facilities and services. Establishes a National Disability Council that will advise the government on eliminating discrimination against disabled people.

In the area of employment, makes it unlawful for an employer with twenty or more employees to treat a disabled person less favourably without a justifiable reason. Requires that employers make reasonable adjustments to the workplace to help overcome the practical effects of a disability.

Disabled people who feel that they have been discriminated against can take their case to an industrial tribunal which will enforce the new legislation.

The Disabled Persons Act, 1944

States that three per cent of the workers in companies with 20 or more employees must be people with disabilities.

The Chronically Sick and Disabled Persons Act, 1970, and the Disabled Persons (Services, Consultation and Representation) Act, 1986

Designed to improve the support and services available for people who are disabled. They strengthen earlier legislation about the information and services which disabled people can expect from their local authorities and give the right to assessment of needs and to the resources to meet them.

The Companies Act, 1985

Requires large companies with more than 250 employees to describe in their annual reports their methods for supporting their disabled employees in the areas of recruitment, training and career development.

Religious and political discrimination

The Fair Employment (Northern Ireland) Act, 1989

Makes it unlawful to discriminate against people in employment situations on the grounds of their political opinions or their religious beliefs.

PORTFOLIO ASSIGNMENT

STEREOTYPING, DISCRIMINATION AND THE LAW

INTRODUCTION

This assignment gives you the opportunity to identify the stereotypes associated with four groups of people who use health or social care services, and to identify the effects that this stereotype may have on them. The second part of the assignment gives you the opportunity to identify the nature of the discrimination that your chosen groups may experience. Finally, you are asked to identify the rights that individuals have through equal opportunities legislation.

TASK 1

Make a list of the client groups which use health and social care services. Try to cover the different age ranges and types of health and social care needs. Choose **FOUR** of these groups to investigate and discuss further.

TASK 2

What are the popular stereotypes of your chosen groups? Make a list of words and phrases that you and other people associate with members of your four chosen client groups. You should:

- think of these for yourself

- ask others for their reactions

- search newspapers and magazines for references to people from your client group.

Collect images of your client groups that express stereotyped views of them. Again, you might like to look at magazines, newspapers, posters and books for photographs and drawings that you could use.

TASK 3

Produce a poster illustrating the stereotyped image of one of your client groups that also explains how such stereotyping can lead to discrimination.

TASK 4

Age, disability, gender, health status, race, religion and sexuality all provide the basis for discrimination. Choose four of these areas and:

- give examples of direct and indirect behaviours that are discriminatory

- identify the possible effects that the discriminatory behaviours may have.

TASK 5

Investigate the individual rights of people in each of your four client groups. Use books, leaflets and other materials covering the following pieces of equality of opportunity legislation to investigate their rights.

- The Sex Discrimination Act (1975)

- Race Relations Act (1976)

- The Disabled Persons Act (1986)

- The Equal Pay Act (1970) and (1983)

Materials are available in many libraries and by writing to organisations which work for equality by representing various social groups. Examples are Age Concern and **MENCAP**.

INVESTIGATE ASPECTS OF WORKING WITH CLIENTS IN HEALTH AND SOCIAL CARE

THE CARING RELATIONSHIP

The relationship between carer and patient or client, (we shall say client from now on) and the way it is developed, is the cornerstone of all the work that is done by care providers. Carers should try to form effective, supportive and empowering relationships with their clients. **Empowerment** involves finding ways of enabling clients to become more independent and able to manage their own lives. This is explained in more detail later.

The relationship between carer and client is different to other relationships that the carer might make in two important ways. We will look at these next.

THE DEPENDENCE OF CLIENTS AND THEIR CARERS ON THE CARE WORKER

Health and social care problems can cause clients to experience varying degrees of incapacity and dependence on carers. The degenerative brain disorder Alzheimer's disease, for example, makes many older people unable to care for themselves independently. The relationship that develops between a care worker and client is centred on the carer trying to meet the needs of the client. Care workers should not expect their own needs to be met.

Clients and their informal carers can develop relationships with care workers in which they become dependent on the care worker. Care workers should avoid making decisions and removing choices that their patients and clients are able to make for themselves. At a basic level clients should be given choices about what to eat, what clothes to wear and what activities they fill their time with.

THE EQUALITY OF THE RELATIONSHIP

Dependence is more likely to occur where there is an obvious power difference between the care worker and the client in their relationship. The relationship between carer and client can be an unequal one. This may be because the carer:

- **knows more about the life and problems of the client through reading their notes and reports**

- **controls access to resources such as welfare benefits and referral to services**

- **has the support and help of fellow workers**

- **has knowledge and information not available to the client.**

It is good practice on the part of carers and care organisations to enable clients to have choices about their care and be able to make their own decisions. Ideally, care workers and clients should develop a partnership relationship.

ADAPTING TO CLIENTS' NEEDS

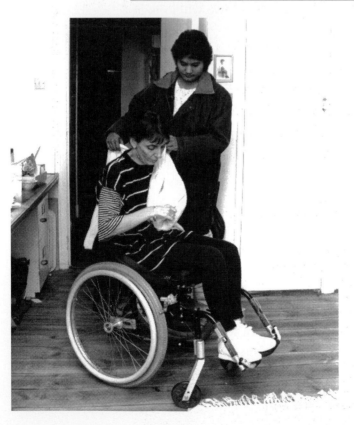

Care workers of all types, from doctors to nurses and social workers to teachers, are trained and employed to be able to identify and respond to their patients' or clients' needs. As all clients are different and have their own unique characteristics and needs care workers have to find ways of being flexible in adapting and responding to them as individuals.

ACTIVITY

Read the case study about Geraldine and then answer the questions that follow.

Caring for Geraldine

Geraldine is 32 years old and a single parent. Since the age of 25 she has suffered from multiple sclerosis. Her condition has left her without the ability to walk, has impaired her eyesight and reduced her energy to care for herself and her two children.

Eddie is 10 years old and Sara is 13 years old. They provide all the home care for their mother when she is too unwell to look after them and herself. These periods are becoming longer as her condition deteriorates. During the week, Eddie and Sara take it in turns to cook, wash the dishes, clean the house, wash and dress their mum, make her comfortable and make sure that she has her medication. They go to school most days. At weekends they take their mum out to see friends, push her around the local park so that she gets fresh air, wash their clothes at the launderette and do the shopping at the supermarket.

Eddie and Sara have got to know Claudette Giddens, the district nurse who comes to see their mum, very well. They try to do the things that she says and ring her when they feel worried about their mum. Geraldine wants to stay at home with her children as long as she can. She feels loved and cared for by her children but now feels that they are under too much pressure to keep meeting her needs. Eddie and Sara say it's tiring but they don't want their mum to go away to hospital.

a **How might Eddie and Sara's relationship with their mother be changed by Geraldine's periods of illness?**

b **List some of the positive and some of the negative feelings and responses that carers like Eddie and Sara may experience while caring for a close relative at home.**

c **What differences might there be in the type of relationship that Claudette, a professional carer, has with Geraldine, compared to the relationship that Eddie and Sara, her informal carers, have with her?**

QUALITIES OF A CARING RELATIONSHIP

Many people who wish to enter the care professions feel that they are suited to such work because they have a 'caring personality' and 'want to work with people'. You may already have said such things at your interview to get on to your health and social care course. There are personality characteristics, practical interests and skills that enable people to be more effective carers. Perhaps one way of expressing your own ideas about what these are is to put yourself in the position of identifying what you would look for in a potential carer employed to look after you or one of your relatives. Try the following activity to do this.

ACTIVITY

At some time in your life you may need to find someone to care for you or to provide care for a member of your family. **Produce an advertisement for a carer that:**

⊗ **identifies the qualities that you are looking for**

⊗ **outlines the main tasks that you will expect them to do**

⊗ **describes briefly the nature of the relationship that you will expect them to develop.**

Choose one of the situations below.

⊗ **Someone to look after your 3-year-old child while you work between 8 am and 4 pm.**

⊗ **A carer for your grandmother who is confused and lives alone.**

⊗ **Full personal care for yourself following a road accident and loss of movement in your legs and right arm.**

Your advertisement should be written in an interesting style (look at adverts in care magazines and newspapers for tips) and should be eye-catching. You should think about using pictures, different lettering styles and the general layout of your advertisement, as well as the written content.

RESPONSES TO CARE RELATIONSHIPS

Caring relationships can have both positive and negative outcomes for clients. People respond to receiving care in different ways.

POSITIVE RESPONSES

Clients respond positively to the caring relationship when it makes them feel:

- **more relaxed in the way that they feel and behave**

- **relieved that they are receiving the help and support that they need**

- **less stressed about the situation and ability to cope.**

Ideally, the care worker builds up a caring relationship to offer the help and support needed to alleviate the client's illness or problems and the client uses this to get better or improve their situation.

QUICK response
Good carers are born and not made. Do you agree? Explain your views.

NEGATIVE RESPONSES

Clients respond negatively to their need for health or social care for a number of reasons. Examples are because:

- **they feel frightened of what might happen to them**

- **they are unable to express their feelings and become withdrawn**

- **they become aggressive or abusive.**

People admitted to hospital or nursing homes are often initially reluctant to talk to staff or fellow patients because they feel vulnerable, powerless and insecure in their unfamiliar setting.

ACTIVITY

Read the following case studies and identify the possible effects of the caring relationships on the clients concerned. Discuss your ideas with others in the class.

Janine is 26 years old. She lives at home with her parents. She has suffered from anorexia nervosa since the age of sixteen. Her parents are very concerned about Janine's health and well-being. They try to encourage her to eat a healthy, balanced diet regularly. They take her to regular out-patient appointments that they have made with her consultant and buy her cuddly toys to cheer her up when she feels down about her appearance. Their biggest concern is that she will neglect herself and die from her illness.

Lizzy is a community psychiatric nurse with twenty-five years' experience of caring for mentally ill people in their own homes. She visits all of her clients at home, every week. On Wednesdays at 10 am she visits Annabelle, whom Lizzy feels is suffering from depression, to wash and put rollers in her hair. They also have a brief chat about how they have both been feeling. At 1 pm Lizzy returns to Annabelle's house to take her rollers out and style her hair. When Lizzy was on annual leave her colleague Dilpesh saw Annabelle and discharged her, saying there was no evidence of a mental health problem. On her return Lizzy put Annabelle back on her case load.

Gerard is a 7-year-old boy who attends a children's unit for emotionally and behaviourally disturbed children. He has recently experienced difficulties at home and school. His mother says that she 'can't control him'. Gerard goes out without telling her and has stolen from shops and from other children at school. His mother says that she would like to buy him more toys and new clothes but that she can't afford to on her income support. His key worker, Erica, explained to Gerard that he is in the unit because he is 'special'. On his birthday she decided to take him to McDonalds and to buy him a personal stereo. Other staff in the unit tried to tell her that it was unit policy to only buy the children a small gift when they were leaving.

BEING SUPPORTIVE THROUGH THE CARER/CLIENT RELATIONSHIP

We all have relationships with other people around us. We tend to live and spend our time with others, in families, work groups and friendship groups for example. To some extent we are dependent on other people, as they are on us. You are probably familiar with being supportive of other people and with receiving support from those you have relationships with. People develop relationships because they are able to meet their needs through them. If you have a need for friendship you will only form such a relationship with a person who can provide what you expect from a friendship.

SUPPORT SYSTEMS

You are probably involved in a range of different relationships in your every-day life. You may not consider some of the contacts that you have with others to be relationships as such. However, our relationships can include regular, reliable contacts or occasional and superficial connections with others. If you were to look at all of your relationships that are supportive you would be identifying your support system. Relationships that you experience as negative and stressful should not be included as part of your support system.

 ACTIVITY

Read through the following case study describing Angela's relationships.

Angela is 34 years old and lives alone. She has lived in Birmingham for the last five years. At work Angela is in charge of an office of five people. She describes her relationships with her staff as 'friendly, but they're not people I see outside work'. She does see one former colleague outside of work. Paul, her former boss, is someone she describes as 'a good friend'. They often go out together for meals and a drink or to see a film.

Angela's parents live in another area of the country, about two hundred miles away. She phones them every few weeks and visits a few times a year. Her brother and sister also pay her a visit about twice a year. She says that she often thinks about them but that because they all live so far away she tends to rely on friends who are nearer for support and company.

Angela has several close female friends she sometimes stays with at weekends. She has known Jane, Fiona and Barbara since her school days and met Felicia when she first moved to Birmingham. They are firm friends and all go out together at the weekends. Angela says that these are her main source of companionship and support.

Produce a diagram showing Angela's relationships and contacts. You should use the following key to describe this.

――――――――― strong, reliable relationship

– – – – – – – superficial relationship or contact

～～～～ personal relationship

Draw a second, more detailed, diagram showing your own support system. You should include your family, friendships, work and other relationships in your diagram. You should try to include as many people as possible who you relate to or have contact with regularly.

SUPPORTING CLIENTS

People who experience health, personal or social problems are offered different kinds of support to help them deal with their difficulties. Support can be divided into five different categories.

1 **Information** – given, for example, in booklets, on posters or in person.

2 **Social** – based, for example, on providing recreation and contact with other people.

3 **Financial** – for example in the form of welfare benefits or loans.

4 **Physical** – helping someone go to the toilet, for example.

5 **Emotional** – for example by giving relatives time away from the demands of caring.

PROVIDING INFORMATION IN CARE SETTINGS

There are many instances where clients rely on being given information when they are in care settings. Effective communication is the key skill that care workers need to develop.

ACTIVITY

Imagine that your GP has informed you that you need to be admitted to hospital next week. Try to think of all the information that you would want to know under the following headings.

- ✪ **Information needed before you go.**

- ✪ **Information needed on arrival.**

- ✪ **Information needed during your stay in hospital.**

It is likely that the hospital would provide you with a lot of information to improve your stay and help you to communicate your needs effectively to staff. Leaflets, direction signs in various languages, newsletters and hospital radio programmes are all used to provide clients with the information they need.

ACTIVITY

Read the following case studies outlining the situations of six clients. Then answer the questions that follow.

Pablo, a 47-year-old Spanish man, has recently lost his sight as the result of an accident at work. The damage to his eyes is irreversible. His wife Maria says that they will need a lot of support over the next few years to help them to come to terms with Pablo's blindness.

Helena is 15 years old. She is six months pregnant. Her parents said that they were ashamed of her and told her to leave home when she informed them of her pregnancy. She has lived in a council home for young people for the last two months in the care of social workers.

Femi, aged 24, is detained in a psychiatric ward. She doesn't want to be there but two doctors, a social worker and her mother have agreed that she must receive treatment in hospital for her serious mental illness. She is very upset and feels betrayed by them all. She complains to the nursing staff that she will lose her job and doesn't understand why she has to be there.

Anne is a 63-year-old widow. She was recently knocked down while crossing the road on her way to the local shops. Anne is now at home with both of her legs and her right arm in plaster. She is still feeling very shaken by the accident and her injuries.

Daniel is 8 years old. He is going into hospital for surgery next week. His parents are concerned that it will be very traumatic for him and are worried that it will affect his confidence and their relationship with him.

Augustine is 25 and has spent the last two years in hospital following a motorcycle accident. He is paralysed from the waist down as a result of the spinal cord damage he suffered. He is due to move to a specially adapted bungalow where he will live with two other paraplegic people and two carers from next week.

a **What types of support do each of these people require? Discuss this with a partner and make some brief notes explaining your ideas and reasoning. You should refer to the five categories of support referred to above.**

b **What practical help could be given to each person to support them though their difficulties? Again, discuss this with a partner and write some notes, giving examples of how the people could be helped and who by.**

EMPOWERING PEOPLE THROUGH EFFECTIVE INTERACTION

Care workers should promote positive working relationships with their clients. A positive working relationship is one in which the client is equally involved and able to make decisions and express their thoughts, feelings and wishes. These kinds of care relationship are **empowering** because they regard individuals as:

- ⊘ **valid and important in their own right**

- ⊘ **having rights and choices appropriate to their age and needs**

- ⊘ **deserving respect regardless of their personal or social characteristics.**

Positive, empowering relationships depend on care workers using communication skills effectively in their interactions with clients. Being sensitive to what other people are saying, thinking and feeling, treating them with respect, and protecting their dignity and rights, are all features of empowering care practice. To be able to do these things, care workers need to be sensitive to the spoken and unspoken communication of their clients. They also need to be aware of how they themselves think, feel and behave in their interactions with clients.

Looking after people is only one part of care work. On its own this approach may result in the client becoming dependent on the carer. Good care practice involves the carer also working to promote the development of the client.

Positive, empowering relationships should have the effect of:

1 **acknowledging the individual's personal beliefs and identity.** This means that you should try to communicate that you accept people for who they are and what they believe in. You may not always share the beliefs and lifestyle of the people you care for but you should show that you accept their individuality. For example, if people have different religious beliefs and practices to your own, give them the opportunity to practise their faith and celebrate their religious festivals where this is important to them.

QUICK response

What do you feel are the limits, if any, on the rights and choices that children should have?

2 **building self-esteem.** This involves improving the clients' positive feelings about themselves. For example, a child who has difficulty learning or who has been unable to keep up with other children in his or her class may feel 'useless' and critical of his or her own abilities. Teachers or nursery workers may use their communication skills (listening, talking, using positive non-verbal messages) to enable such children to express positive things about themselves, their achievements and their future prospects.

3 **building self-confidence.** Personal and social problems and illness can make people feel that they have little belief in their own abilities. A person who has been involved in a road traffic accident and has suffered broken legs will require physiotherapy in order to learn to walk again. An important part of the physiotherapist's role is to build the person's self-confidence so that he or she is able to practise physical exercises and eventually walk unaided.

FIGURE 4.3: Effects of empowering people

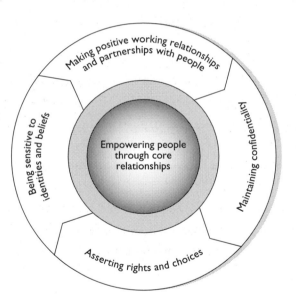

☀ ACTIVITY

Read the case studies of Helena, Daniel, Ann and Augustine again. Explain, for each person, how a care worker could empower them through a caring relationship.

✦ ACTIVITY

We all have expectations of how we should be treated by care workers when we use care services. You have probably had good and bad experiences in your contacts with care workers. This activity requires you to identify why one relationship with a care worker was positive and why another was negative.

Think of two contacts you have had with health or social care workers. One should be a positive experience and the other a negative experience. You might refer to contact with a doctor, a hospital worker, a dentist, a counsellor or social worker who you've seen. You don't have to use their real names or disclose any details about your reasons for seeing them.

Think of all the reasons why one was positive and one was negative, giving examples under the following headings.

- ⊗ How did they empower/disempower you?

- ⊗ How did they acknowledge/fail to acknowledge your personal beliefs?

- ⊗ How did they build-up/reduce your self-esteem?

Discuss your positive and negative experiences in a small group. As a group, discuss the ideas that you all have and bring them together as a list of ten ways to promote a positive relationship with clients. Write your ideas down on a large sheet of paper and explain them to the rest of the class.

VALUES AND ETHICAL ISSUES IN CARE WORK

A **value** is a belief about what is right. Care values refer to the beliefs and principles that care workers try to work with in their relationships with clients. For example, a support worker working with older people might say 'I try to improve the quality of people's lives'. A social worker working with children and families might say ' I try to treat all people equally whoever they are'. We all have beliefs about what is important in care work.

ACTIVITY

Make a list of all those values that you feel should be part of good care practice. Try to come up with lists of examples to illustrate the values that you identify.

The National Council for Vocational Qualifications (NCVQ) is the organisation that works with care sector employers to establish national standards for care work. These standards express a **value base** and principles that care workers should apply in their relationships with clients. The values that all care workers should try to incorporate in their practice include:

1 being anti-discriminatory

2 communicating effectively

3 treating people as individuals

4 respecting people's rights and choices

5 maintaining confidentiality.

The importance of the first four principles has already been discussed. We will look now at the importance of the fifth, maintaining confidentiality.

MAINTAINING CONFIDENTIALITY

People's relationships are based on the **trust** that they have in each other. If you cannot trust another person with your thoughts and feelings then your relationship with them is likely to be quite superficial. The caring relationship is also based on trust and the need for care workers to maintain confidentiality whenever possible.

Confidentiality is an important but very difficult issue in care work. Decisions to breach confidentiality should never be taken lightly and each situation must be thought through individually. Your decision on whether to keep or breach confidentiality can be arrived at by following the guidelines below.

Keeping things to yourself

There are times when it is important to keep confidences and information that you have about clients to yourself. For example, if a child at
the nursery where you do your work placement swore at you and
misbehaved one afternoon, or an elderly resident at a nursing home
refused to bathe after wetting themselves, you would be breaching
confidentiality to reveal these things to your friends. You should not
breach confidentiality in situations where:

- ⊗ **people have a right to privacy**

- ⊗ **their comments or behaviour do not cause anybody harm or
  break the law.**

Where care workers gossip or talk publicly about their clients they are
betraying the trust that has been put in them.

Telling other people

There are other times when you must reveal what you have been told,
or have seen, to a more senior person at work. Where clients request
that you keep what they tell you a secret, this can be over-ridden if:

- ⊗ **what they reveal involves them breaking the law or planning
  to do so**

- ⊗ **they tell you that they intend to harm themselves or another
  person**

- ⊗ **they reveal information that can be used to protect another
  person from harm.**

If an offence is committed that could have been prevented by your
revealing the confidence, you could be brought to court to face
charges.

Care workers should never promise a client that what they say will be
absolutely confidential. They should explain that, depending on what
they are told or observe, there are times when they may have to share
information with their colleagues and other authorities.

QUICK response

**Have you ever revealed
anything to another person
'in confidence'? What did you
expect of them when you had
done so?**

☀ ACTIVITY

Read the following situations.

- ✪ Darren has an appointment with the college nurse for a BCG booster. He's worried about it making him ill. He says that he's just taken some ecstasy and pleads with her not to tell anyone.

- ✪ Jennifer goes to her GP and asks for contraceptive pills. She asks her GP not to tell her parents. She is 14 years old.

- ✪ Eileen has terminal cancer. She tells her district urse that she's had enough of living and is going to end her own life tomorrow. She says it's her choice and asks the district nurse not to interfere.

- ✪ Yasmin tells her new health visitor that her boyfriend is violent and is beating her. She asks the health visitor not to say anything as she is frightened of what might happen. Yasmin and her boyfriend have a 3-month-old baby.

- ✪ Lee turns up at a hostel for the homeless. He says that he has run away from home because his father is beating him. He asks the social worker not to contact his family. He is 16 years old.

- ✪ A social worker phones Terry's teacher to ask whether she knows anything about his home life. The social worker explains that she is worried about Terry's stepfather. Terry is 6 years old.

- ✪ A man with a stab wound arrives at the hospital casualty department. He won't give his name and asks the nurse not to phone the police. He says that he will leave if she does. He is bleeding heavily.

- ✪ Ian is visited in hospital by his local priest. He is recovering from an overdose of tablets. He confesses to the priest that he knocked over a girl on the zebra crossing in town. The girl is still in a coma. Ian says he can't live with himself. The police have appealed for information on the car driver.

Draw a line down the middle of a blank piece of paper. The top end of the line is 'absolute confidentiality', the bottom end is 'complete disclosure'. Write each of the above client's names on the part of the line that indicates the degree of confidentiality you feel is appropriate to each case.

Write a short paragraph on each client explaining:

- ✪ why confidentiality may be important to the client

- ✪ the dilemma facing the care worker

- ✪ the reasons for your decision about confidentiality.

Discuss your answers with other members of your class. Make brief notes on points of view that are different to your own.

PORTFOLIO ASSIGNMENT

CARING FOR OTHER PEOPLE

INTRODUCTION

This assignment helps you to explore the nature of the caring relationship, the role of communication and confidentiality within it, and its possible effects on clients.

The assignment is divided into two parts. The first is concerned with your experiences and ideas about the caring relationship. The second asks you to apply your understanding of care practice and ethical issues to two case studies. It gives you the opportunity to think about and explain how care workers need to use their relationships to protect and support the best interests of the people they look after.

TASK 1

Explain your own reactions to receiving care in two of the following situations.

- **A dental appointment**

- **A visit to your GP**

- **An experience of hospitalisation**

- **A period of illness**

You should include examples of both your positive and negative responses.

TASK 2

Care workers are able to offer different types of support. Give examples of the different types of support that were, or could have been, helpful to you in the two situations you chose above.

TASK 3

Read the following case studies about carer/client interactions.

Mary is 82 years old. She has Alzheimer's disease. She is confused at times but walks well and likes to be with people. She lives alone at home. Her social worker has organised the following care package for her.

- A home care worker will come into her home at 8 am each day to get Mary up, provide personal care and give her breakfast.

- Mary will attend a day centre between 9 am and 4 pm

- A care worker will pick her up at 8.45 am in the day centre minibus.

- The day centre will provide all-day care, including a midday meal, help with personal care, and a range of activities designed to promote awareness of self, others and the environment.

- A care worker will take Mary home at 4 pm in the minibus.

- A home care worker will come to Mary's home at 6 pm to provide personal care, an evening meal, and to put her to bed.

This morning Mary has told a member of the day centre staff that the evening home carer shouts at her and slapped her last night.

PORTFOLIO ASSIGNMENT

Fatima is 23 years old. She is an unmarried Muslim woman, admitted to a mixed medical ward for an exploratory gynaecological operation. Born in Britain, her Islamic background means that she follows the dietary, religious and social rules of her faith. The ward is staffed by doctors and nurses of both sexes, who provide pre- and post-operative care for patients.

Fatima has told a nurse that she had an abortion a month ago. She insists that the nurse must not tell anyone about it. Fatima's father phones up and speaks to the same nurse asking for information on the reasons for her operation.

TASK 4

Write a short report about the two case studies which:

- describes the role of effective interaction in each care relationship

- explains why confidentiality is critically important in health and social care settings

- explains the ethical issues that can arise for care workers when dealing with patients and clients.

✔ MULTIPLE CHOICE QUESTIONS

These questions are designed to test your knowledge and understanding of chapter 4. Answers are given at the back of the book.

1 **Individuals who are unfairly treated because of their social characteristics (e.g. age, race, sexuality, gender or ability) are said to experience:**

A discrimination   C prejudice

B labelling   D socialisation

2 **Paying female staff lower salaries for doing the same job as their male colleagues is an example of:**

A direct discrimination   C indirect discrimination

B prejudice   D scapegoating

3 **Employers who impose an age limit of forty-five on jobs because they feel that older people cannot learn new skills are expressing an attitude that is:**

A sexist   C homophobic

B ageist   D illegal

4 **Feeling hostile towards people because of their skin colour and ethnic origin is an example of:**

A discrimination   C sexism

B stereotyping   D racial prejudice

5 **Which of the following is NOT an example of body language?**

A posture   C eye-contact

B questioning   D gestures

6 **In the Registrar General's scale people's social class is determined by their:**

A wealth   C education

B occupation   D ethnic origin

7 **Putting people in categories and treating individuals who possess a particular characteristic, such as having a visual impairment, as being the 'same' is an example of:**

A orientation   C socialisation

B discrimination   D stereotyping

8 **A group of people of about the same age with similar interests and social background are known as:**

A a peer group   C a social group

B a social class   D a family

9 **A person's status in a group refers to his or her:**

A individual characteristics

B position relative to others

C opinions and values compared to others

D salary level

10 **Which of the following are examples of OPEN questions?**

A What are your feelings about abortion?

B How do you think we can help you?

C How did that happen?

D all of the above

✔ MULTIPLE CHOICE QUESTIONS

11 Which one of the following is an example of a CLOSED question?

  A How are you feeling today?

  B What is your relationship with your parents like?

  C Would you like tea or coffee?

  D What are the characteristics of your ideal partner?

12 The process of judging the quality and effectiveness of your communication skills after interacting with others is known as:

  A summarising   **C** evaluation

  B revision   **D** action planning

13 Clients who tell a social worker of their personal feelings about a difficult and painful experience would expect the social worker to be bound by the principle of:

  A absolute secrecy   **C** equal opportunity

  B confidentiality   **D** philanthropy

14 Should you offer clients absolute confidentiality if they ask you to do so?

  A yes   **C** sometimes

  B no   **D** always

15 People who treat women as inferior to men have attitudes that are:

  A old-fashioned   **C** racist

  B sexist   **D** intellectual

16 Individuals who have been discriminated against may experience:

  A anger and despair   **C** low self-esteem

  B frustration   **D** all of the above

17 Shouting at, hitting or making threats against people because they are members of minority ethnic groups are examples of:

  A direct racial discrimination

  B racial prejudice

  C indirect racial discrimination

  D peer group pressure

18 The level of individual people's self-esteem can be judged by:

  A their popularity

  B the way that they think and feel about themselves as individuals

  C the way that others feel about them

  D their achievements

19 Which one of the following is an example of social support?

  A reassuring a person who is upset and crying

  B helping a person to have a bath

  C going to the cinema with a friend who is lonely

  D a fortnightly security check

20 Which of the following would reduce the effectiveness of communication?

  A listening and attending skills

  B making eye-contact

  C a noisy, poorly lit, uncomfortable room

  D recapping and checking

Answers

1 C
2 D
3 A
4 D
5 B
6 C
7 D
8 C
9 B
10 B
11 C
12 C
13 D
14 C
15 A
16 B
17 A
18 B
19 B
20 D

1 B
2 B
3 D
4 A
5 C
6 A
7 D
8 C
9 B
10 C
11 D
12 A
13 D
14 A
15 A
16 C
17 B
18 A
19 B
20 C

1 B
2 B
3 C
4 B
5 C
6 C
7 A
8 D
9 B
10 D
11 B
12 A
13 C
14 C
15 B
16 C
17 B
18 B
19 A
20 C

1 A
2 A
3 B
4 D
5 B
6 B
7 D
8 A
9 B
10 D
11 C
12 C
13 B
14 B
15 B
16 D
17 A
18 B
19 C
20 C

Glossary

Arthritis
a physical condition which causes pain and stiffness in a person's joints.

Balanced diet
food and fluid intake containing a sufficient quantity and variety of nutrients to promote healthy growth and physical functioning.

Closed questions
questions that limit the way in which the respondent can answer. They are frequently phrased so that the respondent chooses between two possible answers, such as 'Do you want tea or coffee?', or gives a simple piece of information, for example, 'What is your name ?'.

Care manager
social worker who is responsible for planning and purchasing a package of social care to meet a client's individual needs.

Client group
a group of people who share a particular personal, social, psychological or medical characteristic and at whom health and social care services are specifically targeted. For example, mothers and their children under the age of five are the main client group of nurseries and playgroups.

Community psychiatric nurse (CPN)
health care worker who offers care to people who have, or have had, mental health problems. A CPN usually sees people at home or in other community settings rather than when they are in hospital.

Directly managed services
statutory secondary health care services that are still provided by District Health Authorities and which have not yet become NHS Trusts. There are now very few of these in the UK.

Domiciliary care
forms of practical care that are provided in the clients' own home. For example, a home help would provide domiciliary care by helping clients with their cleaning, cooking and personal care in some circumstances.

Empathy
putting yourself in another person's position, trying to appreciate how he or she is feeling or experiencing a situation.

Environment
total physical, cultural and behavioural features that surround and affect an individual.

Funding	the way in which something is paid for or financed. For example, 'voluntary sector funding' simply means the way in which voluntary sector services are paid for.
Fund-holding GPs	general practitioners who are given a sum of money each year by the Regional Health Authority to purchase care directly for patients registered with their practice.
Geriatric	sometimes refers to services for people over the age of 65, and also to the people who fall into this age category. The term is not commonly used now and has been replaced by services for older people, the elderly or elders.
Gland	cell or organ that synthesises chemical substances and secretes them into the body either through a duct or directly into the blood stream.
Haemoglobin	iron-containing, oxygen-carrying pigment in the red blood cells.
Hazard	anything that is considered to be a danger to health, safety or life.
Independent sector	private and voluntary health and social care organisations and individual practitioners who are self-employed rather than employees of statutory organisations.
Internal market	the system where purchasers of health or social care contract with providers of care for a particular care service to be delivered at a particular price and standard.
Menopause	the period during which a woman's ovaries have stopped producing eggs and she stops menstruating.
Open questions	questions that give respondents the opportunity to express themselves in the way that they choose and tend to allow respondents to expand on a topic as opposed to giving a short answer.
Passive smoking	involves breathing in, and being affected by, the tobacco smoke produced by other people smoking in your immediate environment.
Prejudice	involves experiencing negative or hostile feelings and having negative ideas and hostile attitudes towards other individuals or groups of people.
Pressure points	the points in the body where an artery can be compressed

against a bone to stop the blood flowing through the artery to the limb.

Providers   health and social care organisations that provide direct care services to client groups.

Psychiatric   refers to mental health services or problems. For example, a psychiatric social worker is a social worker who deals with the mental health aspects of personal and social care problems.

Purchasers   the organisations, or parts of an organisation, that fund and buy care from provider organisations. Fundholding GPs and District Health Authorities are the main purchasers of health care. Local authorities are the main purchasers of social care.

Risk   the possibility of meeting danger or suffering harm when faced by a hazard.

Socialisation   the process of transferring and learning a society's culture. The family is the main agent of primary socialisation, while school, peer groups and work are sources of secondary socialisation.

Social role   expected patterns of behaviour associated with a particular social status or position. For example, there are particular patterns of behaviour expected of people who occupy the social role of doctor.

Statutory sector   includes health and social care organisations that provide care services funded by central government and which have to be provided by law.

Target group   a group of people at whom a health promotion campaign is specifically aimed, or targeted. For example, anti-drugs campaigns have been aimed at the adolescent target group.

TEC   Training and Enterprise Council.

Venesectionist   medical technician employed in some hospitals to take blood samples; sometimes called phlebotomist.

Index